Learning GDScript by Developing a Game with Godot 4

A fun introduction to programming in GDScript 2.0 and game development using the Godot Engine

Sander Vanhove

Learning GDScript by Developing a Game with Godot 4

Group Product Manager: Rohit Rajkumar

Publishing Product Manager: Kaustubh Manglurkar

Book Project Manager: Sonam Pandey

Senior Editor: Anuradha Joglekar

Technical Editor: K Bimala Singha

Copy Editor: Safis Editing

Proofreader: Anuradha Joglekar

Indexer: Subalakshmi Govindhan

Production Designer: Gokul Raj S.T

DevRel Marketing Coordinators: Anamika Singh and Nivedita Pandey

First published: May 2024

Production reference: 1170424

Published by
Packt Publishing Ltd.
Grosvenor House
11 St Paul's Square
Birmingham
B3 1RB, UK

ISBN 978-1-80461-698-7

www.packtpub.com

To all new Godot Engine users, may your games be great!

- Sander Vanhove

Contributors

About the author

Sander Vanhove is a lead game developer and technical artist at Studio Tolima, a Brussels-based studio working on its first commercial game, Koira.

Creating little games for his friends from the age of 14 led him to pursue a master's degree in computer science, after which he worked as a data analyst for several years.

In 2018, he decided to give the Godot Engine a try and never looked back. With a mountain of jam games, uncountable game experiments, and a few small commercial game releases under his belt, he finally took the plunge of working full time at a game studio, the aforementioned Studio Tolima.

He can always be found working on that next project, learning new game development techniques, or trying to teach people how to use the Godot Engine.

I want to thank my parents, Martine and Gerrit, and close friends who believed in me and this project and would relentlessly inquire about its progress.

About the reviewers

Jesse Glover is a seasoned software consultant with a comprehensive background in both backend and frontend development, specializing in Salesforce and ServiceNow development and administration. Jesse has honed his skills in various technical domains with a particular focus on modern frontend frameworks and tools.

In addition to his professional accomplishments, Jesse is passionate about sharing his knowledge and expertise through his YouTube channel, **GameDevMadeEasy**, where he creates educational content on game and software development.

Jesse was also the author of *Unity 2018 Augmented Reality Projects*, which is available on the Packt website.

Ludovic de Saint-Viance, known on the internet as *theLudovyc*, is a senior developer who likes to use Godot in his free time. He has been creating different projects (you can find them on his Itch.io or GitHub pages) for 6 years. Also, he was the admin of a French Discord server about Godot: Espace Godot.

I thank Nikita Raghani from Packt, who invited me to review this book, and my manager, Sonam Pandey. I am also very thankful to the author of this book, Sander, and Packt for being part of this incredible journey. To quote Sander, "I want to respect Packt rules, but it feels strange to introduce myself like on a Wikipedia page. If someone reads those lines to the end, my favorite pizza is the one with pineapple."

Table of Contents

3

Grouping Information in Arrays, Loops, and Dictionaries   53

4

Bringing Structure with Methods and Classes   73

5

How and Why to Keep Your Code Clean   101

Part 2: Making a Game in Godot Engine

6

7

8

Splitting and Reusing Scenes   171

9

Cameras, Collisions, and Collectibles   179

10

Creating Menus, Making Enemies, and Using Autoloads   203

11

Playing Together with Multiplayer   247

Part 3: Deepening Our Knowledge

12

Exporting to Multiple Platforms   277

13

OOP Continued and Advanced Topics   297

14

Advanced Programming Patterns   309

15

Using the File System 325

16

What Next? 333

Preface

Godot Engine is the most popular free open-source game engine on the market. With the advent of Godot 4.0 and the release of many hit games made in Godot, such as *Dome Keeper*, *Brotato*, and *Case of the Golden Idol*, this popularity only grew. There is no better time to learn how to use this wonderful game development tool than now.

Learning how to program and use a new game engine can be a daunting task. However, this book will guide you step by step through all the aspects of creating your own game from scratch, from the basics of writing our first scripts in GDScript to more advanced topics.

We'll learn how to program in GDScript, the custom language of the Godot Engine, which is easy to learn yet very capable and performant for game development. Then, we'll go over all the ins and outs of the engine's intuitive graphical interface and discover everything about its flexible node-based approach to game development.

Who this book is for

This book is for programmers, game designers, game developers, and game artists who want to start creating games in Godot 4. If you're new to coding or game development, looking for a new creative outlet, and want to give Godot 4 and GDScript 2.0 a try, this book is for you. While no prior knowledge of programming or Godot is required, this book gradually introduces more complex concepts as you advance through the chapters.

What this book covers

Chapter 1, *Setting Up the Environment*, starts off the book by setting up everything we need to create games in the Godot Engine and gives a brief overview of the engine and how to write scripts.

Chapter 2, *Getting Familiar with Variables and Control Flow*, explains the major concepts of what variables are and how we can store data within them. From here, we go over different control flows that help us make decisions during the execution of our game.

Chapter 3, *Grouping Information in Arrays, Loops, and Dictionaries*, teaches about two new data types: arrays and dictionaries. These will help us group data in a more structured format. Along the way, we will learn about the two different kinds of loops with which we can loop over different sets of data.

Chapter 4, *Bringing Structure with Methods and Classes*, delves into writing reusable pieces of code using methods and how to structure variables and methods into classes.

Chapter 5, How and Why to Keep Your Code Clean, introduces many concepts around writing clean code, which will help us create code that is reusable and understandable by others as well as ourselves.

Chapter 6, Creating a World of Your Own in Godot, will kick off our own game project. We'll start by defining what kind of game we will be making and progress to making the base of a player character and the environment in which they will be moving around.

Chapter 7, Making the Character Move, offers a refresher on vector math, which is integral to moving entities around in two-dimensional space. Then, we'll write the physics code to make our layer character move and go into debugging the game while it is running.

Chapter 8, Splitting and Reusing Scenes, shows how we can easily split up our game into multiple smaller scenes that are easier to manage and maintain, followed by how we can organize all the scene and script files in tidy folders within the project.

Chapter 9, Cameras, Collisions, and Collectibles, starts by making a smooth camera that will follow the player character without making the real-life player nauseous. After this, we'll move on to handling collisions with the terrain and creating collectible items.

Chapter 10, Creating Menus, Making Enemies, and Using Autoloads, finishes up our single-player game by teaching us about the menu system of the Godot Engine, followed by the creation of enemies that can navigate through the world and projectiles with which the player can shoot these enemies. We conclude this chapter with an introduction to autoloads, with which we can store the high score.

Chapter 11, Playing Together with Multiplayer, converts our single-player experience into a multiplayer one. We start with a crash course in computer networking. After this, we will learn about `MultiplayerSpawner` and `MultiplayerSynchronizer` to be able to play our game with others over a network.

Chapter 12, Exporting to Multiple Platforms, shows how we can export the game for different platforms such as Windows, macOS, Linux, and even the web. We will conclude the chapter by uploading our game to Itch.io, a popular platform for indie games.

Chapter 13, OOP Continued and Advanced Topics, introduces the more advanced **object-oriented programming** (**OOP**) topics such as the `super` keyword, static variables, enumerations, lambda functions, the different ways of passing values to methods, and the `tool` keyword.

Chapter 14, Advanced Programming Patterns, gives us a basis for programming patterns and explores the Event Bus, Object Pool, and State Machine patterns so that we can use them in our next project.

Chapter 15, Using the File System, introduces the file system of the Godot Engine and shows us how we can save and load data in our game.

Chapter 16, What Next?, leaves us with some last techniques and resources to start the next game project as well as introduce the game development community we can be part of.

To get the most out of this book

You don't need any prior knowledge about programming or game development. The only prerequisite is that you are open to learning and willing to improve. During the book, I propose multiple experiments you could do and have included quizzes to test your knowledge. It's important that you take the time to do these so that the knowledge gets cemented in your brain.

We'll cover how to download and set up the Godot Engine in the first chapter of this book but you could already download Godot 4.2.1 or later if you're feeling impatient. All the examples in the book were tested on Godot 4.2.1 but should work in future versions too.

Software/hardware covered in the book	Operating system requirements
Godot 4.2.1	Windows, macOS, or Linux
GDScript 2.0	

The Godot Engine is a very light piece of software that easily runs on older, outdated hardware but it doesn't hurt to check out the minimum specifications and make sure your computer is able to meet them: `https://docs.godotengine.org/en/stable/about/system_requirements.html`.

If you are using the digital version of this book, we advise you to type the code yourself or access the code from the book's GitHub repository (a link is available in the next section). Doing so will help you avoid any potential errors related to the copying and pasting of code.

Download the example code files

You can download the example code files for this book from GitHub at `https://github.com/PacktPublishing/Learning-GDScript-by-Developing-a-Game-with-Godot-4`. If there's an update to the code, it will be updated in the GitHub repository.

We also have other code bundles from our rich catalog of books and videos available at `https://github.com/PacktPublishing/`. Check them out!

Conventions used

There are a number of text conventions used throughout this book.

`Code in text`: Indicates code words in text, database table names, folder names, filenames, file extensions, pathnames, dummy URLs, user input, and Twitter handles. Here is an example: "In *Chapter 1*, we learned to write code with the `_ready` method of a node."

A block of code is set as follows:

```
func deal_damage(amount: float) -> void:
    player_health -= amount


func heal(amount: float) -> void:
    player_health += amount
```

When we wish to draw your attention to a particular part of a code block, the relevant lines or items are set in bold:

```
func minimum(number1, number2):
    if number1 < number2:
        return number1
    else:
        return number2
```

Any command-line input or output is written as follows:

```
unzip Godot_v4.2.1-stable_linux.x86_64.zip -d Godot
```

Bold: Indicates a new term, an important word, or words that you see onscreen. For instance, words in menus or dialog boxes appear in **bold**. Here is an example: "You can access the user:// folder for a given project by opening up the **Project** menu and choosing **Open User Data Folder**."

> **Containers**
>
> We call an array a **container** because we can store and retrieve pieces of data of other data types within them, like integers, strings, booleans, and such. An array contains other data.
>
> Containers structure other data so it is easier to work with.

Get in touch

Feedback from our readers is always welcome.

General feedback: If you have questions about any aspect of this book, email us at customercare@ packtpub.com and mention the book title in the subject of your message.

Errata: Although we have taken every care to ensure the accuracy of our content, mistakes do happen. If you have found a mistake in this book, we would be grateful if you would report this to us. Please visit www.packtpub.com/support/errata and fill in the form.

Piracy: If you come across any illegal copies of our works in any form on the internet, we would be grateful if you would provide us with the location address or website name. Please contact us at copyright@packtpub.com with a link to the material.

If you are interested in becoming an author: If there is a topic that you have expertise in and you are interested in either writing or contributing to a book, please visit authors.packtpub.com.

Share Your Thoughts

Once you've read *Learning GDScript by developing a game with Godot 4*, we'd love to hear your thoughts! Scan the QR code below to go straight to the Amazon review page for this book and share your feedback.

https://packt.link/r/1-804-61698-2

Your review is important to us and the tech community and will help us make sure we're delivering excellent quality content.

Download a free PDF copy of this book

Thanks for purchasing this book!

Do you like to read on the go but are unable to carry your print books everywhere?

Is your eBook purchase not compatible with the device of your choice?

Don't worry, now with every Packt book you get a DRM-free PDF version of that book at no cost.

Read anywhere, any place, on any device. Search, copy, and paste code from your favorite technical books directly into your application.

The perks don't stop there, you can get exclusive access to discounts, newsletters, and great free content in your inbox daily

Follow these simple steps to get the benefits:

1.   Scan the QR code or visit the link below

https://packt.link/free-ebook/978-1-80461-698-7

2.   Submit your proof of purchase

3.   That's it! We'll send your free PDF and other benefits to your email directly

Part 1:
Learning How to Program

In this part, we'll start off by downloading the free and open-source Godot Engine and setting up the environment in which we will be developing our very own game from scratch. Before we come on to creating a game, though, we'll build strong fundamentals in programming using the GDScript programming language.

By the end of this part, you will know all about variables, control flows, different data and container types, methods, and classes. We will conclude this part with a chapter on clean coding.

This part has the following chapters:

- *Chapter 1, Setting Up the Environment*
- *Chapter 2, Getting Familiar with Variables and Control Flow*
- *Chapter 3, Grouping Information in Arrays, Loops, and Dictionaries*
- *Chapter 4, Bringing Structure with Methods and Classes*
- *Chapter 5, How and Why to Keep Your Code Clean*

1

Setting Up the Environment

Game development is becoming more accessible as game engines become more powerful. Tools and pipelines that were only available to big companies and wealthy individuals are now freely available to everyone with a computer. Anyone can feel the satisfaction of creating their own game and having others play it.

This is exactly what we are going to achieve in this book. We will go from knowing absolutely nothing about programming or developing games to creating our very first game and even a little beyond.

During the first part of this book, we will learn all about setting up Godot and programming. This might be a little more abstract, but I'll try to give clear examples and keep you engaged with exercises and experiments you can do for yourself.

The second part of this book will be way more practical as we will dive neck-deep into creating our very own video game! We'll learn how to use the Godot editor to create interesting game scenes and scenarios.

In the last part of this book, we'll take our programming skills to the next level and learn all about advanced topics, such as more powerful concepts, programming patterns, the filesystem, and much more.

But before we get there, nothing is more satisfying than starting a new project! It represents a blank slate with endless possibilities. By the end of this chapter, we'll have created our very own blank slate and written our first lines of code. But first, I'd like to take some time to introduce the Godot game engine and open-source software in general.

In this chapter, we're going to cover the following main topics:

- Godot Engine and open-source software
- Downloading the engine from the official website
- Creating our first project
- How to join the community

Technical requirements

As this book aims to get you from knowing nothing about programming and game development to an intermediate level, there are no technical requirements. So, instead, I'll guide you through all (or at least most) of the steps required for creating games.

> **Example project and code**
>
> You can find the example project and code for this book in this book's GitHub repository: `https://github.com/PacktPublishing/Learning-GDScript-by-Developing-a-Game-with-Godot-4/tree/main/chapter01`.

Godot game engine and open-source software

We'll be using the Godot game engine, which I presume you already know exists as this is a book specifically about that engine. But let me give you some more insight into its history and what open-source means.

Some background on the engine

Godot Engine is a piece of open-source software that lets people from all experience levels and walks of life create games. The project was started in 2007 by Juan Linietsky and Ariel Manzur as an in-house engine for several Argentinian game studios. In late 2014, the engine got open-sourced, giving everyone free access to the code. Since then, it has gained lots of traction and is currently one of the most used game engines on the market. Many commercial games have been released or are under development using the engine. Examples of released games are Brotato, Dome Keeper, Case of the Golden Idol, and Cassette Beasts.

For those of you wondering, yes, the engine is named after the theatrical piece *Waiting for Godot*, by Samuel Beckett. This choice of name is because people will always be waiting for the next version or new feature, resulting in an endless cycle of waiting.

While on the topic of the engine's name, let's also get the pronunciation out of the way. In short, there is no standard way of pronouncing Godot. Because of the association with the play's title, which is written in French, some people say it should be "go-do," without emphasis on any syllable. But most English speakers would say "GOH-doh" and stress the first syllable. Then, there is the stream of people that pronounce it "go-DOT," mainly because it sounds similar to the word "robot" and the engine's logo is a blue robot. But I notice that I say Godot differently each time. So, to cut a long story short, pronounce it however you like. Just use roughly the same letters.

What is open-source software?

As mentioned earlier, Godot is open-source, meaning the engine's source code is freely available. Because everyone has access, people can alter this code to their liking. Once they have tweaked enough parameters or developed a new feature, they can ask the creator of the software to include these tweaks or features in the original project. The creator will then review what the other person has done, alter it a bit if needed, and then add it to the code of the original software. This process creates a virtuous circle that results in a win-win situation for everyone:

- *The software's creator* can grow the code faster because everyone chips in
- *People with technical knowledge* can add the features they miss, making it fit their needs
- *The end user* gets a much better and more stable end product

But not every open-source project is created equal. Each **free open-source software** (**FOSS**) comes with its respective license. This license dictates how you can or should use the software. Some of these are pretty restrictive, but in the case of Godot Engine, we are in luck: we can do anything without significant restrictions. We only have to attribute the creators on the credit page of our games.

Alright – we know what Godot Engine is, how to pronounce its name (or not), and why FOSS is so awesome. Let's dive right into preparing our development environment!

Getting and preparing Godot

Before we can do any programming, we'll need to set up the development environment. That is what we will do in this section, beginning with downloading the engine and creating a new project.

Downloading the engine

Getting the engine is relatively easy and only requires a few steps:

1. First, we'll need to download a copy of the software. We can do this at `https://godotengine.org/download`.

Figure 1.1 – The download page of Godot Engine 4.0 for the Windows platform

2. Usually, the page will automatically direct you to the download page of the operating system you are using to browse the website and you can press the big blue button in the middle of the page to download the engine. If it doesn't, you'll need to select your computer's platform (Windows, macOS, Linux, and so on) when scrolling down the page.

Figure 1.2 – Select your computer's platform if the download page was not able to detect it

3. The download page should also detect whether you're using a 64- or 32-bit system. If it did not do this correctly, then you can find the other versions under the **All downloads** section:

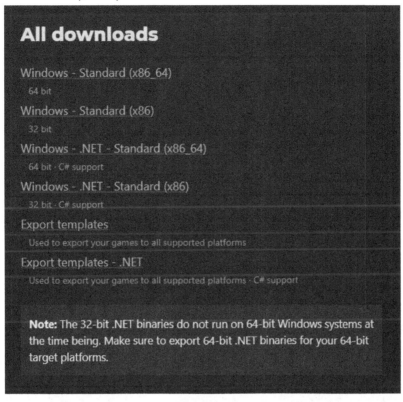

Figure 1.3 – The All Downloads section, where you can find different versions of the engine

4. What we downloaded is a ZIP file. So, unzip it to get to the actual engine.

    -   On Windows: Right-click the zip file and select **Extract All...**. Now follow the prompt that pops up to choose a location.

    -   On macOS: Double-click the zip file, the file will be unzipped into a new folder.

    -   On Linux: Run the following command in the terminal:

        ```
        unzip Godot_v4.2.1-stable_linux.x86_64.zip -d Godot
        ```

5. Put the extracted files somewhere on your computer where it will be safe, such as the desktop, applications, or any other location besides the Downloads folder. Otherwise, if you are anything like me, you might accidentally remove it in a clean-up spree of the Downloads folder.

For this book, we will be using version 4.0.0, as it just came out. But any version with a 4 at the beginning should work fine. Unfortunately, this is not a guarantee. We'll do our best to keep this book's content up to date, but open-source software can move quickly.

The download size of Godot Engine is tiny, about 30 to 100 MB, depending on your platform. This small package is all we need to create awesome games. Compare this to Unity's 10 GB and Unreal Engine's whopping 34 GB! Of course, these all come without any assets, such as visuals or audio.

That's it for getting the engine. You don't need to install anything else to use it.

> **Other versions of the engine**
>
> Because Godot Engine is open-source, there are also a lot of complete game projects that are open-source too. If you ever want to run one of those game projects on your machine, make sure you use the correct version of Godot; otherwise, the game could crash and weird things might happen. You can find and download all official versions of Godot from `https://godotengine.org/download/`.

Creating a new project

Now, let's go ahead and create our first Godot Engine project, hopefully with many others to come in the future!

1. First, open the engine by double-clicking the file we downloaded in the *Downloading the engine* section. A screen like this will greet you:

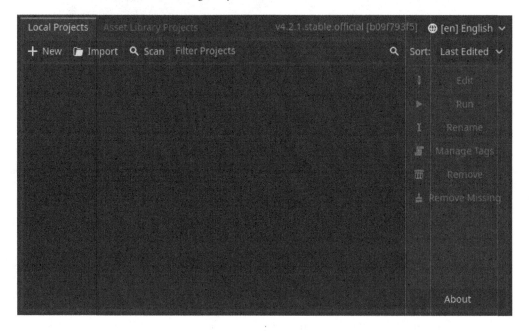

Figure 1.4 – Creating a new project by pressing the New button

2. Choose + **New**; a new window will pop up:

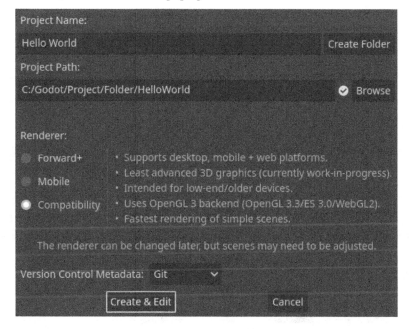

Figure 1.5 – Setting up the new project

3. Call the project `Hello World`.

4. Select a **Project Path** area to put the project. Create a new folder by using the **Create Folder** button or use an existing one but note that this folder should preferably be empty. Although the folder you select can contain files already, starting from a clean directory will keep everything we do more organized.

5. Select **Compatibility** under the **Renderer** category. The compatibility renderer is made to make sure that our game can run on a wide variety of hardware and supports older graphics cards and web exports. The Forward+ renderer is used for cutting-edge graphics but demands a better graphics card, while the mobile renderer is optimized for mobile devices. For what we are doing, the compatibility renderer is more than capable enough and it makes sure that we can export to the biggest amount of platforms possible.

6. Finally, press **Create & Edit**!

Godot will now set up the basic structure of our project within the selected folder and, after a few seconds, show us the editor:

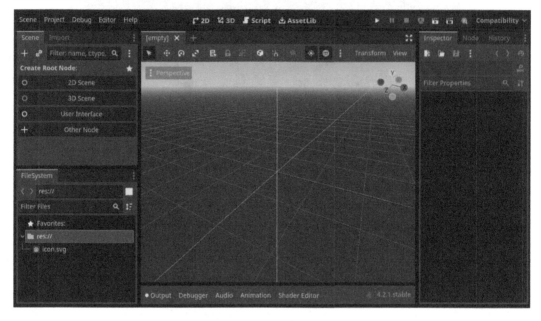

Figure 1.6 – The Godot Engine 4.0 editor

At first sight, this may look quite daunting – little windows everywhere, multiple controls here and there, and a giant 3D space in the middle. Don't worry. By the end of this book, you'll know the ins and outs of almost everything that lies before you. You're in good hands.

> **Fun fact**
>
> The Godot developers used Godot Engine to create the editor itself. Try to wrap your brain around that! They did this to easily extend and maintain the editor.

Light mode

Because of the limitations of printed media, dark screenshots might look grainy and unsharp. That is why, from this point on, we'll switch to the light version of Godot. There is no difference but the appearance of the editor.

If you also want to follow along in light mode, perform these optional steps:

1. Go to **Editor | Editor Settings…** at the top of the screen:

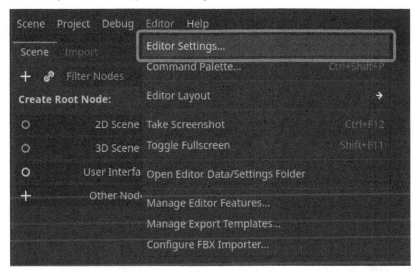

Figure 1.7 – The Editor Settings… option in the Editor menu

2. Find the **Theme** settings.

3.   Select the **Light** theme within the **Preset** dropdown:

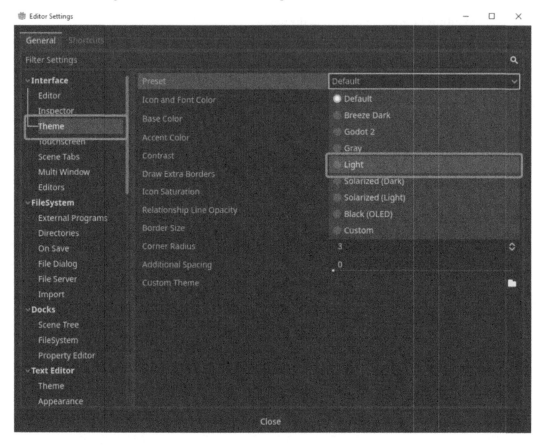

Figure 1.8 – Selecting the Light theme preset in the Theme settings

Now, the editor will look like what's shown in *Figure 1.9*:

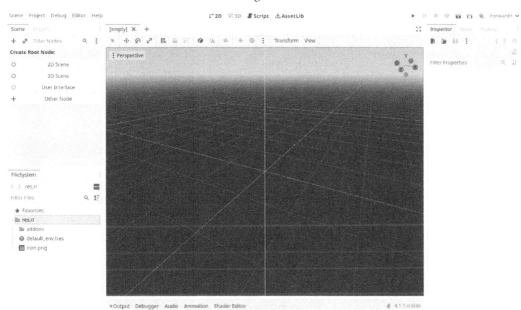

Figure 1.9 – The Godot Engine editor with the Light theme applied

With that out of the way, let's get back to creating a game by learning how to create a scene.

Creating the main scene

Let's continue by setting up our first scene:

1. In the leftmost panel of *Figure 1.10*, which shows the **Scene** panel, select **2D Scene**. This button will set up the scene for a 2D game, as shown here:

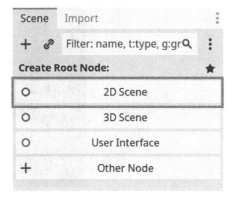

Figure 1.10 – Selecting 2D Scene in the left panel

You'll see that there is one node in the **Scene** panel called **Node2D** and that the 3D space in the middle window got replaced with a 2D plane.

2. Right-click the node called **Node2D** and rename it `Main`. This node will be our main node to work with for now:

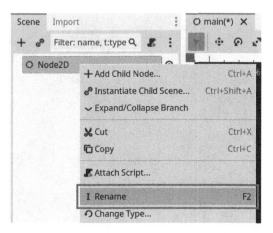

Figure 1.11 – Renaming the Node2D node to Main

3. Save the scene by going to **Scene | Save Scene** or by pressing *Ctrl/Cmd + S*:

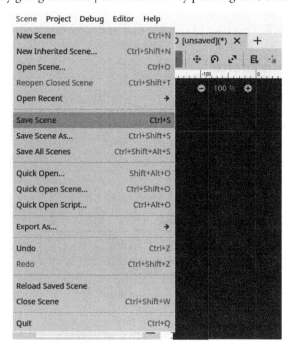

Figure 1.12 – Saving the scene

4. We'll be asked where we wish to save the scene. Choose the project's root folder and name the file main.tscn:

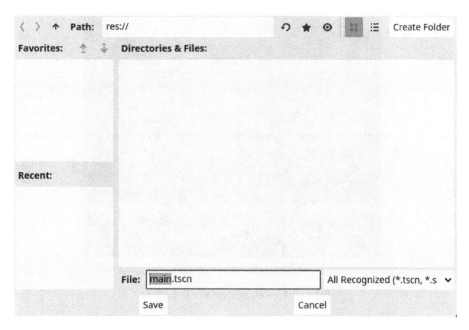

Figure 1.13 – Selecting the root folder to save the scene and naming it main.tscn

That's all for creating our first scene. What we just added is a node. These nodes represent everything in Godot. Images, sounds, menus, special effects – everything is a node. You can think of them as game objects, each having a separate function in the game. The player could be a node, just like enemies or coins.

On the other hand, scenes are collections of nodes or collections of game objects. For now, you can think of scenes as levels. For a level, you need a player node, some enemy nodes, and a bunch of coin nodes; the collection of these is a scene. It's like nodes are the paint and scenes are our canvases.

We'll come back to nodes and scenes throughout this book.

A brief UI overview

Now would be a great time to review some of the more prominent features of the editor's UI. As we saw earlier, it looks something like this:

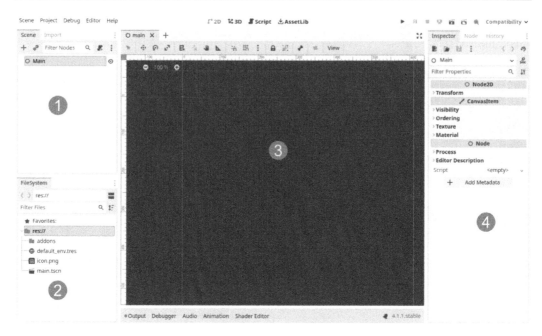

Figure 1.14 – An overview of the editor

The prominent elements of the editor are as follows:

1. The **Scene Tree** area shows all the nodes in the current scene. For now, there is only one.

2. The **FileSystem** area provides access to the files within the project folder.

3. The middle window is the **currently active main editor**. For now, we can see the 2D editor, which will allow us to place nodes in 2D space within the scene.

4. The **Inspector** area can be found entirely to the right and shows the properties for the currently selected node. If you open some accordion menus, such as the **Transform** section, you will find multiple settings associated with the selected node.

Nodes by themselves don't do much. They provide us with specific functionalities, such as showing an image, playing a sound, and more, but they still need some higher logic to bind them into the actual game. That's why we can extend their functionality and behavior with scripts.

Writing our first script

A **script** is a piece of code that adds logic to a node, such as moving an image or deciding when to play that sound.

We'll create our first script now. Right-click the Main node again and choose **Attach Script**:

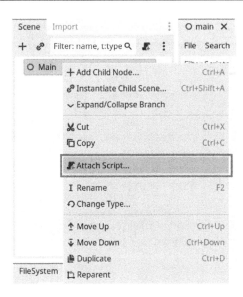

Figure 1.15 – Attaching a script to the Main node

A pop-up window will appear. Keep everything as-is. The important thing to note is that the selected language is **GDScript**, the programming language we'll learn throughout this book. The rest is not very important for now. It even pre-filled the script's name after the node's name, which will attach this script. Press **Create**:

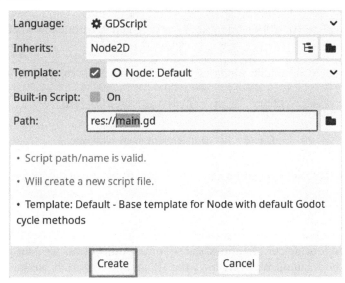

Figure 1.16 – Pressing Create to create the script

The middle panel, where the 2D plane used to be, is replaced with a new window:

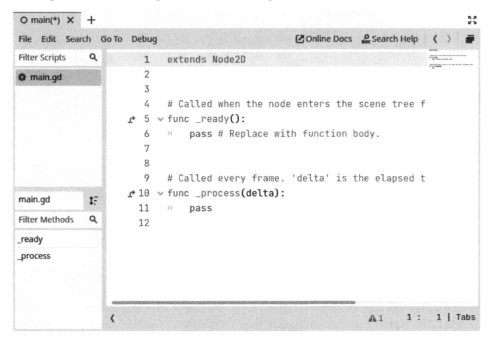

Figure 1.17 – A fresh script

This is the **Script** editor. We will spend most of our time here learning how to program during the first part of this book.

As you may have noticed, the middle window is context-dependent. It can be a **2D**, **3D**, or **Script** editor:

2D   3D   Script   AssetLib

Figure 1.18 – The different main windows

To switch between these different editors, use the buttons at the top of the screen.

> **AssetLib**
>
> The last tab, **AssetLib**, is useful for getting pre-made assets from the Asset Library of Godot. This library can provide custom nodes, scripts, or any other assets for your project directly from within Godot Editor. We won't cover the 3D editor or AssetLib, but it is good to know they are there.
>
> All of the assets on **AssetLib** are open-source and thus completely free to use! Hurray for FOSS!

If you have tried to change to the different editors, return to the **Script** editor so that we can create our first script and ensure everything is ready. The code within the script looks like this for the moment:

```
extends Node2D


# Called when the node enters the scene tree for the first time.
func _ready():
    pass # Replace with function body.


# Called every frame. 'delta' is the elapsed time since the previous
frame.
func _process(delta):
    pass
```

Again, don't worry about all the different commands and specific syntax here. We will cover everything in due time. For now, it's enough to know that this is a script written in GDScript, the scripting language of Godot.

To create the classic **"Hello, World"** program, which is a staple for beginner programmers, all we must do is change the line containing `pass # Replace with function body.` to the following:

```
    print("Hello, World")
```

This line of code will show the text `"Hello, World;"` it will not use a printer to print out anything. We can also throw away a bunch of the code we don't need. The whole script should now look like this:

```
extends Node2D


func _ready():
    print("Hello, World")
```

Notice that there must be a *tab* in front of the `print` statement we added. We add this *tab* because it shows that the line of code belongs to the `_ready` function. We call the practice of adding *tabs* in front of lines **indentation**.

> **Important note**
>
> Throughout this book, we haven't used tabs in the text due to editorial reasons. We will use three spaces to represent one tab. This is why you're better off not copying and pasting code from this book into the editor. The complete code for this book can be accessed and copied from this book's GitHub repository (link in the *Technical requirements* section).

All the lines within the _ready function will run when the node is ready, we'll see what this means in more detail later. For now, it suffices to know that this function gets executed when the node is ready to be used.

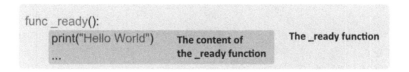

Figure 1.19 – A function contains a code block

Functions are small groups of code a computer can execute. A function is always introduced by the func keyword, followed by the name of the function.

You can see that the pre-filled script also provided us with a _process function, which we will not use for now, so we deleted it. We'll return to functions in *Chapter 4*. Remember that every line of code within the _ready function will execute from the moment our game runs and that a *tab* must precede these lines.

Use the *Tab* key to insert these tabs. The symbol on your keyboard looks like this: ⇆

The last line of interest in the script says extends Node2D. This simply says that we are using **Node2D**, the type of node we added to the scene, as a base for the script to start from. Everything in the script is an extension of the functionality that **Node2D** completes. We'll learn more about extending scripts and classes in *Chapter 4*.

Now, press the play button in the top right to run our project:

Figure 1.20 – The play button is used to run the project

A popup will ask us which scene we want to use as the main scene. Choose **Select Current** to set the current scene as the main one:

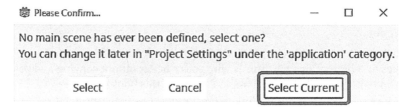

Figure 1.21 – Godot Editor will ask us to define a main scene. We can just select the current one

An empty, gray screen will pop up. We did not add anything visually to our game yet. Later, there will be a sprawling and exciting game here. But this gray screen is what we should expect for now:

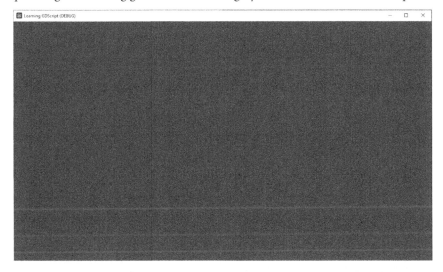

Figure 1.22 – An empty game window

The actual exciting part is happening in the editor window itself. You'll see a new little window unfolding from the bottom where the text **Hello, World** is printed out:

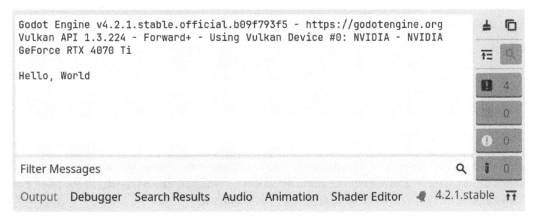

Figure 1.23 – The output of the game shows Hello, World

Success! We wrote our first script!

As an experiment, try changing the text within the double quotes of *step 4* and rerun the program. You should see the new text printed in the output window:

Figure 1.24 – The output of the game after changing the printed text

Those were our first steps in creating a scene and script within the Godot game engine. Throughout this book, we'll learn everything we need to know to create a whole game from scratch, but we'll leave it here for now. Next, we'll take a quick look at joining the game development community.

The Godot Engine Documentation

If you ever feel lost, there is also the official **Godot Engine Documentation**. This is a very exhaustive source of information on all the different classes and nodes and contains manuals on all the different subsystems related to the engine.

You can access the documentation here: `https://docs.godotengine.org/`.

Whenever you are searching how to use a certain part of the engine or something in the book is not 100% clear, you could consult the documentation.

Join our community!

As the last part of this chapter, I invite you to join our community! If you need any help, encounter a bug, or just want to chat with other game developers, come and find us on any of the platforms mentioned at `https://godotengine.org/community`.

I also encourage you to post your progress on X, Facebook, Instagram, Mastodon, or any other social media platform. Getting feedback and extra eyes on your projects is always fun! If you decide to do so, don't forget to use these hashtags: `#GodotEngine`, `#indiedev`, and `#gamedev`.

Want to reach out to me personally? Check out my site for the most up-to-date contact information: `www.sandervanhove.com`.

In the last part of this book, I'll go into more detail about the community and how you can join and maybe even help. But for now, let's focus on learning the trade ourselves!

Summary

In this chapter, we learned about Godot Engine, which is a FOSS. Then, we downloaded the engine for ourselves and created our first project. Lastly, we saw that the built-in programming language is GDScript and made our first `"Hello, World"` script.

In the next chapter, we'll start our journey of learning how to program. See you there!

Quiz time

- What does the acronym FOSS mean and where is it used?
- Is the Godot engine an open-source project?
- What line of code did we add to show *"Hello, World"* in the Output? Why did we add a *tab* at the beginning of this line?
- What are *nodes* in Godot Engine and how do they relate to *scenes*?

2

Getting Familiar with Variables and Control Flow

Programming is all about manipulating data. In games, this data can be the position of the player, the amount of health they have, or what items they possess. These pieces of data are called **variables**, and in this chapter, we will learn how these variables work and how we can manipulate them.

In the second part of this chapter, we'll learn how to use these variables to make decisions during the game. For example, if the health of the player goes to zero, we end the game. This concept is called **control flow** because we control the flow throughout the code.

In this chapter, we will cover the following main topics:

- What are variables?
- Data types – Integers, floats, and strings
- What are constants?
- Getting started with control flow
- Commenting in code

Technical requirements

We have prepared everything we need for *Chapter 2*. Check out the `chapter02` folder in the repository of code examples if you get stuck anywhere. You can find the repository here: `https://github.com/PacktPublishing/Learning-GDScript-by-Developing-a-Game-with-Godot-4/tree/main/chapter02`.

What are variables?

Secretly, under the hood, games are all about data. The position of the player character, the names of your teammates in an online match, the volume amount in the setting window, or the maximum distance a fireball can travel – these are all pieces of data that the game works with to create an experience users like to play.

For example, a player character's position can change during play by pressing the arrow keys on a keyboard. The computer will take this input, calculate the new position, and show the player where their character is within the virtual world. The computer will do this in some capacity for every piece of data within the game. We will learn a lot more about how the computer does all of these calculations throughout the book, but first, we'll have to learn about these little pieces of data, where they get stored on the computer, and how they are used while the game is running.

Within the code of a game, each of these pieces of data gets represented by a variable. Let's take a closer look at variables in the following section.

Variables – Drawers in a filing cabinet full of data

An excellent way to conceptualize variables is to see them as drawers in a filing cabinet. Each drawer is one variable and contains the data for that variable. If we want to change some of that data, we pull open the right drawer, change the value, and put the result back into the drawer. Of course, we need to know which drawer contains the data for the player's position and which contains the number of lives the player has left. Mixing those up would lead to very confusing situations. Smart archivists solved this problem by putting name tags on each drawer so that they could see what data each contains at just a glance.

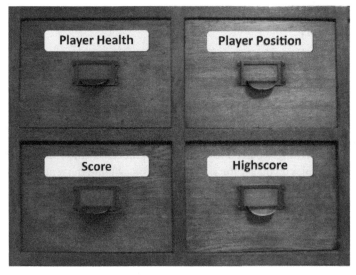

Figure 2.1 – Conceptualizing variables as the drawers of a cabinet

The same principle applies to variables. When creating a variable, we start by giving it a name. The creation process reserves a *drawer*, a little bit of space in the computer's memory, which we can call upon using the name we gave it. We can then use this name to retrieve the value of that variable from memory and store new values in the same drawer.

Naming variables

We have already talked about the importance of a variable's name to reserve space and retrieve the data of a variable. They should be named in such a way that we can use them easily. However, there are some extra guidelines that variable names need to adhere to for them to be valid.

Using the correct characters

Variable names in GDScript cannot contain spaces. They can only consist of alphanumerical or underscore characters. Other characters will result in errors. So, the safe characters to use are abcdefghijklmnopqrstuvwxyzABCDEFGHIJKLMNOPQRSTUVWXYZ1234567890_.

Note that the name cannot begin with a number. You also cannot choose any of the built-in keywords of the programming language as a variable's name, since this would be tremendously confusing for both you and the interpreter.

> **Important notes**
>
> **Keywords**: Some words have special meanings within GDScript. They execute specific commands – for example, creating a variable. We call these words **keywords**. We'll see a lot more of them throughout the book. Variable names cannot be existing keywords in GDScript.
>
> **Interpreter**: The part of the engine that runs the code is called the **interpreter**. It goes down the GDScript code, line by line, and interprets it as machine-readable code. We'll talk more about this in *Chapter 4*.

The convention of naming variables in GDScript is not to use capital letters and use underscores to separate words; this way of naming variables is called **snake case**, or **snake_case**. I know, I know – I just told you that capital letters are valid characters to use in variable names. But the GDScript convention is to (almost) never use these because they get used in different cases, such as the names of constants and classes. I'll explain different naming and coding conventions further in *Chapter 5*. For now, it's good to know that a coding convention is a guideline for how to style your code. It doesn't say anything about the code's logic, just how it is written.

Using descriptive names

Smart programmers give each variable a descriptive name so that we can see at a glance what data it contains. Use a variable name such as number_of_lives over something such as nol, l, or lives. Although when creating the variable you will know what data it contains, you will forget when you come back to the same code a month or even just a week later. Don't worry about the length of a variable's name. Knowing what kind of data it contains and how it is used matters more.

In short, good variable names should look like this:

```
var player_position
var car_acceleration
var distance_to_goal
```

They should not look like this:

```
var a
var thing
var PLaYerpOsition
var distancetogoal
```

Now that we know how to name variables, let's see how we can create and assign variables in GDScript in the next section.

Variables in GDScript

Let's take a closer look at a variable in a script. Creating and assigning a variable in GDScript looks like this:

```
var number_of_lives = 3
```

In this example, there are four crucial steps:

1. First, we specify that we are creating a new variable by using the var keyword.
2. Second, we specify the name we want this variable to have – in our case, number_of_lives. Because of its name, we know that the data contained within the variable should be the number of lives.
3. Third, we use an equals sign to indicate that we want to assign a value to our freshly created variable.
4. Lastly, after the equals sign, we specify what data to put into the variable – in this example, the number 3.

It's good to note that the assignments work from right to left. This means that the value on the right (3 in this case) will be assigned to the variable on the left (number_of_lives).

> **Important note**
>
> Note that assigning a variable is not the same as a mathematical equation. A mathematical equation, $x = 3$ for example, signifies that both sides are equal. While a variable assignment, `number_of_lives = 3` for example, really stores the value on the right side in the variable on the left.

In the next section, we'll see how we can print variables.

Printing out variables

Until now, my explanation of variables has been abstract. So, let's take some time to create a first script that uses variables!

Open the `main.gd` script we created in *Chapter 1*, and add a line that creates a variable for the number of lives after the line we used to print out *Hello, World*, at *line 7*, like so:

```
var number_of_lives = 3
```

Again, ensure to include the tab at the start of the line. Usually, the editor will add it automatically.

If we run this program, you won't see much of a difference from when we ran it in *Chapter 1*. That is because creating variables doesn't change anything in the execution of the game until we do something with them.

I hear you think, "But can't we use the `print()` command from earlier to print out the variable's value?" We can, so let's do that:

```
print(number_of_lives)
```

The complete code looks like this now:

```
3
4  v func _ready():
5    >|    print("Hello World")
6    >|
7    >|    var number_of_lives = 3
8    >|    print(number_of_lives)
9
```

Figure 2.2 – Printing out the number_of_lives variable can be done easily with the print function

When we run the program, we see the following:

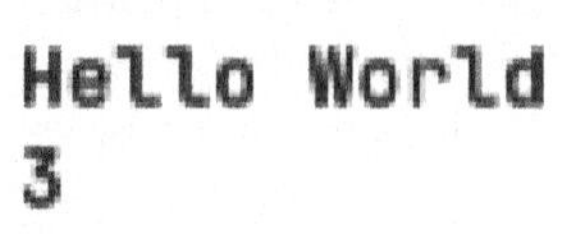

Hello World
3

Figure 2.3 – The result after printing out the number_of_lives variable

This result is already great, but we can do more! We can pass multiple pieces of data to the same `print()` command, and it will print all of them on the same line in the order we provided them; try this line out in our script:

```
print("The number of lives is: ", number_of_lives)
```

Ensure that you put a comma between each piece of data when providing them to the `print()` command. We call a piece of data that we provide to a function an **argument**.

The `printt()` command will print all values, just like the regular `print()` command, but will put a tab between each value. This command is one of my go-to debug techniques, but there'll be more on that in *Chapter 3*:

```
printt("The player has", number_of_lives, "out of", 10, "lives left")
```

As an experiment, try printing something with the `prints()` command. You can use it in the same way as the normal `print()` and `printt()` commands. However, in what way do they differ?

If you did the experiment, you'll see that `prints()` functions the same as `printt()`, but it now puts a space between each passed argument.

Now that we know how to print out variables to observe their values, let's have a look at how to change the values these variables hold.

Changing a variable's value

Unlike data in filing cabinets, data in a video game tends to be updated often, very often, and sometimes hundreds of times per second. Luckily, the syntax to update a variable is even simpler than creating one:

```
var number_of_lives = 3
number_of_lives = 4 + 1
```

The preceding code creates the `number_of_lives` variable and assigns it the value 3, just like before. The step-by-step breakdown of what happens next is as follows:

1. First, we specify what variable we are using so that the computer knows what drawer of its filing cabinet to open up.

2. Next, we use the assignment operator, the equals sign, which signals that we want to change that variable's value to a new one.

3. Lastly, we specify the new value – in this case, the result of 4 + 1. The computer will do the math for us, conclude the result is 5, and assign that value to the variable.

To summarize these two lines of code, we created a variable called `number_of_lives`, assigned it the value 3, and, in the following line, assigned this same variable the value 5.

To take this a step further, you can also use other variables or even the same variable in an assignment like this:

```
var number_of_lives = 3
var fireball_damage = 2
number_of_lives = number_of_lives - fireball_damage
```

At the end of this code, `number_of_lives` will contain the value 1. What happens after the equals sign on line three is as follows:

The computer sees two variable names, looks them up, and substitutes them with their values. It will replace `number_of_lives - fire_ball_damage` with 3 - 2.

As in the preceding example, the computer does the math, concludes the result is 1, and assigns this value to the `number_of_lives` variable.

Extend our script with the preceding example and print out `number_of_lives` again to see the result:

```
 3
 4  ⌄ func _ready():
 5    ⊁    print("Hello World")
 6    ⊁
 7    ⊁    var number_of_lives = 3
 8    ⊁    print(number_of_lives)
 9    ⊁
10    ⊁    var fire_ball_damage = 2
11    ⊁    number_of_lives = number_of_lives - fire_ball_damage
12    ⊁    print("The number of lives is: ", number_of_lives)
13
```

Figure 2.4 – Calculating the new number of lives that the player possesses when hit by a fireball

Okay, we can change the value of a variable now. In the next section, we'll look at what mathematical operations are available to us.

Mathematical operators

In the previous examples, we saw some mathematical operators, adding and subtracting numbers using the + and - operators. We call symbols such as + and – operators because they take data, such as numbers, and operate on them. GDScript provides us with all the expected mathematical operators, which work much the same and in the same order as in regular mathematics.

Operator	Name	Example	Result
**	Power	5 ** 3	125
*	Multiplication	8 * 2	16
/	Division	16 / 8	2
%	Modulo, the rest of a division	5 % 3	2
+	Addition	2 + 4	6
-	Subtraction	6 - 2	4

Table 2.1 – Mathematical operators in the order of how they get applied while executing

Like in ordinary mathematics, we can use parenthesis to execute parts of equations first – for example, (4 + 3) * 7.

> **Learn more**
>
> Want to learn more about the operators in GDScript? Check out the official documentation: https://docs.godotengine.org/en/stable/tutorials/scripting/gdscript/gdscript_basics.html#operators

As an experiment, try dividing a number by zero and see what happens. If you can't close the game window while running the program now, you can click the **Stop Running Project** button (see *Figure 2.5*) to force it to stop.

Figure 2.5 – The Stop Running Project button

Mathematical operators are the backbone of all data manipulation in programming. There is a way to write these mathematical equations more compactly. Let's look at one of those methods next.

Other assignment operators

We have assigned new valuesv to variables using the assignment operator (=), but there are other variations on this operator. Often, you want to add a number to a variable and store the result back in the same variable – for example, tracking the number of lives after a player heals from damage:

```
number_of_lives = number_of_lives + 2
```

This is such a frequently returning use case that there are special operators for this – +=, -=, *=, /=, %=, and **=. If we rewrite the previous example with one of these operators, we get this:

```
number_of_lives += 2
```

This code says, take the value of number_of_lives, add the number 2 to that, and assign the result back to number_of_lives.

The other assignment operators follow the same structure, just with other operations such as subtraction, multiplication, division, modulo, and power. Note that you cannot use these special assignment operators while creating the variable because it will not exist yet.

As an experiment, try using one of these special assignments while creating a variable and see what error pops up.

If we use the -= operator to subtract the fireball damage from the number of lives, we get this code:

```
3
4   func _ready():
5       print("Hello World")
6
7       var number_of_lives = 3
8       print(number_of_lives)
9
10      var fire_ball_damage = 2
11      number_of_lives -= number_of_lives
12      print("The number of lives is: ", number_of_lives)
13
```

Figure 2.6 – Using the -= assignment operator to subtract the fireball damage from a player's health

We learned all about variables and how to change them during the execution of our game. In the next section, we'll take a look at the different types of data we can store in these variables.

Data types – Integers, floats, and strings

Until now, we've only worked with numbers, but variables can hold many different data types. In this section, we'll go over three of the most used data types. Throughout the book, we'll see even more types whenever they are applicable.

Integers

Integers are whole numbers, such as 1, -422 or 10983457. They do not contain a decimal point. They work very well for counting the number of lives or bullets. An integer in the GDScript can be any value between -9223372036854775808 and 9223372036854775807. This is a limit that is imposed by the way numbers are represented within the computer using bits; it's not an arbitrary number imposed by Godot itself. The number will wrap around and switch from very, very high to very, very low if you cross this barrier in any direction, which is not recommended. Luckily, this range gives us more numbers than the number of stars in our galaxy by a few magnitudes, so we should be safe:

```
var big_number = 9223372036854775807
big_number = big_number + 1
```

After running this code, our variable, `big_number`, will contain the smallest number possible in a GDScript integer!

Floats

Floats, also known as **floating point numbers**, are numbers containing a decimal point (also known as a **floating point**), such as 3.41, -1978.8791, or 1.0. They are very well-suited to handle more specific numbers, speeds, positions, or estimations of real numbers, such as pi for example. A float in GDScript has a precision of up to 14 decimal digits.

> **Important note**
> Integers can be stored in a float, as long as they are small enough, without problems. However, when we store a float in an integer, everything after the decimal point will be thrown away! This is called **implicit type conversion**, because we implicitly convert the float to an integer.

A curious thing to know is that computers are very bad at dealing with floating-point numbers. Because of the way computers work, they cannot accurately represent every possible number and, thus, will have to round them off at some point. This results in minute deviations from what you would expect the result of a calculation to be. We will not have to worry about this too much, but it comes up sometimes and is good to remember.

For example, the next line of code sums `0.1` and `0.1`. You would expect the result to be `0.2`, but what do you actually observe? Don't worry about the weird string at the beginning; this makes sure it prints the result with `20` digits behind the decimal point. What matters is the summation between the parenthesis:

```
print("%.20f" % (0.1 + 0.1))
```

The result might be different on different computers – for me, this line prints out `0.20000000000000001000`.

And although the difference between `0.2` and `0.20000000000000001` is very, very small, they are two different numbers for the computer.

Of course, programming languages can also handle data that is not a number. Let's have a look at text.

Strings

Ah, our first non-numerical data type. **Strings** are basically text. They are called strings because they represent a series (string) of characters. We already dealt with a string in *Chapter 1*, when we printed out *Hello, World*. Everything within double (`"`) or single (`'`) quotes is a string. You can store a string in a variable like so:

```
var character_name = "Erik"
```

Strings in GDScript can contain any **Unicode character**, which is basically any character from any global language all over the world and more! Strings can have any length, as long as you don't run out of memory on your computer.

As previously mentioned, you can use double or single quotes to create a string, as they'll both work; just make sure you begin and end the string with the same kind of quote. The convention in GDScript is to use double quotes:

```
"One string, using double quotes, as is convention in GDScript"
'Another string, using single quotes'
```

We had a look at three basic data types within programming languages. In the next section, we'll talk about a special kind of variable that never changes its value – the constant.

What are constants?

We've talked extensively about variables, but there is a second type of container to put data in – **constants**. A constant is a special kind of variable. It also stores any kind of data type, just like variables, but you are not able to change it during the execution of a program; it stays constant. Otherwise, it is exactly the same as a variable and has the same restrictions on its name.

Constants in GDScript

Let's take a closer look at a constant in a script. To define a constant, you need to use the `const` keyword, like so:

```
const MAX_NUMBER_OF_BULLETS = 100
```

Note that the name of this constant is `MAX_NUMBER_OF_BULLETS`. Unlike normal variables, using all capitals is the convention for constants; this is known as **screaming snake case**, or **SCREAMING_ SNAKE_CASE**. This way, we know that we will not be able to change them in our code.

Using a constant is exactly the same as using a variable. Try this out in your code:

```
const FIREBALL_DAMAGE = 2
number_of_lives = number_of_lives - FIREBALL_DAMAGE
print("The number of lives is: ", number_of_lives)
```

This snippet of code should print out the following:

```
The number of lives is 3.
```

As an experiment, try to assign a new value to a constant and see what error pops up:

```
const FIREBALL_DAMAGE = 2
FIREBALL_DAMAGE = 10
```

The interpreter will throw the following error:

```
Cannot assign a new value to a constant
```

You can see the result in *Figure 2.7*:

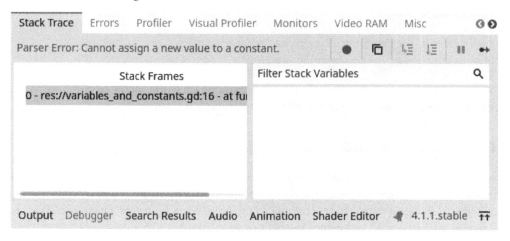

Figure 2.7 – Changing a constant will result in an error

Next to defining values that cannot change, constants also help us by associating a name to the value so that we don't have to use raw values. The name of a constant helps us give context to what the value of the constant represents. Let's look why this important with magic numbers next.

Magic numbers

Lastly, constants are used to remove **magic numbers**. In programming, we call a number a magic number when it is just a number within code without any context, such as the following:

```
number_of_lives += 5
```

From this snippet of code, you wouldn't be able to deduce why I added 5 to the number of lives, but with a properly named constant, we can clarify this, like so:

```
const LIVES_RESTORED_BY_HEALTH_POTION = 5
number_of_lives += LIVES_RESTORED_BY_HEALTH_POTION
```

Magic numbers are generally bad and make your code harder to read and follow.

Constants are used a lot to keep code clean; they show us what values should never change. They are also useful during debugging because you know they will never change, and you don't have to trace what their value is throughout the execution of the game.

So far, we have covered all the basic concepts related to variables and constants. Now, let's have a look at how we can create new scenes before diving into control flows.

Creating new scenes

We have been experimenting with the same scene and script file for now. Working like this was okay for now, but we need a way to create different scripts for different topics and solutions to separate all lessons. This way, we don't have to throw away all our previous experiments and can have a clean scene every time.

Luckily, we can easily make a new scene and use a different script. We can even name the scene to identify what happens within.

> **Important note**
>
> Remember that a scene is a separate file that can be executed. It contains a collection of nodes. For now, we only use one root node. Later, from *Chapter 6*, we will work with more intricate scenes that contain more nodes.

To create a new scene, follow these steps:

1. Right-click anywhere in the **FileSystem** window and choose **New Scene…**.

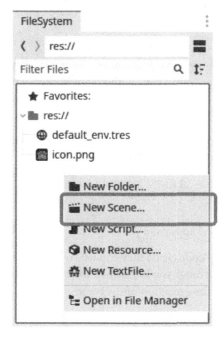

Figure 2.8 – We can select the option to create a new scene by right-clicking in the file manager

2. The new scene will load into the Editor.

3. Choose a 2D scene, just like we did in *Chapter 1*.

4. Name the root node appropriately, such as `ControlFlowTest`.

5. Save the scene.

6. Attach a script to the root node, like in *Chapter 1*. You can leave the name as the default generated from the node's name.

You should repeat these steps for every exercise you do to ensure an orderly project. Want extra plus points? Create folders to organize your code and scenes. They'll be more on organizing projects in *Chapter 5*.

It is possible to move scripts and scenes around to different directories; just make sure you do so within the **FileSystem** dock of Godot Engine itself. This way, the engine tracks where the files move to and ensures everything keeps working.

If you want to run the currently opened scene, click the **Run Current Scene** button (see *Figure 2.9*). The normal **Run** button runs the main scene of the project, while the **Run Current Scene** button runs the currently opened scene.

Figure 2.9 – The Run Current Scene button can be found at the top-right

Alright, we are able to a new scene for each chapter or experiment. Let's make a new scene for the next section and learn about how programs can make decisions using control flows.

Getting started with control flow

By themselves, computers are pretty dumb. They don't know what to do or how to reason independently. In this part of the chapter, we'll learn how to instruct a computer to make decisions based on the data it receives.

Computers do exactly what we tell them to. As you'll come to understand while learning to code, this is a blessing and a curse at the same time. It means that we must be very precise in formulating what we desire from them. Luckily, there are multiple structures to provide these instructions.

The if statement

The easiest way to make decisions, on a computer or otherwise, is by using an `if` statement. An `if` statement looks like this: *If the player's health is below zero, end the game.* We could generalize this as *if a certain condition is true, perform an action.* The code to make this decision could look like this:

```
if number_of_lives < 0:
    print("You died!")
```

This code can be read as a sentence: *if the number of lives is below 0, print out You died!.* The separate parts of the code are:

- The `if` keyword indicates that we start an `if` statement.

- A condition – in this case, `numbers_of_lives < 0`.

- The condition is followed by a colon (`:`), indicating the beginning of the code block that will get executed *if* the condition is true. In the English language, a comma often performs the split between the two.

The general structure of an `if` statement goes like this:

```
if <condition>:
    <code block>
```

Note that the code block is indented once to the right using one tab.

The simplest conditions just compare two values against each other. In GDScript, the operators to compare values are listed in *Table 2.2*:

Operator	Name	Example	Result
==	Equal	2 == 3 - 1	true
!=	Not equal	2 != 2	false
>	Greater than	5 > 2	true
<	Smaller than	4 < 1	false
>=	Greater than or equal to	2 >= 6 - 1	false
<=	Smaller than or equal to	5 + 1 <= 2	true

Table 2.2 – Operators to compare values in GDScript

> **Important note**
>
> The equal operator uses two equal signs (==). It will be interpreted as an assignment operator if you use a single equal sign (=).

As an experiment, try printing the result of the following: `print(10 == 5)` or `print(3 >= 1)`.

If you did the previous experiment, you would see that the `true` and `false` values were printed in the console. These indicate whether the condition was evaluated as `true` or `false` by the computer. This is a new data type we call a **Boolean**. You can put a Boolean in a variable, just like any other data type:

```
var player_died = number_of_lives < 0
var a_true_boolean = true
```

A variable containing a Boolean value can then be used in an `if`-statement as a substitute for the whole condition:

```
if player_died:
    print("You died!")
```

Unlike other data types, which could have millions or billions of different possible values, Booleans only have two possible values, `true` or `false`. You can also use these values directly, without storing them.

In the following code, we see a Boolean value used directly in an `if` statement and as a value in a variable:

```
if true:
    print("This code will always be executed")

var always_false = false
if always_false:
    print("This code will never be executed")
```

We learned that `if` statements evaluate conditions and only execute their code block when a condition turns out to be `true`. We also learned about the Boolean data type, which can have a `true` or `false` value. But what if we want to execute another code block if the condition is `false`? Let's find out in the next section.

The if-else statement

We use `if` statements in everyday conversations all the time. An extension to this structure, which we also use very frequently, is the `if-else` statement. Let's say a player needs to acquire points within a game, and at the end, they win if they have at least 50 points. *If the player's score is higher than or equal to 50, they win the game; otherwise, they lose*. We can generalize this again as *if a certain condition is true, perform one action; if this condition is false, perform another action*.

In GDScript, we express the `if-else` statement like so:

```
if score >= 50:
    print("You Win!")
else:
    print("You Lose!")
```

The general structure of an `if-else` statement goes like this:

```
if <condition>:
    <code block>
else:
    <code block>
```

The `if` statement gets extended with an `else` statement that is at the same level as the `if`. Note the colon (`:`) after the `else` keyword and further indentation, signaling the beginning of a new code block.

Note that you can write two `if` statements that have the exact same behavior as an `if-else` statement. The condition of the second `if` statement just has to cover everything the first one didn't:

```
if number_of_lives < 0:
    print("You died!")
if number_of_lives >= 0:
    print("You live!")
```

You usually will not do this, as a standard `if-else` structure is more straightforward in the code.

As an experiment, create a new scene and rewrite the previous code snippet with an `if-else` statement.

The elif statement

Sometimes, you want more than two different outcomes. Luckily, we can extend an `if`-statement with as many `elif`s as we like. `elif` is an abbreviation of *else if* and functions much the same as a normal `if` statement, except that it always comes after an `if` statement:

```
if number_of_lives < 0:
    print("You died!")
elif number_of_lives <= 1:
    print("You could die with only one blow!")
elif number_of_lives <= 3:
    print("You don't have a lot of lives left.")
else:
    print("You LIVE!")
```

First, the computer will evaluate the first `if` statement. If it is `true`, it will run its code and stop there. If it returns `false`, it will go to the next `elif` statement. If that one is `true`, it will run its code and stop there. If it is `false`, it will go to the next `elif` and so on. If none of these return `true`, the computer will default to the code within the `else` statement, if there is one.

Note that if you tested a condition in a previous `elif`, you can be sure it is `false` in consecutive `elif` conditions. This is because if it would have been `true`, the computer would have stopped there and executed that `elif`'s code block. Therefore, you don't have to recheck previous conditions again.

The general structure of an `if-elif-else` statement goes like this:

```
if <condition>:
    <code block>
elif <condition>:
    <code block>
<more elif statements>
else:
    <code block>
```

That concludes our exploration of the different if statements. Now, let's have a look at how we can add commentary to our code to clarify what we are trying to achieve.

Commenting in code

Like writing a book, code can get complex as it grows in length. On top of that, although you may understand what a piece of code does while writing it, you can forget what it actually does when returning to it after weeks or months. We have been naming our variables correctly, which is one of the best ways of combating this issue, but there is another powerful method – **comments**.

Comments are text in your code that is not executed while running the game. So, they are purely there for somebody reading the code to understand what it does.

Comments in GDScript start with the hash sign (#). Everything after a hash symbol will be ignored by the GDScript interpreter, such as the following:

```
# This is a comment and will be ignored by Godot
var number_of_lives = 2 # This is also a comment
```

From now on, I'll start using comments in code examples to give extra context, and I encourage you to do the same! I'll also use comments to summarize and substitute actual code, leaving the exact implementation as an exercise for you.

Another interesting use for comments is to comment out certain lines of code when you don't need them momentarily but don't want to remove them completely from the code. That could look like this:

```
# var number_of_lives = 2
var number_of_lives = 5 # Let's try 5 lives instead of 2
```

The shortcuts to comment out pieces of code in the Godot Editor is *Ctrl + K* for Windows and Linux and *Cmd + K* for MacOS. Try selecting some code and using these shortcuts to comment out lines here and there.

> **Important note**
> Although comments are pretty great, it's always better to name your variables properly, so don't slack off on that.

Indentation

Consecutive lines of code with the same amount of whitespace on their left belong to the same code block. We call this whitespace **indentation** because we indent the code toward the right.

As an experiment, try not indenting the code block after an `if` statement and see what error pops up.

We can even nest code blocks. We already do this with functions and `if` statements, but it's also possible to nest an `if` statement within another `if` statement, like so:

```
var number_of_lives = 0
var damage_type = "fire"

if number_of_lives <= 0:
    print("You died!")
    if damage_type == "fire":
        print("By going up in flames")
    elif damage_type == "water":
        print("By drowning")
```

You can see indentation as a pyramid; each layer builds upon the previous one, and each time, we go one layer deeper. So far, we have seen that functions and `if`-statements require a code block, but shortly, we'll see more structures that will need one.

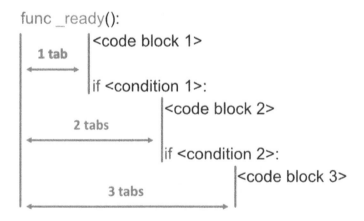

Figure 2.10 – Indentation separates different code blocks

Indentation in GDScript is critical.

> **Important note**
> Indentation is also important in Python, a language that has a lot of similarities with GDScript. Most other programming languages don't really care about indentation, but they use other methods to delimit code blocks, such as the renowned curly brackets ({ }).

For each code block, the type of whitespace *and* how much should be the same. We have been using one tab per indentation layer as we go deeper. The other kind of whitespace you could use are regular space characters, such as the ones between the words of a sentence. There is a whole debate on whether tabs or spaces are the best. I like tabs, but if you want to use spaces, use at least four of them to signal a new code block.

> **Important note**
>
> The code in this book does not use tabs for layout reasons; that is why I advise against copy-pasting code into your game. You can use the complete code available in the GitHub repo of the book here: `https://github.com/PacktPublishing/Learning-GDScript-by-Developing-a-Game-with-Godot-4`

As an experiment, try to use tabs in one line and spaces in another line of code of the same code block to see what error pops up.

If you look closely at your script in the Script editor, you'll see that it visualizes indentation using the tab symbol, as demonstrated in *Figure 2.11*.

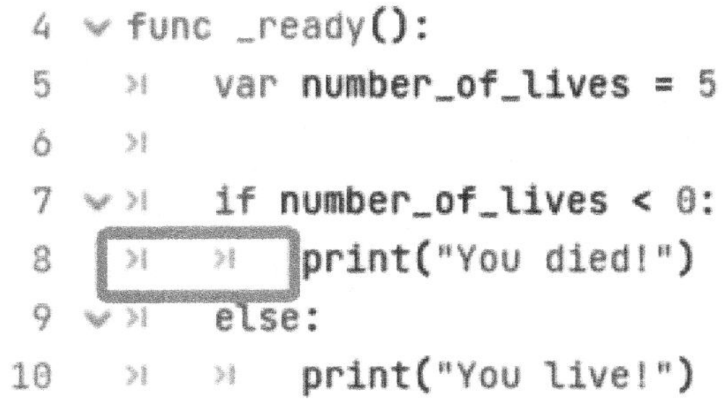

```
4  ⌄ func _ready():
5    ⊐|   var number_of_lives = 5
6    ⊐|
7  ⌄ ⊐|   if number_of_lives < 0:
8    ⊐|    ⊐|  print("You died!")
9  ⌄ ⊐|   else:
10   ⊐|    ⊐|  print("You live!")
```

Figure 2.11 – The Script editor shows tabs within the code

In this chapter, we saw that GDScript expects a code block to be present after an `if` statement. In *Chapter 3*, we'll learn about more structures that require code blocks.

Boolean logic

Computers don't understand ambiguity. Conversely, human language is very ambiguous. We can do this because we regard the full context of a conversation. For example, the sentence *"Do you like coffee or tea?"* could be interpreted in two different ways:

- It could enquire whether you like one over the other
- It could enquire whether you like either of them

Depending on the context, both *Tea* or *Coffee* and *Yes* or *No* are possible answers to that question. Computers, however, only know about what you tell them at any given moment. So, a computer would be happier with the sentence "*If you needed to choose any of the two options, do you like coffee or tea?*" But then again, how do you express all this in code?

To deal with this, an intelligent mathematician came up with **Boolean logic**, named after that intelligent mathematician himself, George Boole. This small, unambiguous language makes it easier to talk to computers. It concerns getting a *true* or *false* answer from statements, just the thing we need to plug into `if` statements. Boolean logic has three major components:

- **Statements**: We used these earlier, such as `number_of_lives == 2` or `5 < 1`.

- **Operators**: These combine statements to create more extensive statements. The most used operators, and the ones we are interested in, are `and`, `or`, and `not`.

- **Parentheses**: Like in regular math, parentheses change the order in which a computer evaluates statements.

These three elements combined are very powerful. A statement in Boolean logic looks like this:

```
number_of_lives < 2 and is_hit
```

Here, I use the `and` operator to combine two statements into a single big one. The statement will return `true` if, and only if, both the smaller statements it combines return `true` – that is, if `number_of_lives` is smaller than 2 *and* `is_hit` is `true`. In all other cases, this will return `false`.

Another statement in Boolean logic could look like this:

```
number_of_lives < 2 or damage >= 6
```

In this sentence, we use the `or` operator. The statement will return `true` if `number_of_lives` is smaller than 2 *or* the amount of damage is larger or equal to 6. So, there is only one case in which the statement returns `false` – when the number of lives is 2 or higher *and* the damage is smaller than 6.

To visualize these relationships of the operators, have a look at the following tables, called truth tables. *Table 2.3* shows the results of the `or` operator for all the possible values of the two conditions it combines.

P or Q		
P	**Q**	**Result**
True	True	True
True	False	True
False	True	True
False	False	False

Table 2.3 – The possible outcomes of the or operator

Table 2.4 shows the results of the and operator for all possible values of the two conditions it combines.

P and Q		
P	**Q**	**Result**
True	True	True
True	False	False
False	True	False
False	False	False

Table 2.4 – The possible outcomes of the and operator

The and and or operators can also be combined into one statement to make it as long and complex as we want:

```
number_of_lives < 2 and damage >= 6 or is_hit
```

In such a case, the and operator will always get evaluated first, followed by the or operator. This means that number_of_lives < 2 and damage will get evaluated first, after which the result will be combined with or is_hit.

To overrule this behavior, you can use parentheses. For example, if you want to evaluate damage >= 6 or is_hit first, you can use parentheses, like so:

```
number_of_lives < 2 and (damage >= 6 or is_hit)
```

The last operator that interests us is the not operator. This one negates statements, transforming a true statement into a false one, and vice versa, such as the following:

```
not damage >= 6
```

This statement returns true if the damage is smaller than 6 and false if it is larger or equal to 6. Note that the not operator doesn't combine two statements but works on only one.

You can also use not in front of the parentheses to negate a whole group of statements, like so:

```
number_of_lives < 2 and not (damage >= 6 or is_hit)
```

To visualize the result of the `not` operator, see the following table:

not P	
P	**Result**
true	false
false	true

Table 2.5 – The possible outcomes of the not operator

> **Important note**
>
> In older programming languages, such as C++ and Java, the and, or, and not operators were portrayed by different symbols (&&, ||, and !, respectively). Luckily, in GDScript, we spell them out entirely. You can still use the symbols in GDScript if you like, but the spelled-out ones make statements easy to read and understand. Just read out a statement, and it should make sense in human words, although less ambiguous.

With Boolean logic under our belt, let's have a look at some more control flow structures.

The match statement

In one of the previous examples, we used the `damage_type` variable, which can hold all the different kinds of damage in a game (fire, water, electricity, etc.). If we wanted to do something specific for each type, we could use a whole bunch of `if-elif` statements, like so:

```
if damage_type == "fire":
    # Do something with fire
elif damage_type == "water":
    # Do something with water
# And so on …
else:
    # No damage type matched
```

However, there is a nicer and more powerful way of doing this! Enter the **match statement**. The same piece of code using a `match` statement would look like this:

```
match damage_type:
    "fire":
        # Do something with fire
    "water":
        # Do something with water
# And so on ...
```

```
    _:
        # No damage type matched
```

In this example, you can see that we check whether the `damage_type` variable matches any of the following values. If it does, we execute the block of code underneath it. If none match, we execute the code under the "`_`" case, which you can see as `else` in an `if-else` statement. This case with the underscore is called the wildcard or default case.

The general structure of a `match` statement looks like this:

```
match <variable>:
    <pattern>:
        <code block>
    <pattern>:
        <code block>
    _:
        <code block>
```

Note that the underscore is not mandatory; you can leave it out if you want, as we do in the next example.

The values we match against can also be another data type, such as numbers. We can even have multiple different values for the same case if we separate them using a comma:

```
match a_variable:
    "fire", "water":
        # a_variable had the value "fire" or "water"
    1, 2:
        # a_variable had the value 1 or 2
```

This example shows that the `fire` and `water` values will make the `match` statement execute the first code block, while the values 1 and 2 will make it execute the second one.

> **Important note**
>
> These are not all the kinds of patterns that a `match` statement can work on. For a more exhaustive list, check out the official Godot documentation on the `match` statement at `https://docs.godotengine.org/en/stable/tutorials/scripting/gdscript/gdscript_basics.html#match`.

The `match` and `if-elif-else` statements can be pretty big; let's have a look at a construction that is a bit more compact – the `ternary-if` statement.

The ternary-if statement

The last control flow structure in this chapter is the **ternary-if statement**. We'll touch upon it quickly because a standard `if-else` statement is a more readable way of writing the same behavior, but it's good to know this kind of control flow exists.

Sometimes, you may want to do something like this:

```
var amount_of_damage
if damage_type == "fire":
    amount_of_damage = 5
else:
    amount_of_damage = 1
```

We create a variable, `amount_of_damage`, and assign it the value 5 if the `damage_type` is `"fire"`, and 1 in all other cases. A `ternary-if` statement condenses this whole structure to one line:

```
var amount_of_damage = 5 if damage_type == "fire" else 1
```

This line will have the exact same effect as the preceding code snippet. It's just a lot more compact. The confusing part of a `ternary-if` statement is that it starts with the value that gets returned if the condition is `true`. You should read this as "return 5 if the `damage_type` is equal to `"fire"`; else, return 1."

The general structure of a `ternery-if` statement is as follows:

```
<value> if <condition> else <value>
```

There is a way to chain `ternary-if` statements to create something that functions like an `if-elif-else` structure. However, I would advise against overusing this and would always use a regular `if-elif-else` statement in such a scenario, as it is easier to read and comprehend.

Additional exercises – Sharpening the axe

Want some extra practice? Try out the following exercises in a **new scene and script**:

1. Take the following script and add an `if` statement that checks whether the player has enough money to buy an item. If so, use the variables to print out *"You bought a Potion for 10 gold coins"*. If the player does not have enough money, print out *"You don't have enough money"*. Bonus points if you calculate and print the player's new amount of money after buying the item. The line that says `randi() % 6 + 5` just generates a random `item_cost` between 5 and 10:

    ```
    extends Node

    func _ready():
        var amount_of_player_money = 5
    ```

```
var item_cost = randi() % 6 + 5

var item_name = "Potion"

# Your code
```

2. Complete the following script with all the possible combinations of `true` and `false` for the `and`, `or` and `not` operators:

```
extends Node

func _ready():
    print(true and true)
    print(true and false)
    # Other combinations for the and-operator

    print(true or true)
    # Other combinations for the or-operator

    print(not true)
    # Other combinations for the not-operator
```

3. Rewrite the following code snippet to use an `if-elif-else` statement:

```
var number_of_lives = 1

if number_of_lives >= 10:
    print("You have full health")
if number_of_lives < 10 and number_of_lives > 2:
    print("You still have some life left")
if number_of_lives <= 2:
    print("You are running low on health")
```

4. Rewrite the following code snippet with a `match` statement:

```
var name = "John"

if name == "Eric" or name == "Maria":
    print("Welcome ", name)
elif name == "John":
    print("How are you doing, John?")
else:
    print("Hi ", name)
```

Summary

In this chapter, we learned the basic building blocks upon which all programs are built. Variables are essential to store and manipulate data, while control flow structures give us the ability to make decisions based on Boolean logic.

In the next chapter, we'll extend both concepts. We'll look at more complex variable types (arrays and dictionaries) and two new control flow types (`for` and `while` loops).

Quiz time

- How can we conceptually think about variables in a computer system?
- Which of the following variable names are formatted correctly and descriptively?

    - `var target_position`

    - `var PlayerHealth`

    - `var inventory`

    - `var high score`

    - `var x`

    - `var enemy_name`

- What are the resulting values of the following Boolean expressions?

    - `true` and `true`

    - `false` and `true`

    - `false` or not `false`

    - Not (`true` and `false`) and `true`

    - `false` or not $100 < 500$

- What is indentation and why do we need to indent our code in GDScript?
- What does the following code snippet print out?

    ```
    var number_of_lives = 0
    Print("You live" if number_of_lives > 0
    ```

3

Grouping Information in Arrays, Loops, and Dictionaries

In *Chapter 2*, we learned about the all-important basics of programming: variables and control flow. Although these building blocks may seem rudimentary and limiting, they are already Turing-complete, meaning you can create any program you've ever used with them. I'm not saying that you should or that it would be easy, but you could.

In this chapter, we'll learn about new data structures and more advanced control flows to make our lives easier when dealing with large quantities of data. First, we'll see how arrays can help us create lists of data. Then, we'll learn all about loops, a very powerful control flow structure to execute code blocks multiple times instead of just once. Lastly, we'll learn about dictionaries, a data structure that helps us group other pieces of data in little packages.

In this chapter, we will cover the following main topics:

- Arrays
- Loops
- Dictionaries
- Debugging
- Null

Technical requirements

If you get stuck anywhere, don't forget that you can find an example of everything we do in this chapter in the `chapter03` folder of the repository. You can find the repository here: `https://github.com/PacktPublishing/Learning-GDScript-by-Developing-a-Game-with-Godot-4/tree/main/chapter03`.

Arrays

Often, we want to work with a list of data, such as a list of items the player possesses. An **array** is precisely the data structure we want to use for such occasions: it is a list that can contain elements from other data types; it is a container type.

> **Containers**
>
> We call an array a **container** because we can store and retrieve pieces of data of other data types within them, such as integers, strings, Booleans, and such. An array contains other data.
>
> Containers structure other data so that it is easier to work with.

Let's have a look at what an array is in code and how we can create one and access its elements.

Creating an array

Creating an array looks like this:

```
var inventory = ["Key", "Potion", "Red Flower", "Boots"]
```

Here, we created an array – a list of four strings – and put it in the `inventory` variable. Notice that all the elements of the array are contained within square brackets, `[]`, and that each element is separated by a *comma*.

Creating an array in one line like we did just now is often fine. But sometimes, it can make the line of code too long. Luckily, we can also put every element on a separate line; this promotes readability and makes it easier to edit the array later if we want to add or remove an element:

```
var inventory = [
    "Key",
    "Potion",
    "Red Flower",
    "Boots"
]
```

This snippet of code will create the same array as the one at the start of this section, but with the added benefit that each element is nicely formatted on a new line and thus easier to read.

> **Important note**
>
> Note that we don't have to indent the elements of the array with a tab, but the general convention is to do so and I urge you to do the same. This is part of the clean code philosophy makes it extra clear that these elements are part of the array. We'll talk more about writing clean code in *Chapter 5*.

As an experiment, try printing out a variable that contains an array.

Accessing values

Now that we have our list – the array – we want to be able to access its elements. To do this, we must specify the number of the element we want to retrieve within the square brackets, right behind the name of the variable. To get the first element of our array, for example, we must write the following:

```
print( inventory[0] )
# Prints out: Key
```

But what is this? I told you we were retrieving the first element in the array, but I used the number 0 to do so. That is because, unlike human counting, arrays are 0-based, meaning that they start counting from 0. By extension, the second element can be accessed by using 1 and so on:

Contents of inventory	
Index	**Value**
0	Key
1	Potion
2	Red Flower
3	Boots

Table 3.1 – The contents of the inventory array

Zero-based counting makes a lot of sense within the context of mathematic concepts and computer algorithms, so we better get used to it.

We call the position an element is at in an array its **index**.

As an experiment, instead of directly using a number to retrieve an element, try putting a variable that contains a number between the square brackets like so:

```
var index = 3
print(inventory[index])
```

You can also try accessing an element that is not in the array, such as element 1000, and see what errors pop up. Try negative numbers too.

Accessing elements backward

You might have noticed something strange if you tried out one of the earlier experiments where I asked you to access an array's element using negative numbers. Although negative numbers don't always give an error, some return elements from the array.

This is because if you use negative numbers, you access elements within the array from the back! So, the element with index -1 is the last, -2 is the second last, and so on:

```
var inventory = ["Key", "Potion"]
prints("The last item in your inventory is a: ", inventory[-1])
# Prints out: Potion
```

This indexing trick will prove to be very useful.

Changing the elements of an array

An interesting property of arrays is that we can treat each element as a regular variable. To assign a new value to an element, for example, we can just assign it a new value:

```
inventory[3] = "Helmet"
```

We can also use one of the special assignment operators, such as += or -=, that we learned about in *Chapter 2* to directly change one of the values in the array:

```
var array_of_numbers = [1, 4, -74, 0]
array_of_numbers[3] += 4
```

In this previous example, we added 4 to the third element in our `array_of_numbers`, 0, so that the value is now 4.

Using the assignment operator (=) makes it easy to change the elements in an array.

Data types in arrays

Arrays can hold any data type. You can even put multiple different data types in the same array, like so:

```
var an_array = [
    5,              # An Integer
    "seven",        # A string
    8.9,            # A float
    True            # A boolean
]
```

This is bad practice because when you want to access one of the elements, you don't know what you are dealing with. That is why I advise you to always use one data type for all the elements in an array.

Strings are secretly arrays

If you think back to *Chapter 2*, when I said that strings are called that way because they are *strings of characters*, then this might not seem like a big surprise. But a string can be thought of as an array of characters. So, we can get one specific character, just like we would get one particular element in an array:

```
var player_name = "Eric"
print(player_name[0])
# Prints out: E
```

In practice, we use this less often, but it is good to know how strings work under the hood.

Manipulating arrays

So far, we have created arrays, accessed their elements, and even changed those elements. But there are so many more things that arrays can do. Unlike the standard data types we've already encountered, arrays provide functions to us that we could use. Functions are little pieces of code, just like the _ready() function we have been writing for each scene, that provides functionality and can do things for us.

For example, one of these functions can append an extra element at the end of an array:

```
var inventory = ["Key", "Potion"]
inventory.append("Sword")
```

Try printing out this variable; it will show [Key, Potion, Sword]. Cool, right?

As you can see, to call a function of an array, add a point (.), followed by the name of that function, to the name of that array. This also applies to other data types.

But what if we want to append one array to another one? Well, there is a function for that too:

```
var loot = ["Gold Coin", "Dagger"]
inventory.append_array(loot)
```

Now, the whole loot array will be appended at the end of the inventory.

But wait, there's more! What if you need to remove an element? You use the remove_at() function. This function removes an element of the array at a certain index:

```
inventory.remove_at(1)
```

This will remove the element at index 1. But what if you don't know the position the element is at? You can always find it!

```
var index_of_sword = inventory.find("Sword")
inventory.remove_at(index_of_sword)
```

The `find()` function will return the index of the element we were looking for. If it finds nothing, it will return the number -1. So, it's best to check if the number it returns is equal to or larger than 0; otherwise, you might remove the wrong element.

The `remove_at()` and `find()` functions are very useful in their own right, but there is also a function that combines the two into one! This is the `erase()` function, and it can be used like this:

```
inventory.erase("Sword")
```

This last line of code will give the same result as the snippet of the two lines before because it removes the first instance of `"Sword"` it finds within the array.

Arrays are an important concept in programming. They dynamically hold an arbitrary number of elements.

After a small detour into debugging in the next section, we'll learn how we can loop over these elements and run code for each of them separately using the `for` and `while` keywords.

Don't be scared of errors or warnings

We've encountered errors here and there while writing code, especially during some of the experiments. These errors often contain valuable information about the problem and how to solve it. Let's examine the following piece of code:

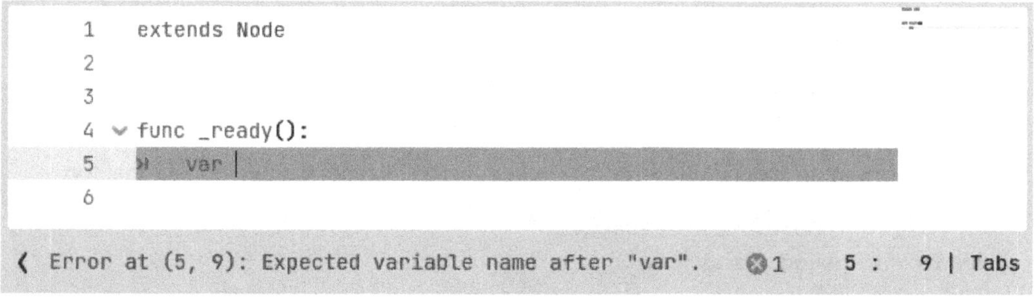

```
1    extends Node
2
3
4  ⌄ func _ready():
5  ≫   var |
6
```

```
❮  Error at (5, 9): Expected variable name after "var".    ⊗1    5 :    9 | Tabs
```

Figure 3.1 – An error tells us that the var keyword should be followed by the new variable's name

Here, I stopped typing halfway while defining a variable. The code editor immediately gave me an error. As shown at the bottom, it is telling me it expected a variable's name. Thanks for the hint, engine!

Let's look at an error that the engine can't predict before running the code:

```
func _ready():
    var inventory = [
        "Boots",
        "Bananas",
        "Bees"
```

```
]

print(inventory[100])
```

At first glance, this code might look okay, but if you put it in a script and run it, you'll see the following error pop up:

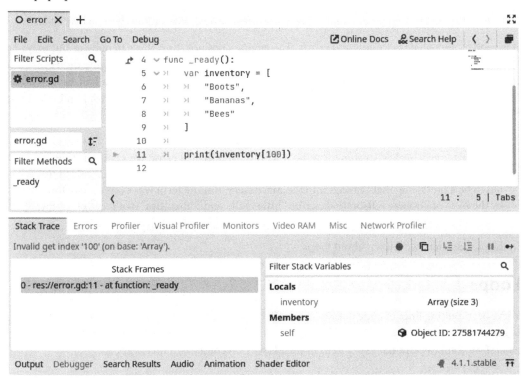

Figure 3.2 – After running this code, the interpreter warns us that
the inventory array does not have a 101st element

The **Debugger** panel opened up, clearly stating that there was an *Invalid get index '100' (on base: 'Array')* error. This means we used an invalid index to retrieve an element from an array. We can also see a yellow arrow showing the exact line where the error occurred. From this, we can conclude that the inventory array does not have a 101st element and thus, we should not try to print it out.

Some errors and warnings already pop up while writing the code, such as the first one we saw in this section. This makes it easy to ensure what we write will run. Unfortunately, writing code that does not contain errors or warnings at this stage does not guarantee that executing this code will be error and warning-free. This is because, from the moment we run a piece of code, it can encounter scenarios the code parser could never have considered.

These runtime errors and warnings occur because GDScript is a weakly typed language, meaning that any variable can have any type and could even switch types mid-execution. Here's a simple example:

```
var my_vairable = 5
my_variable = "Hello, World"
```

But this means that during execution, a piece of code could crash. In *Chapter 4*, you'll learn how to deal with this uncertainty in an elegant way that keeps the flexibility of loosely typed variables.

It is good to appreciate warnings and errors. The engine does not show these to bully us but to nudge us in the right direction to create a better, more solid piece of software. If the engine didn't care and didn't crash the game when an error occurred, for example, then we might ship a half-broken game. This is not what we want! We want the best experience for our players with the lowest number of bugs!

> **Bugs**
>
> When a game is broken in some way, be it a crash or a logical error, we say it has **bugs**. This terminology comes from one of the first times a computer malfunctioned and the culprit turned out to be a literal bug that crawled into the machinery. But the term was even used before that by the likes of Thomas Edison to describe "little faults and difficulties" in a piece of hardware.

In the next section, we'll learn about loops.

Loops

We've been putting lines of code one after the other and Godot Engine executed them nicely from top to bottom. But there comes a time when we want to repeat one or multiple lines of code. For example, what if we want to print out every item in the player's inventory in a nice way?

We could do something like that with the following code:

```
var inventory = ["Boots", "Bananas", "Bandages"]
for item in inventory:
    print("You possess ", item)
```

This is called a **loop**; this specific one is a **for loop**. We'll have a look at the two kinds of loops that are present in GDScript in the next few sections.

For loops

 A **for loop** will repeat its code block for every element of an array. In the case of the example provided in the introduction, this element will be available in the variable that is only valid within the `for` loop called **item**. Of course, we can use the same structure for other arrays and call the temporary variable differently. I chose the name *items* because that is what an inventory contains. Another suitable name could be *item_name*.

We can visualize the `for` loop with the following flow chart:

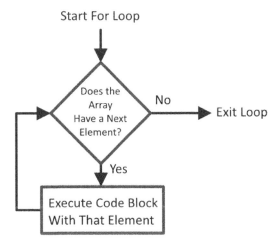

Figure 3.3 – The flow of a for loop during the execution of the code

As shown in *Figure 3.3*, we start the loop from the top. If there is a first element, we follow the *Yes* and execute the code block within the loop for that element. Then, we check if there is a next element. If so, we execute the code block again, now for that element, and so on until there are no more elements left.

The **syntax** – that is, the general structure – of a `for` loop looks like this:

```
for <temporary_variable_name> in <array>:
    <code_block>
```

> **Syntax**
> The preceding structure is also called the syntax of the language. It captures the rules of what is possible and how things should be specified in the language.

A `for` loop is a very powerful control flow structure. Let's have a look at some other use cases in which we can use it.

Range function

Sometimes, you will want to iterate over all indexes within an array. To do so, you can use the `range()` function, which is built into the engine. This function returns an array from 0 to a specified number. Here's an example:

```
var numbers_from_0_to_5 = range(6)
print(numbers_from_0_to_5 )
```

This code will print out [0, 1, 2, 3, 4, 5].

Notice that we gave the number 6 to the function but that the array stops at the number 5.

We can use the range() function like so:

```
var inventory = ["Boots", "Bananas", "Bandages"]
for index in range(inventory.size()):
    print("The item at index ", index, " is ", inventory[index])
```

Here, I called the size() function on the inventory array; this returns the size of the array, which we then can plug right into the range() function.

The range() function can even do more than this. If you provide it with two numbers, it will create an array that starts from the first number and goes up to the second one, excluding it again. Try this:

```
for number in range(10, 20):
    print(number)
```

As an experiment, try constructing a for loop with the preceding range() function and print the result – that is, range(16, 26, 2).

You'll see that we go from 16 to 26 as expected. But this time, the interval between each number is 2. So, we should get the numbers 16, 18, 20, 22 and 24.

The third argument that's given to a range command defines the size of the step we take between numbers.

Now that we have the for loop and range() function under our belt, let's take a look at the while loop.

While loops

The second kind of loop in GDScript is the **while loop**. This loop works a bit like an if statement – we give it a condition and repeat its code block, so long as the condition evaluates to true. Here's an example:

```
var inventory = ["Boots", "Bananas", "Bandages", "Warm Gloves",
"Goggles"]
while inventory.size() > 3:
    inventory.remove_at(0)
```

Here, we remove the first element of the inventory array as long, so the array has a length of more than three elements.

The syntax of a while loop looks as follows:

```
while <condition>:
    <code_block>
```

When Godot encounters a `while` statement, it follows these steps:

1.   First, it evaluates the condition statement. If it is true, it will go to *step 2*; otherwise. it will skip the code block completely and go to *step 4*.

2.   Second, the code block will be executed.

3.   Third, it will go back to *step 1* to evaluate the condition again and see if it has changed.

4.   Finally, it will execute the rest of the code.

So `while` loops will loop so long as the condition we defined returns a `true` value.

We can visualize a `while` loop with the following flow chart:

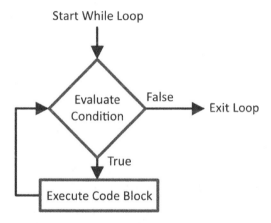

Figure 3.4 – The flow of a while loop during the execution of the code

In *Figure 3.4*, we start the loop by evaluating the condition we specified. If it results in a `true` value, we execute the code block of the loop. If this value is not evaluated to be `true`, we exit the loop.

Infinite loops

The code block within a `while` statement must work toward getting the condition to evaluate false. Otherwise, this will result in an **infinite loop**. Luckily, Godot ensures this does not crash our computer, but it could freeze up your game and make that crash instead!

So far, we have learned about the two basic loops within GDScript. Now, let's have a look at how we can have more control over these loops with some special keywords that we can only use within these loops.

Continuing or breaking a loop

Two keywords can only be used within a loop: **continue** and **break**. Using them excessively or abusing them is not a best practice; you can avoid both if you construct your loop correctly. But they are still essential to know.

The continue keyword

The **continue** keyword can be used within a loop to directly skip back to the beginning. In a `for` loop, this means we go to the next element in the array. In a `while` loop, this means we go back to evaluating the condition:

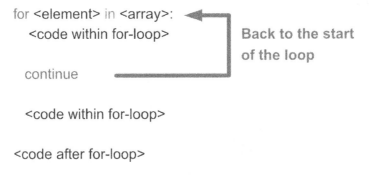

Figure 3.5 – The continue keyword will skip all subsequent code and go back to the start of the loop for the next element in the array

For example, the following code will print out all items in the inventory but skip Banana:

```
var inventory = ["Boots", "Banana", "Bandages"]
for item in inventory.size():
    if item == "Banana":
        continue
    print(item)
```

The result of this loop will be as follows:

```
Boots
Bandages
```

The `continue` keyword is quite useful when you want to skip elements, but what if you want to halt the execution of the loop altogether? That is where the `break` keyword comes in. Let's look at that now.

The break keyword

Sometimes, you'll want to stop the execution of a loop prematurely. In such a case, we can use the **break** keyword:

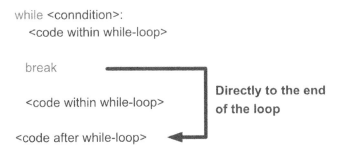

Figure 3.6 – The break keyword will skip all subsequent code and stop executing the loop

The interpreter will drop everything it was doing within the loop and go to the code after it. Here's an example:

```
var inventory = ["Boots", "Bandages", "Bananas", "Warm Gloves",
"Goggles"]

while inventory.size() > 3:
    if inventory[0] == "Bananas":
        break
    prints("Removing :", inventory[0])
    inventory.remove_at(0)
```

This snippet will print out the following:

```
Removing Boots
Removing Bandages
```

Then, it will see that the first item in the inventory is Bananas, so the if statement evaluates to true and we break the loop, stopping it completely.

With that, we've seen how to use continue and break, but as I said earlier, it is possible to write the same loop without these keywords. As an experiment, try rewriting both examples using the **continue** and **break** keywords so that they have the same behavior, but don't use the **continue** or **break** keywords.

Loops allow us to run code for an undefined number of elements, making our code more flexible and dynamic. We will use them throughout this book. Now, let's take a look at another container data type: dictionaries.

Dictionaries

A **dictionary** is another data container, just like an array. But unlike arrays, which store data in a certain order, dictionaries store data using a **key-value pair**. Instead of associating each element with a predetermined number, like in an array, we associate them with a key that we define ourselves. Because we must define our own keys, there is a more rigid structure in a dictionary than in an array.

Creating a dictionary

Let's say that we want to store the name, price, and weight of an item in our game. We can do this using a dictionary:

```
var item = {
    "name": "Boots",
    "price": 5,
    "weight": 3.9
}
```

Here, we use curly brackets, { }, to define a dictionary. Then, we define a key and its associated value within the curly brackets. For example, the `"name"` key is associated with the `"Boots"` value. Each key-value pair must be separated by a comma:

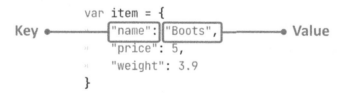

Figure 3.7 – Dictionaries consist of one or more key-value pairs

As an experiment, try printing the preceding dictionary like so:

```
print({
    "name": "Boots",
    "price": 5,
    "weight": 3.9
})
```

Dictionaries help us in organizing the data together in a more structured form. Now, let's have a look at what data we can put in a dictionary.

Data types in dictionaries

What data types can we use for keys and values?

The values within a dictionary can be any data type we like, even arrays or other dictionaries!

The keys, on the other hand, cannot. We can only use simple data types as keys in a dictionary. Strings, floats and integers are valid. More complex data types, such as arrays or dictionaries, are not allowed.

It's good to note that the type of the keys and values don't need to be the same over the whole dictionary. You can use different data types throughout:

```
var a_mess_dictionary = {
    "string_key": [4, 6, 9],
    3.14: "Pi",
    123: {
        "sub_key": "This is a sub-dictionary"
    }
}
```

As you can see, dictionaries are very powerful structures for organizing data.

Accessing and changing values

Accessing and changing a dictionary's values is very similar to how we access the values of an array. Instead of specifying the index of the element within the square brackets, we specify the key of the value we want:

```
var item = {
    "name": "Boots",
    "price": 5,
    "weight": 3.9
}
print(item["name"])
item["price"] += 10
```

We can even use a stored key from within a variable:

```
var key_variable = "name"
print(item[key_variable])
```

Lastly, if the key you are trying to access is a string, you can also get to its value using the following syntax:

```
print(item.name)
```

Just use a dot behind the dictionary's name and then the key. This will not work if the key is anything other than a string, like a number.

Creating a new key-value pair

A remarkable feature of dictionaries is that we can easily add new key-value pairs after the dictionary is created. We can simply do this by assigning a value to a non-existing key:

```
item["color"] = "blue"
```

Here, we added a new key-value pair to the item dictionary with `"color"` as the key and `"blue"` as the value.

Useful functions

Just like arrays, dictionaries have some useful functions that come in handy occasionally.

has

Sometimes, we need to know if a dictionary contains a certain key. In such a case, we can count on the `has()` function:

```
var item = { "name": "Banana" }
if item.has("name"):
    print(item.name)
```

Because the `item` dictionary has a key called *name*, this code will print that name.

erase

We only saw how to add key-value pairs to a dictionary. But with `erase()`, we can also remove a pair:

```
var item = { "name": "Banana" }
item.erase("name")
```

The item dictionary will be empty at the end of this snippet.

As an experiment, try printing out the item dictionary after you erase all keys.

Looping through dictionaries

It might be surprising, but you can loop through dictionaries, just like arrays. For example, if we want to print out all the information in an item dictionary, we could do something like this:

```
var item = {
    "name": "Boots",
    "price": 5,
    "weight": 3.9
}
```

```
for key in item:
    prints(key, "is", item[key])
```

As you can see, the temporary variable, key, carries the keys of the dictionary one for one.

We can also directly iterate over all the values of a dictionary instead of first having to get the keys:

```
for value in item.values():
    print(value)
```

This loop will print out all the values within the dictionary.

> **Important note**
>
> Looping over an array or other data structure can also be called *iterating* over it.

As an experiment, try printing out the values of a dictionary with item.values(): print(item.values())

Nested loops

If you want to have more fun with loops, you can also nest them. By this, we mean you can use a loop within another loop. For example, let's say we have an inventory that is an array of item dictionaries and we want to print out the information of each item in a nice way. We could do something like this:

```
var inventory = [
    {
        "name": "Boots",
        "price": 5,
    },
    {
        "name": "Magical Gloves",
        "price": 10
    },
    {
        "name": "Cool Glasses",
        "price": 58
    }
]

for item_index in inventory.size():
    print("Stats of item ", item_index, ":")
```

```
var item = inventory[item_index]
for key in item:
  printt(key, item[key])
```

First, we iterate over all the elements of the array, which gives us each item dictionary. Then, we iterate on all the keys of that item and print the key and its value.

Of course, you can also combine `while` and `for` loops freely. There are no limits!

With that, we've learned all about the two main looping control flows and the two main container data types in GDScript. In the next section, we'll learn about a new data type: `null`.

Null

Lastly, let me introduce you to a new data type: **null**. This type only has one value: `null`. It carries no information, cannot be changed, and has no functions you can call. So, what is it good for? It is a variable's value when we don't give it one from the start. Try out the following snippet of code:

```
var inventory
print(inventory)
```

You'll see that it will print out `null`. Sometimes, you'll want to do this to ensure a variable exists but don't want to initiate it with a value yet. In the filing cabinet metaphor from *Chapter 2*, this would mean that we reserved a drawer and a name for the variable but haven't filled it with data yet.

Using a variable in any way while it is null will result in an error. For example, the next two operations will result in an error while running the code:

```
var inventory
inventory.append("Boots")

var number_of_lives
number_of_lives -= 2
```

So, it is best to check whether a variable is `null` if you are not sure that the variable is initialized:

```
var number_of_lives
if number_of_lives != null:
  number_of_lives -= 2
```

Some operators or functions return `null` when they cannot complete their task as expected. For example, if you access a key in a dictionary that doesn't exist, it will return the `null` value:

```
var item = {
  "name": "Boots",
  "price": 5,
```

```
    "weight": 3.9
}
print(item["height"])
```

The preceding example will print out `null`.

Additional exercises – Sharpening the axe

1. Write a script that finds and prints out the name of the most expensive item in the following array using a `for` loop. You will need to keep two variables `most_expensive_item` and `max_price`. The `max_price` variable starts out at 0. Now, every time you come across a more expensive item you save that item in the `most_expensive_item` variable and update the new `max_price`. The most expensive item in the following array should be the *Ring of Might*:

```
var inventory = [
    { "name": "Banana", "price": 5 },
    { "name": "Ring of Might", "price": 100 },
    { "name": "Potion of Healing", "price": 58 },
    { "name": "Helmet", "price": 44 },
]
```

2. Write a script that checks whether a specific string is a palindrome; this means that the string should look the same whether you're reading it forward or backward. For example, *rotator* is a palindrome, while *bee* is not. To do this, you'll have to iterate over the string in two directions simultaneously.

Summary

In this chapter, we looked at two new container types, arrays and dictionaries, and two types of loops, `for` and `while` loops. We also learned about useful functions in the string data type and got acquainted with the `null` value.

In the next chapter, we'll learn all about classes, which are custom data types that we can define ourselves.

Quiz time

- What are two container types we learned about in this chapter?

- What is the difference between arrays and dictionaries?

- How do you access the 4th value in the following array?

```
var grocery list = ["Appels", "Flour", "Lettuce", "Jelly",
"Soap"]
```

- How do you access the value of the height in the following dictionary?

```
var person = {
    "name": "Mike",
    "eye_color": "brown",
    "hair_color": "blonde",
    "height": 184,
}
```

- What does range(2, 9) return?

- What is the difference between a for and a while loop?

- When we use one loop inside of another loop, do we call this a nested loop?

- What value does the following variable have?

```
var number_of_lives
```

4

Bringing Structure with Methods and Classes

In *Chapter 3*, we learned about collection types and loops. These powerful concepts helped us to structure our data and run code an arbitrary number of times.

Being able to reuse code in a loop is great, but what if we want to reuse this code at any arbitrary moment in time? And what if we want to reuse whole structures of code and data, such as – for example – enemies or vehicles?

Methods and classes are exactly the concepts that will help us achieve this level of reuse!

Over the course of this chapter, we'll see the last few basic concepts of programming. By the end, we will have learned everything that is needed to call ourselves real programmers.

In this chapter, we cover the following main topics:

- Functions
- Classes
- Type hinting
- Object-oriented programming (OOP)

Technical requirements

If you get stuck anywhere, don't forget that you can find an example of everything we do in this chapter in the `chapter04` folder of the repository. You can find the repository here: `https://github.com/PacktPublishing/Learning-GDScript-by-Developing-a-Game-with-Godot-4/tree/main/chapter04`.

Methods are reusable bits of code

In *Chapter 1*, we learned to write code with the `_ready()` method of a node. We saw that the code contained in this function would be executed from the moment our game started to run. Now, let's look closer at what functions are and how we can use them.

> **Method versus function**
>
> The terminologies *method* and *function* are often used interchangeably. They denote two very similar concepts but applied in different ways. In this book, we'll use both interchangeably.

What is a function?

A **function** bundles a code block as one unit so that we can use and reuse it without having to rewrite the same code. We've already been using functions all over the place. For example, to find the index of an element within an array, we used the `find()` function:

```
var inventory = ["Amulet", "Bananas", "Candles"]
print(inventory.find("Bananas"))
```

Under the hood, the interpreter looks up the code block that is associated with the `find` function, executes it with the `Bananas` string as input, and then returns the result to us.

In the preceding case, we would print out the result. Note that the `print` statement we use in that code is also just a function!

The input data we give to a function is called **arguments**.

To oversimplify the technical aspects, a function is just a detour that our program makes from its normal path of execution – a sidetrack through another code block.

Defining a function

Let's have a look at a function that lowers the player's health:

```
func lower_player_health(amount):
    player_health -= amount
```

As you can see, to define a function, we need the following parts:

- The `func` keyword. This indicates to GDScript that we are about to define a new function, such as the `var` keyword for variables.

- A name. This is the name we will be using to call the function, `lower_player_health()` in this case. Make sure you select a descriptive name, just like with variable names.

- A list of parameters that are separated by commas and surrounded by parentheses; in this case, we only have one parameter: `amount`. These are the pieces of data we want the user of the function to provide us. It is not mandatory to have any parameters.

- The code block that gets executed when we call the function. Within this code block, we can use the parameters of the function as if they were normal variables.

Arguments and parameters

Attentive readers might have noticed that when we call a function, the input data is called **arguments**, and while inside the function, we call them **parameters**. Parameters are basically the input variables of a function, while arguments are specific values with which we call upon the function.

But don't worry about mixing the terminology up; almost every programmer does, and everyone will know what you are talking about.

The basic syntax of a function looks like this:

```
func <function_name>(<parameter1>, <parameter2>):
    <code_block>
```

It's good to note that the number of defined parameters can vary. In the syntax example, we defined two parameters, but we could define none or even a hundred.

As an example, here is a function that simply prints out `Hello, World`:

```
func say_hello():
    print("Hello, World")
```

Naming a function

Function names have the same constraints as variable names:

- They contain only alphanumerical characters.

- There should be no spaces.

- They can't begin with a number.

- They should not be named after existing keywords.

But unlike variable names, it is important that a function's name reflects what the code within the function does. This way, you know what to expect when running a function.

Here are some examples of good function names:

```
calculate_player_health()
apply_velocity()
prepare_race()
```

And here are some examples of bad function names:

```
do_the_thing()
calculate()
a()
```

Naming functions, just like naming anything while programming, is difficult but important. But it is necessary to give everything clear descriptive names.

The return keyword

In `for` and `while` loops, we used the `break` keyword to prematurely exit the loop. In functions, we have a very similar keyword: `return`. This keyword will make the execution exit the function immediately. And to be fair, if you put a `return` statement within a loop, it will also stop that loop because we are no longer executing the function in general.

Put it anywhere in a function and we can return to where we called the function, even if that means there is certain code that will never be executed:

```
func a_cool_function():
    print("This piece of code will be executed")
    return
    print("This piece of code will NEVER EVER be executed")
```

Functions can also return values, just like we saw with the `find()` function for arrays, which returned the index of the value we were searching for. To return a value, we use the `return` keyword again, but this time, we specify the value we want to return right after it:

```
func minimum(number1, number2):
    if number1 < number2:
        return number1
    else:
        return number2
```

We could now utilize this `minimum()` function to get the smallest of the two values:

```
print(minimum(5, 2))
var lowest_number = minimum(1, 300)
```

Running this snippet of code will print the number 2 and will populate the `lowest_number` variable with the number 1.

In this section, we implemented our own `minimum()` function, but this function actually already exists in the engine, called `min()`. So, from now on, you can use the one that the engine provides to find the smallest number.

The pass keyword

When creating a new script, we've already seen the `_ready()` function structured like this:

```
func _ready():
    pass
```

This is effectively an empty function, waiting to be filled in by the programmer. It does nothing. But we still need a code block within the function; otherwise, the engine will throw an error. That is where the `pass` keyword comes in. It is a line of code that does nothing at all. We can thus use it to create a code block that carries no logic. This way, we can create empty functions.

Empty functions are very useful in OOP, which we will talk about in *Chapter 5*.

Optional parameters

To make a function more flexible, you can decide to specify some parameters as optional. This way, you can later choose to provide the arguments or not. To do this, we must provide a default value for that argument.

If you don't give a value for these parameters while calling the function, GDScript will take the default values we specified.

We can use this technique to extend our previous function about removing life from the health total of the player:

```
extends Node

var player_health = 2

func lower_player_health(amount = 1):
    player_health -= amount
```

In the preceding example, the `lower_player_health()` function has one parameter, `amount`, which is optional. We know it is optional because we give it a default value within the definition using the equals sign. If we call this function and give it an argument, it will use that argument to fill in the amount. If we don't give it any argument, it will default to 1 as the value for the amount. We can use this function like so:

```
lower_player_health(5) # Will subtract 5 from the player's health
lower_player_health(2) # Will subtract 2 from the player's health
lower_player_health() # Will subtract 1 from the player's health
```

If a function has multiple parameters, of which one or more are optional, the optional parameters should always come last in the definition. This is because if you leave out one of the arguments, GDScript cannot guess which one and just assumes it is the last one. If we accidentally misorder the parameters, we'll get an error from the code editor to tell us to properly order them.

Let's say we have to write a function that moves the player at a certain angle, with a certain speed, and we also have to specify if the player is running and can collide with things in the world:

```
func move_player(angle, is_running, speed = 20, can_collide = true):
    # function body
```

This `move_player()` function can be used in more diverse ways than the `lower_player_health()` function:

```
move_player(.5, true) # Fill none of the optional parameters
move_player(.5, true, 100) # Fill one of the optional parameters
move_player(.5, true, 1, false) # Fill two of the optional parameters
```

As you can see, we can choose which optional parameters to fill out, as long as we always give them in the order they were specified in the function definition.

Functions are the basis of all programming. Many programs work with just the data types we have learned about until now and functions. But let's take it one step further and learn how we can group data and functions into one cohesive unit using classes.

Classes group code and data together

Finally, we made it to one of the most important revolutions in computer science, something that shook the world of programming languages in the mid-60s: **classes**.

Some smart computer engineers thought about how we use data and functions and saw that we often use a select set of functions on a select set of data. This led them to group these two together so that they would live very closely with one another. Such a group is called a class.

In games, classes often model specific separate entities. We could have a class for the following:

- The player
- Enemies
- Collectibles
- Obstacles

Each of these classes contains and manages its own data. The player class could manage the health and inventory of the player, while the collectibles manage what kind of collectibles they are and what effect they have on the player.

In essence, each class is a custom data type, just like the ones we saw before. But now, we put in the data and functions ourselves! This is a very powerful concept, so let's get started!

Defining a class

To create a simple class, we just use the `class` keyword with the name we would like the class to have. After that, we can start putting the class together by defining the variables and methods that it encompasses:

```
class Enemy:
    var damage = 5
    var health = 10

    func take_damage(amount):
        health -= amount
        if health <= 0:
            die()

    func die():
        print("Aaargh I died!")
```

Here, we see a class called `Enemy`; it has two member variables, `damage` and `health`, and two member methods, `take_damage()` and `die()`.

Instancing a class

You can see the class as a blueprint or template of our custom data type. So, once we have a class with member variables and functions defined, we can make a new instance from it. We call this instance an **object**. Each object stands on its own. This means that there is no data shared between them. To create a new object, we specify the class name and call the `.new()` function on it:

```
var enemy = Enemy.new()
```

Now, this variable contains an object of our very own Enemy class! With this object, we can access its member variables and call its functions:

```
print(enemy.damage)
enemy.take_damage(20)
```

We can also use this object in container types such as arrays and dictionaries and can pass it as an argument to functions:

```
var list_of_enemies = [
    Enemy.new(),
    Enemy.new(),
]
var dict_of_enemies = {
    "Enemy1": Enemy.new(),
}

var enemy = Enemy.new()
any_function(enemy)
```

You can see that instances of a class can be used just like any other kind of variable.

Naming a class

Classes need names, just like variables and methods. Although the name of a class has the same restrictions as that of a variable, the convention is to glue the words within the name against each other and capitalize the first letter of each. We call this **Pascal case** or **PascalCase** because it was popularized in Pascal, a programming language from 1970. Here are a few examples:

```
Enemy
HealthTracker
InventoryItem
```

These are all great class names. In *Chapter 5*, we'll go over some more tips about naming classes.

Extending a class

We can also create a new class by extending an already existing one. This is called **inheritance** because we inherit all the data and logic from a parent class into a child class and extend upon it with new data and logic.

To create a new enemy based on the previous one, for example, we follow this structure:

```
class BuffEnemy extends Enemy:
    func _init():
```

```
        health = 100

    func die():
        print("How did you defeat me?!?")
```

You can see that we follow the new class's name with the `extends` keyword and then the class we want to inherit from. To overwrite the variables of the original class, we have to set them within the `_init()` function. This is a special function, called the **constructor**, that gets called from the moment an object of this `BuffEnemy` class is created. The constructor should initialize the object so that it is ready to be used.

You can also see that we can redefine methods, as I overwrite the `die` function to print out a different string. When the `BuffEnemy` class takes damage and dies, it will call the `die` function of the inherited class and not of the parent class.

If we create an object of the `BuffEnemy` class, we can see that its health is indeed `100` and it will not die from `20` points of damage, and when the enemy dies, it will print out the new string from the overwritten function:

```
var buff_enemy = BuffEnemy.new()

print(buff_enemy.damage)
buff_enemy.take_damage(20)

print(buff_enemy.health)

buff_enemy.take_damage(80)
```

As an experiment, try creating a new enemy by extending the Enemy class yourself.

Each script is a class!

I'll let you in on a little secret. Each script we have written until now is already a class! You might already have realized this after reading the *Extending a class* section because the first line of each script we have written was to extend the Node class! This class is the base class for each type of node in the Godot engine.

This Node class has a bunch of boilerplate data and code that Godot needs to use it during the game. Most of this is not of interest to us at the moment. But some that are of interest include the following:

- **Life-cycle methods**: These are methods that get executed at certain times within the node's life cycle – when it gets created, destroyed, or updated, for example.

- **The child and parent nodes**: In Godot, nodes follow a hierarchical structure, and each node has a reference to its children and parent nodes. Having access to these helps a lot when dealing with a given hierarchical structure.

The node we attach the script to gets paired with that script, and so with the script's data and logic, and is basically an instanced object of the script.

In *Chapter 7*, we'll also learn to extend more specific nodes, such as Node2D or Sprite.

While normal classes are required to have a name, the class that is derived from a script does not, although it is possible to do so. Just use the class_name keyword at the top of the script:

```
class_name MyCustomNode
extends Node
# Rest of the class
```

Godot makes it easy for us to start a new class.

When are certain variables available?

You may have already noticed, but the variables we define are not accessible from everywhere. Each variable has a certain domain within which you can use it. Let's take a closer look at the following piece of code:

```
func _ready():
    var player_health = 5
    if player_health > 2:
        var damage = 2
    player_health -= damage
```

If you type this code out in the script editor, which I encourage you to do, you'll see an error pop up at the last line saying that the variable called damage is not in scope. This means that the variable is not available to us and we cannot use it.

In general, there are five scenarios in which a variable is available to us:

- The variable was defined within the same code block as where we use the variable, like so:

```
var player_health = 2
print(player_health)
```

- The variable was defined in a code block that is a parent to the current code block, like so:

```
var player_health = 2
if player_health > 1:
    print(player_health)
```

- The variable was defined within the current class, like so:

```
extends Node

var player_health = 2

func _ready():
    print(player_health)
```

- The variable was defined globally. We'll learn more about this kind of variable in *Chapter 10*. But it suffices to say that this kind of variable is available anywhere any time, in any script, even in the editor itself. This kind of variable is very useful for storing information used by many different processes. We call these **autoloads**.

- The variable was built into the engine. These variables are exposed to us on a global level; we did not define them ourselves. You can find a list of these global constants and functions here: `https://docs.godotengine.org/en/stable/classes/class_%40globalscope.html`.

Here are a few examples:

```
PI # Carries the constant of pi, about 3.1415
Time
OS
```

The domain within which a variable is accessible is called its **scope**.

While it is not possible to define two variables with the same name within the same scope, it is possible to define two variables with the same name when one is outside the current function and the other inside it. We call this **shadowing** because one lives in the shadow of the other. For example, one variable is defined within the class as a member variable and the other within a function, like so:

```
extends Node

var damage = 3

func a_function():
    var damage = 100
    print(damage)
```

If you run the preceding code, you will see it print out 100, because when in doubt, GDScript will always take the closest defined variable:

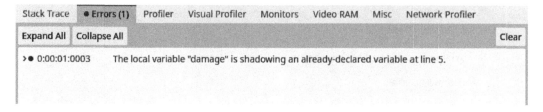

Figure 4.1 – A warning that tells us the damage variable is defined within the script and within the function

However, as shown in *Figure 4.1*, you will also see that the engine throws a warning telling us about the double usage of the variable name, which could lead to confusion for us as developers.

The scope of a function

Functions also have a certain scope, though a little more restricted than the scope of a variable. You can use a function in the following scenarios:

- The function was defined within the class we are using.

- The function was defined within any parent class that our class inherits from.

- The function was built into the engine; these are available from anywhere. Here's an example:

```
print("Hey")
max(5, 3) # Returns the highest of the two numbers
sin(PI) # Returns the sinus value for an angle
```

But, as we saw earlier, we can also call a class function of an object. This way, the scope of that function is as big as the object's scope.

Types help us to know how to use a variable

We saw different data types and even know how to create our own. But there was one big problem! Variables could change type mid-execution. This is particularly annoying because if we use the wrong type of data in a certain situation, the game will crash!

```
var number_of_lives = 5
number_of_lives += 1

number_of_lives = {
    player_lives = 5,
    enemie_lives = 1,
```

```
}
number_of_lives += 1
```

In the preceding code, the first marked line will work, but the second one crashes the game! This crash happens because, in the first instance, we add 1 to the value 5, another number, while in the second instance, we try to add 1 to a whole dictionary. This operation is not supported and thus crashes the game.

Luckily, there is a way we can leverage our knowledge of what data type we expect for certain operations or functions. This is what we will learn over the course of this section.

What is type hinting?

Other popular languages such as C++, C#, Java, Golang, and Rust solve the problem of not knowing what data type a variable is by implicitly specifying what type it will carry from the moment it is defined. There is (almost) no way of defining a variable without locking it to a certain type. Also, the type of a variable, unlike in GDScript, cannot be changed over the course of a program in those other languages.

In GDScript, there is a system to do something such as this too, but less restrictive. This system is called **type hinting** because we give a hint of what type we would like a variable to be in. This helps GDScript to determine beforehand if an operation will work or is going to crash the game.

Let's have a look at different ways to type hint in GDScript.

Type hinting variables

For example, if we want to specify that the player's number of lives will always be a whole number, aka an *integer*, we can give a hint of this variable's type, like so:

```
var number_of_lives: int = 5
```

We can do the same for different data types as well:

```
var player_name: String = "Erik"
var inventory: Array = ["Cool glasses", "Drinks"]
```

If we try to assign a value of a different type to a type-hinted variable, as in the following example, the code editor will give us a warning before we run the game and an error while running it:

```
var inventory: Array = ["Cool glasses", "Drinks"]
inventory = 100
```

Note that we can only type hint a variable while defining it. After the definition, we can freely use the variable, and the engine needs to know if it is a specific type. That is why we cannot just add a type or change it later on.

Type hinting helps us to catch bugs before they happen!

Type hinting arrays

On top of specifying that a certain variable is an `Array` type, we can also specify the type of values we can find within this array. This is very useful and makes it easy for us to know what kind of data to expect within an array.

To specify what data types can be found within an array, just mention this type within square brackets after the `Array` type, like so:

```
var cool_numbers: Array[float] = [3.1415, 6.282, 2.71828]
```

The preceding snippet explicitly specifies that `cool_numbers` is an array of floating-point numbers, and thus every element of this array should be treated as a floating-point number.

As an experiment, try the following line of code. It will error; why?

```
var inventory: Array[String] = ["Cool glasses", "Drinks", 100]
```

If you try it out, you'll see this will error because we are hinting that the `inventory` variable is an array filled with strings. But one of the values within the array is a number. The engine will see this and give an error.

Learning about the Variant type

In the background, GDScript will use `Variant` as, almost, every variable's type. The `Variant` class can hold almost any other data type; that is why we can switch the type of a variable mid-execution when we don't specify a type at its creation.

Also, variables that we type hinted are `Variant` types. But they have extra type requirements attached to them, such as that their value should be an integer or a dictionary.

In GDScript, we never deal directly with the functionality of the `Variant` class. GDScript wraps it nicely around whatever value we assign it, and thus we don't have to worry about the `Variant` type. We can just reason about the data type of the data we are storing in the variable.

Type hinting function parameters

In addition to hinting the type of a variable, we can also hint the type of the parameters of a function in the same manner:

```
func take_damage(amount: int):
    player_health -= amount
```

Now, if you try to call this function with an argument that is not an integer, the editor will warn you that you are making a mistake. For example, take a look at the following line of code, which uses the `take_damage()` function from the previous code snippet:

```
take_damage("Two")
```

Here, the engine will throw an error because the `take_damage()` function expects an integer value, and a string is not compatible with an integer.

> **Automatic conversion of variables**
>
> When you try `take_damage(1.5)`, you'll see that the editor doesn't show a warning or throw an error. This is because GDScript automatically converts certain variables from one type to another. This is called **implicit conversion**.
>
> One of these conversions happens between floating-point and integer numbers. In this case, GDScript will round the floating-point number down to the nearest integer value. For our little example at the start of this callout, this means that `1.5` will be rounded down to an integer value of `1`.

Type hinting can also be combined with a default value for the parameter; just put the type hint first and specify the default value after:

```
func take_damage(amount: int = 1):
    player_health -= amount
```

The `take_damage()` function now takes one parameter, `amount`, which is type hinted as an integer and has a default value of `1`.

Type hinting function returns

We can also type hint the value that will be returned by a function. This is very useful because it gives us a lot of information about what to expect from that function. The way to do this is like so:

```
func minimum(number_1: float, number_2: float) -> float:
    if number_1 < number_2:
        return number_1
    else:
        return number_2
```

This `minimum()` function will always have to return a floating-point number, no matter which `return` statement does so.

As an experiment, try returning nothing in a function that is type hinted to return a floating-point number; you'll see that we get an error thrown at us by the engine.

Using void as a function return

Sometimes, a function does not return a value at all. In that case, we can type hint the return value of that function using the void type. void cannot be used for variables, only in function definitions. So, void indicates that the function does not return anything:

```
var player_health: int = 5

func subtract_amount_from_health(amount: int) -> void:
    player_health -= amount
```

However, most people will omit the void type hint when a function doesn't return anything and only type hint the function when it actually does return something. It is good to know that the void type hint exists when you encounter it somewhere.

Inferred types

There is a second way of typing a variable without explicitly giving it a type. This method leverages the type recognition of the engine itself. We can namely use the type of the first value assigned to the variable as the type of that variable for the rest of the execution. We can do that like so:

```
var number_of_lives := 5
```

This looks very similar to a regular, untyped, variable definition. But this time, we put a colon before the equals sign. This will lock the type of the variable to the type of the value we are assigning to it.

This technique is called **type inferring** because GDScript is just taking the type of the value we are passing it during assignment.

Note that, just like with normal variable type hinting, we can only infer a variable's type while defining it. So, the following code will not work:

```
var number_of_lives
number_of_lives := 5 # This will error
```

Type inferring can make it easier for us to type hint variables without having to think about the actual type in advance.

null can be any type

Knowing what type a variable carries does not mean we don't have to look out for variables that are
null. null can be assigned to any kind of variable that is not a basic type (int, float, String,
and so on). So, arrays, dictionaries, self-defined classes, and the like can still be null if they are
not initialized:

```
var inventory: Array[String] = ["Bananas", "Cinder", "Drake"]
inventory = null # This is legal
inventory.find("Drake") # This will crash the game
```

null is often used to reset variables to an empty state.

Autocompletion

Another great perk of typing our variables is that the text editor will help us out when we want to call
a function or get to a member variable of a class by providing autocompletion. For example, if we have
a string and we start typing to call a function on it, a little popup will show all the possible functions
we are trying to get to. We can then just keep typing or use the arrow keys to select the right function
and press *Enter* to select one. This helps tremendously if you know what you want to do but are not
completely sure what the function was called, or just to speed up typing out long function names:

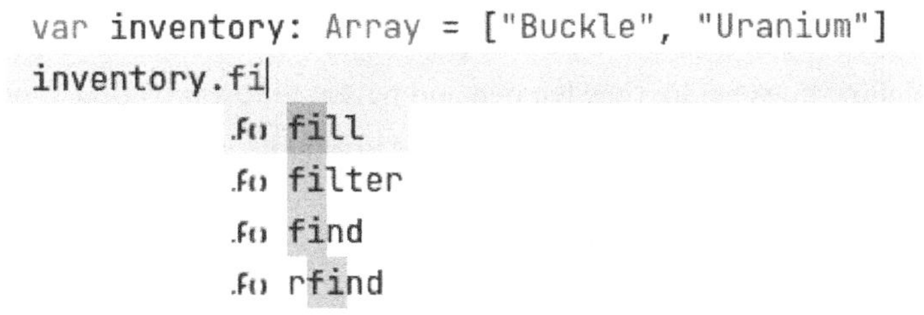

```
var inventory: Array = ["Buckle", "Uranium"]
inventory.fi
            .fo fill
            .fo filter
            .fo find
            .fo rfind
```

Figure 4.2 – The code editor will help us out with autocompletion when using type hinting

Autocomplete is our friend in general, so making the autocomplete, well, more complete will only
help us out in the long run.

Using type hinting for named classes

In addition to built-in types, we can also type hint our own custom classes. But for that, we first have to register a name for the type of our class. To register the name, we can use the `class_name` keyword followed by the name we would like the data type of our class to have at the top of the file, like so:

```
class_name Player
extends Node

var player_health = 2

func _ready():
   print(player_health)
```

Here, we see that we name our class `Player`. We can now use this type to type hint variables of the `Player` class and even use it to initiate a new instance of the class, like so:

```
var player: Player = Player.new()
player.player_health += 1
```

Naming classes is an easy way to type hint variables with instances of our custom classes.

Performance

In addition to catching bugs before they happen and having autocompletion, type hinting has one last big advantage up its sleeve. If you type the variables in your game, the engine will be able to work with them way easier, resulting in better performance.

Because the engine doesn't need to check if a variable will be able to perform certain operations, it can do more of these operations per second. In some cases, this will make your code twice as fast!

Editor adding type hints

As a last tip around type hinting, I would like to show you that the editor can help you out too! If you go into **Editor Settings | Text Editor | Completion**, there is a setting called **Add Type Hints**. This setting will let the editor autocomplete certain parts of your code with type hints. I recommend you turn it on:

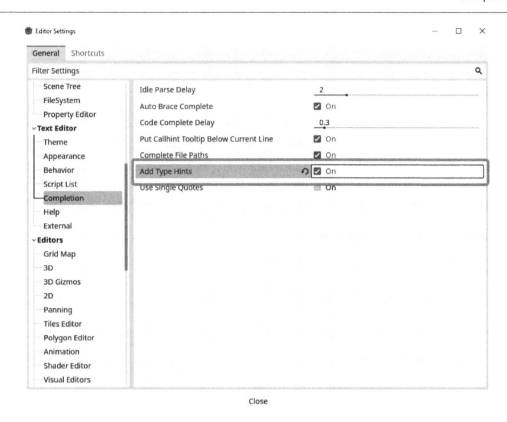

Figure 4.3 – The Add Type Hints setting

With this setting enabled, the editor will automatically fill out type hints whenever it has to generate any code for us – for example, when generating an empty script.

In this section, we learned a lot about type hinting and saw how it can enhance our coding experience. Next, let's take a look at a very important concepts in programming: OOP.

OOP primer

So far in this chapter, we have learned about functions, classes, and objects. These concepts are very powerful: they give us a completely different way of working with data and the logic that accompanies it.

In programming, there are multiple different paradigms of structuring code and data, one of them is **Object Oriented Programming (OOP)**. GDScript is an **object-oriented (OO)** and **imperative** programming language, which means that we group data and its accompanying logic within classes and objects. The logic we write consists of statements that tell the computer fairly exactly what to do and how to do it for us. Each statement changes the internal state of the program. Most game engines and their accompanying programming languages are OO and imperative.

OOP is built upon four key principles: inheritance, abstraction, encapsulation, and polymorphism. So, let's have a look at these.

Inheritance

OOP allows classes to inherit from one another. This means that we get all the functionality from the parent class for free and can extend it with extra logic. This makes reusing code very easy.

For example, while there could be a lot of different enemies within a game, most of those would share some quite common code, and more common code would then differentiate them. Pathfinding, dealing damage, health management, inventory management, and so on would be shared by almost any enemy. So, we could define one class, Enemy, that encapsulates all of these functionalities and from which all other enemies can inherit.

From here, we can define enemies that do the following:

1. Walk up to the player and use melee attacks.
2. Stay at a distance and shoot projectiles at the player.
3. Move around a lot and heal other enemies.
4. And so forth…

This list is non-exhaustive and shows that we can base a diverse cast of enemies on the same base Enemy class.

We can visually represent this inheritance, just like we do with humans and their families, using an inheritance tree:

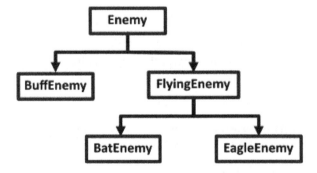

Figure 4.4 – Different kinds of enemies can easily be derived from the base Enemy class

Figure 4.4 clearly shows how certain classes are related and/or differ from one another.

Abstraction

A class hides its internal implementation, abstracting its functionality only by exposing higher-level functions. The user of the class doesn't care how certain results are accomplished; for all the outside world knows, the actual process to get certain results could be pure magic.

For the Enemy class example from earlier, this could mean that we can ask an enemy to move toward a certain point in the world, but not how. We have no business in how the enemy does its pathfinding or how it moves around the world. That is the enemy's business:

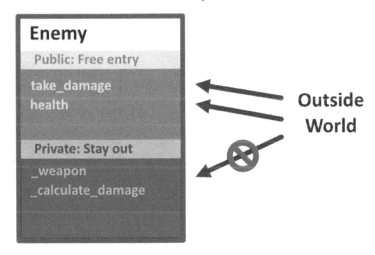

Figure 4.5 – Public and private member variables and methods
tell the outside world how to interact with a class

In most programming languages, abstraction comes in the form of public and private member functions and variables. They work like this:

- **Public**: The outside world can access variables and functions that are marked as public and used to interact with the object.

- **Private**: Variables and functions marked as private are inaccessible by the outside world and can only be used by the class itself. These support the internal functionality of the class.

In GDScript, however, there is no way to explicitly mark variables or functions as public or private. Everything is public by default and accessible to the outside world. But there is a convention that GDScript developers took over from Python developers: we put an underscore (_) in front of variable and function names that are supposed to be private. This way, we can signal that a variable or method is supposed to be private and should not be used by anything outside of the class:

```
extends Node

var health: int = 2 # Public variable
var _weapon: String = "Sword" # Private variable
```

```
func take_damage(amount: float): # Public function
    # Take damage in some way

func _calculate_damage() -> float: # Private function
    # Calculate damage in some way
```

The engine will not enforce such private members, so you can still call them, but this is a very bad practice. You can see this distinction between public and private members built into the scripts we've already written with functions that are already present in the nodes, such as _ready() and _update().

Abstraction has multiple advantages:

- **Security**: Because the user of the class knows only to use public methods and variables, there is a lower chance of them accidentally misusing the class.

- **Maintainability**: Because the functionality of the class is hidden behind a few public functions, we can easily rewrite that functionality if needed without breaking other pieces of code.

  This protects against other classes or pieces of code meddling too much with the internals of a class. Because what if we rewrite the pathfinding of enemies? If we properly encapsulate this code, there is no problem, but if other pieces of code call upon the enemies' pathfinding directly, we will have to rewrite all of these as well.

- **Hiding complexity**: Some code can be very complex, but by using classes, we can hide this behind easy-to-use methods and member variables.

Now that we learned about abstraction, let's look at the last principle: encapsulation.

Encapsulation

A well-written class should encapsulate all important information within itself so that the user of the class doesn't have to worry about the nitty-gritty details. This means that a class should only expose select information to the outside world.

Encapsulation is an extension of abstraction but homed in on a class's data. The less the outside world has to deal with member variables of a class directly and the more with member functions, the better.

Polymorphism

The last principle of OOP is polymorphism, which says that objects and methods can morph into multiple different forms. In GDScript, this happens in two distinct ways: over objects and over methods.

Object polymorphism

Let's say we have a class structure such as the one in the earlier example: a base enemy from which other enemies inherit. The code could look something like this:

```
class Enemy:
    var damage: float
    var health: float

class BuffEnemy extends Enemy:
    var attack_distance: float = 50

    func _ready():
        damage = 2
        health = 10

class StrongEnemy extends Enemy:
    func _ready():
        damage = 10
        health = 1
```

Now, when we make instances of the BuffEnemy and StrongEnemy classes, we can type hint them as such, but we can also type hint them as their base class, Enemy:

```
var buff_enemy: BuffEnemy = BuffEnemy.new()
print(buff_enemy.damage)

var enemy: Enemy = buff_enemy
print(enemy.damage)
```

This works because everything that inherits from the Enemy class should have the same member variables and functions at its core, so it can be put in a variable of the parent class.

But you cannot assign an object from the Enemy type to a variable that is typed as one of its child classes. So, the next line will error:

```
var buff_enemy: BuffEnemy = Enemy.new()
```

The two child classes are also not compatible. So, the next line will error too:

```
var buff_enemy: BuffEnemy = StrongEnemy.new()
```

These preceding two examples don't work because you are not guaranteed that the member variables and functions within the Enemy and StrongEnemy classes will be the same as those in the BuffEnemy class. And indeed, we can see that the BuffEnemy class has another member variable, attack_distance, that the Enemy and StrongEnemy classes do not have.

A good analogy for the concept of polymorphism is vehicles in the real world. Let's say we have three vehicles:

- Cars

- Bikes

- Trucks

Although all three vehicles can move you from one point to another, have a certain number of wheels, and are made of metal, there is a certain hierarchy:

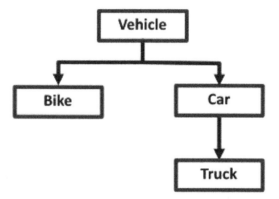

Figure 4.6 – The class structure of simple vehicles

A bike needs somebody to power it, while a car and a truck have motors. Furthermore, we could take the car as a template for the truck and say that the truck is a kind of long, big car.

The truck is also unique from the car because it has a place to transport larger cargo. This makes it so that we can say a truck is a car, but a car is not a truck.

Method overriding

Then, there is also the possibility to override methods from the parent class. This will completely replace the original function with a new one, but only for the given child class. This is very useful when the child class needs some logic to be slightly or even drastically different from that of the parent class. To do this in GDScript, the method in the child class should adhere to the following conventions:

- Have the same name

- Have the same number of parameters

- If the parameters are typed, have the same types

- Have exactly the same default values, if any

You see that we need to be exact when we want to override a method. If we are not, the engine will recognize it as a separate function or error because the overriding was done incorrectly.

Let's look at two classes that demonstrate this. A base class, Enemy, has a function called die() that prints out "Aaargh!". This die function just prints out an exclamation when the enemy dies. Then, we inherit the BuffEnemy class from this base and override the die() function to print out "How did you defeat me?!?":

```
class Enemy:
    func die():
        print("Aaargh!")

class BuffEnemy extends Enemy:
    func die():
        print("How did you defeat me?!?")
```

If you call the die() function of each enemy type, you'll see that they each have their own implementation of the function:

```
var enemy: Enemy = Enemy.new()
enemy.die()
```

The preceding code will print out "Aaargh!", as expected. Now for the BuffEnemy class:

```
var buff_enemy: BuffEnemy = BuffEnemy.new()
buff_enemy.die()
```

Now, we execute the overridden die() function, and the printout will read "How did you defeat me?!?".

Even if you put the BuffEnemy object in an Enemy variable, it will still use the overridden function from the BuffEnemy class:

```
var enemy: Enemy = BuffEnemy.new()
enemy.die()
```

Again, we'll see "How did you defeat me?!?" printed out. This is because the BuffEnemy class inherits from Enemy and thus is of type Enemy, but the implementation of its functions can still be overridden.

We learned a lot about OOP and its principles. It's a very interesting but complex subject. Don't worry too much about getting all principles perfect directly. Knowing they exist is already half the work. Let's wrap the chapter up with some extra exercises in the next section.

Additional exercises – Sharpening the axe

1. Write a function, `limit_inventory()`, that takes an array representing an inventory and an integer. The function checks if the array is longer than the provided integer; if it is, it should remove all items that are too much. Lastly, the function returns the resulting array:

```
var inventory: Array = ["Boots", "Sword", "Grapes", "Cuffs",
"Potion"]
var limited_inventory: Array = limit_inventory(inventory, 2)
print(limited_inventory)
```

This example should print out `["Boots", "Sword"]`.

2. Rewrite the previous function so that the integer it takes has a default value of 3 for the following code to work:

```
var inventory: Array = ["Boots", "Sword", "Grapes", "Cuffs",
"Potion"]
var limited_inventory: Array = limit_inventory(inventory)
print(limited_inventory)
```

This should print out `["Boots", "Sword", "Grapes"]`.

3. Rewrite this code so that it does not error anymore:

```
func _ready():
    var player_health = 5
    if player_health > 2:
        var damage = 2
    player_health -= damage
```

4. Write `Player` and `Enemy` classes that make the following code work. In this code, the player and enemy will damage each other until one of them has a health that is equal to or less than zero. See it as a primitive battle:

```
var player: Player = Player.new()
var enemy: Enemy = Enemy.new()

while player.health > 0 and enemy.health > 0:
    enemy.take_damage(player.damage)
    player.take_damage(enemy.damage)
```

5. Rewrite the `Player` and `Enemy` classes from the previous exercise to inherit from the same base class.

Summary

With functions, classes, and type hinting in our toolkit, we have finally learned all the basic building blocks of programming! From now on, the possibilities are endless!

In the next chapter, we will learn how to write and structure our code in a clean way so that it's easy to use and understand for others.

Quiz time

- Why do we use functions and classes?
- For which two purposes can the `return` keyword be used in functions?
- What is the scope of a variable? What are the different tiers?
- What is the scope of a function?
- Is a class a group of variables and functions?
- Given the following code, how do we make a new instance of the Enemy class?

```
class Enemy:
    var damage: int = 5
    # Rest of the class

var new_enemy: Enemy = ...
```

- How do we call the instance of a class?
- What is type hinting?
- Add type hinting to the following variables:
  - `var player_health = 5`
  - `var can_take_damage = true`
  - `var sword = { "damage_type": "fire", "damage": 6 }`
- In addition to autocompletion and increased performances, what is the final benefit of using type hinting?

5

How and Why to Keep Your Code Clean

In *Chapters 1* to *4*, we learned all the basics of programming and are about to dive deep into developing our very own game.

But before we do so, we must realize that the code base for games can grow very large. This means that the code and systems we write one day can be buried under other code and systems. As a result, returning to our earlier work can be a hassle because we forget how or why we coded certain things in a certain way.

That is why now is the ideal moment to stand still and think about how to keep our code clean and understandable even months after writing it. Most of the things in this chapter were learned through making mistakes myself and having to find a solution in books and articles.

Although most of the tips can feel like critical thinking and will bring you to the same point (which they probably will), it always helps to voice them and explain why programmers employ them.

Holding them in the back of your mind while programming will give you a big step up from other starting programmers.

In this chapter, we will cover the following main topics:

- Naming things (again)
- Writing good functions
- Why use private variables and functions
- Don't repeat yourself (DRY)
- Defensive programming
- Coding style guides

Technical requirements

Check out the `chapter05` folder in the repository of code examples if you get stuck anywhere. You can find the repository here: `https://github.com/PacktPublishing/Learning-GDScript-by-Developing-a-Game-with-Godot-4/tree/main/chapter05`.

Back to naming things

Let's have another look at how to name variables, functions, and classes. Picking the right name for any of these is very important as it will make understanding the code way easier.

Naming conventions

As we saw in *Chapters 3* and *4*, variable, function, and class names have different constraints. We used specific rules to name each. These ways are called **naming conventions**. They give a term to how we want to constrain the formation of names. The three main naming conventions that are recommended in the GDScript style guide are as follows:

- **snake_case**: We have used this naming convention to name all our variables and methods. It is called **snake_case** because each word is connected by an underscore, which looks like a little snake. Example names could be the following: `player_health`, `movement_speed`, and `weekly_highscore`.

- **SCREAMING_SNAKE_CASE**: This is the convention we use to name constants. It is exactly the same as snake case, only all the alphabetical characters are uppercase. Example names could be the following: `BUTTON_SIZE`, `PI`, and `TEAM_A_COLOR`.

- **PascalCase**: We have used this naming convention to name classes and nodes in the scene. It is called **PascalCase** because it was popularized in the programming language **Pascal**. In this convention, we start every word within the name with a capital letter and the rest are lowercase. Example names could be the following: `BackgroundColor`, `PlayerWeapon`, and `GameStartTimer`.

There are a bunch of other, more exotic conventions, like the following: **kebab-case**, **camelCase**, **flatcase**, and so on. But these are not used in GDScript.

General naming tips

Now, let me be clear: naming things is not easy. It is, in fact, one of the hardest things in programming. So, if you have the naming right, you'll always be able to return to any code quickly.

Here are some tips to make you a naming master.

Use meaningful and descriptive names

In the early days, programmers had to work with computers that didn't have a lot of computational power and memory, and they also prided themselves in creating the shortest script to solve a problem. This resulted in code where variables were given one or two-letter names such as a or c5. Optimizing a piece of code to be as short as possible is very satisfying. However, these pieces of code are very incomprehensible. Even the person who wrote the script is not able to read it anymore after some time has passed.

That is why descriptive variable names are a big plus. Sure, they take a few extra seconds to type out, but that is nothing compared to spending minutes or even hours figuring out why a variable exists and how it should be used; and, anyway, autocomplete will always help us out.

Some people even go as far as to say that short variable names result in a better-performing game. This is not true at all. A programming language will tokenize the variables in the code, making any variable name perform equally fast, no matter how long.

The trick is making a variable's, method's, or class's name meaningful and descriptive. To do this, you can ask yourself these questions for the different types:

- **Variables**:

    - What kind of data will the variable contain?

    - How should this data be used?

- **Functions**:

    - What does the function do?

    - What data does the function return?

    - What kind of parameters does the function require to work?

- **Classes**:

    - What will the class be used for?

    - What data is the class responsible for?

Using these questions will guide your decision making while coming up with names for variables, functions, and classes.

Avoid filler words

Although long descriptive names are the way to go, we also don't want to obscure the name with filler or unnecessary words such as the following:

- The

- A
- Object

Such words just bog down the name and make it unnecessarily long while providing no extra meaning.

Keep names pronounceable

Good code should be easily readable. This means that you should be able to read it like a book and it should make sense without you having to look at the content of the function or the data type of the variables.

This also means that we should keep names pronounceable. Use complete words or very common abbreviations if we decide to abbreviate one.

Be consistent

Now, for the most important tip: be consistent in your naming. This way, you can count on your own style of naming and make assumptions about the variables, functions, and classes you write. If you break any of the rules, at least break them consistently, and don't just do something different every time.

Public and private class members

In *Chapter 4*, we learned that **abstraction** and **encapsulation** are two key components of **object-oriented programming**. This means that code outside of a class should not need to worry about how that class gets results. For all the outside world is concerned, it could be magic or, even worse, manual labor.

To signify that a particular variable or method is meant for internal use by the class alone, GDScript took over the convention popularized in Python: putting an underscore before the name of that variable or function.

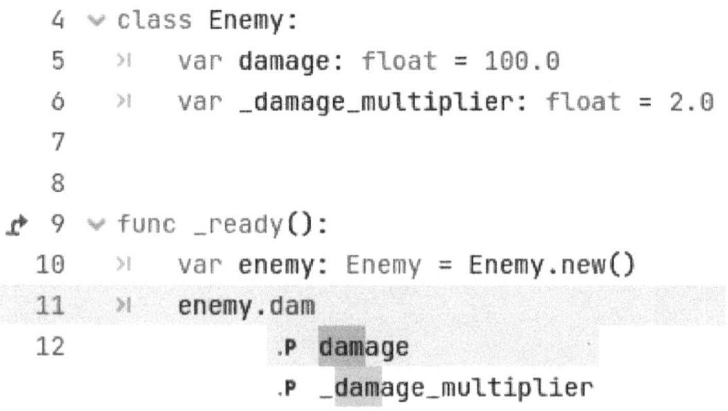

```
 4 ˅ class Enemy:
 5   ⇥    var damage: float = 100.0
 6   ⇥    var _damage_multiplier: float = 2.0
 7
 8
 9 ˅ func _ready():
10   ⇥    var enemy: Enemy = Enemy.new()
11   ⇥  enemy.dam
12              .P damage
                .P _damage_multiplier
```

Figure 5.1 – The auto-complete still suggests private variables

However, as shown in *Figure 5.1*, you'll notice that the auto-complete still suggests private class members. It is still very important to indicate which members of the class are private and should not be accessed. This will help you or any other programmer coming after you by using the class itself.

Make short functions

The more a function tries to do, the more code there is within that function and the harder it is to understand what it is doing. So, to keep functions easily understandable, a great rule of thumb is to keep the number of lines under 20. This lets you quickly understand what is happening and how to use the function effectively.

Of course, you can call different functions. Splitting long functions into multiple smaller ones with a good descriptive name will save you many hours of figuring out what code does.

DRY

There are two acronyms that almost every programming student will have heard of. The first is DRY. This acronym urges us to write a piece of code only once and then reuse it as much as possible. If we create small, generic functions, we can prevent copy-pasting the same few lines over our whole code base.

But I should also warn you not to overdo it. Sometimes, it is okay to have a little bit of duplicate code that is better tailored to a particular scenario than to hack multiple scenarios into one piece of code. Use your best judgment.

Do one thing (KISS)

The second acronym everyone knows about is **KISS**, which stands for **keep it simple, stupid**. This could be interpreted in two ways:

- Keep the solution to the bare minimum, which means you don't solve problems that do not exist yet. This way, you don't develop features that are not needed and don't spend time creating something nobody will use.

- Don't make your code complex. Complex code is notoriously hard to maintain and understand. That is why it's better to keep any solution simple, so you always know what is happening.

Simple code is always easier to read, comprehend, and maintain. So, keep it simple, stupid!

Defensive programming

The last principle I want to show you is **defensive programming**. In this paradigm, you try to play it safe by checking as many things and edge cases in code as possible. In a function, for example, you can check at the start of the function whether the parameters are correct. This way, you will prevent a lot of crashes in the long run.

For example, if you have a function that should return the item within an inventory at a certain index, you could write it non-defensively and defensively like this:

```
func get_inventory_item(index: int):
    return inventory[index]

func  get_inventory_item (index: int):
    if index < 0 or index >= inventory.size():
        return
    return inventory[index]
```

The second version of the function is defensive because it checks first if the index of the item we want is within the range of the inventory. We do this because if the index is outside of this range, we crash the game.

Programming style guides

Lastly, I would like to go over what programming style guides are. These are guides that tell you how to structure your code. These guides never say anything about the content of the code but more about how to style it.

You can compare these guides to the style of this book. I could put all the sentences in one long line without styling, headers, or images. But in the end, this would make the content very hard to comprehend.

Next to making code more readable, these style guides also get whole teams of coders on one line, so each person's code looks more alike and people don't have to keep switching between different coding styles when trying to comprehend the code base of a project.

Most companies have their internal style guide, and yes, there is an official GDScript style guide! You can read it over here: `https://docs.godotengine.org/en/stable/tutorials/scripting/gdscript/gdscript_styleguide.html`.

I don't recommend you read the whole thing and try to apply it all at once. Instead, you could read some snippets here and there and once you have those guidelines down, read some more and try to fit these in your own coding style.

Don't get mistaken. Even with these style guides, there is still room for a personal touch while coding. These guides will just be within a framework that makes your code nicer and easier to understand for other programmers working within the same programming language and framework.

For the rest of this chapter, I would like to review some of the tips from the official GDScript style guide. Namely, the following few:

- White spacing
- Blank lines
- Line length

So let's dive right into these style recommendations of the Godot Engine developers themselves.

White spacing

Except for indentation, which we discussed in *Chapter 2*, GDScript doesn't care about white space within lines of code. The next two lines are functionally the same:

```
var total_damage:float=100+get_damage()*0.5
var total_damage: float = 100 + get_damage() * 0.5
```

However, the second line is way more readable for humans because each part has room to breathe. That is why it's essential to always use a space between numbers, function calls, and operators. This way, a line doesn't just become a jumble of characters.

In arrays, we also want to add a space between elements to clearly show that each is a separate entity:

```
inventory = ["Boots","Sword","Potion"]
inventory = ["Boots", "Sword", "Potion"]
```

The opposite can also be true. Inserting unnecessary spaces could obscure certain operators, for example, accessing a key in a dictionary:

```
dictionary ["key"] = 100
dictionary["key"] = 100
```

In the preceding example, it is more apparent that the square brackets are there to access a key from the dictionary and not to define an array.

Two other examples where no space shows a clear relation between the elements are the function name and its parameter list:

```
print ("Hello")
print("Hello")
```

Also, we can see this when accessing a member variable or function from an object:

```
object . function()
object.function()
```

In general, it is very important to use white space within a line of code to show when things are separate entities or belong together. This will improve readability tremendously.

Blank lines

The other kind of white space we can use to make code more readable is blank lines. A blank line is simply a line that contains nothing. The style guide suggests using two blank lines to separate functions and class definitions. This way, it is clear which pieces of text belong together as a function:

```
func deal_damage(amount: float) -> void:
    player_health -= amount


func heal(amount: float) -> void:
    player_health += amount
```

In addition to separating functions and classes with two blank lines, the guide advises us to use one blank line to separate lines of code that are logically grouped. For example, if we have code that calculates the damage from an attack and then applies that damage to all enemies, we can nicely group this logic into the following:

- Determining the damage
- Calculating the total damage
- Applying the damage to all enemies

We can see this in the following code:

```
var weapon_damage: float = 10
var damage_type: String = "Fire"

var total_damage: float = weapon_damage
if damage_type == "Electricity":
    total_damage *= 2

for enemy in enemies:
    enemy.deal_damage(total_damage)
```

You will see me sin against the blank lines guide rules here and there throughout the book. I do this mainly to make the code more compact to fit the pages, but that doesn't make the rule less important!

Line length

In the early days, computer monitors were tiny. They often couldn't hold more than 70 to 90 characters in one line of text before it scrolled off the end or wrapped around. That is why code was best written in lines with, at most, this length. Nowadays, my ultra-wide computer monitor can hold over 500 characters on one line without a problem. Well, not a technical problem anyway. Working with text this wide makes it very hard to read for humans!

This is why people still restrict their line lengths while programming, to keep everything nice and easy to read. While, of course, not everyone agrees on the perfect line length, the GDScript defaults are 80 characters as a soft limit and 100 as a hard limit.

It is advised to keep your lines under this amount of characters. If you do run into them, you can always subdivide your line by storing intermediate results in separate variables. For example, the next snippet of code checks if the player's health is between 0 and 100 and whether the player has a potion in their inventory:

```
if player_health > 0 and player_health < 100 and inventory.
has("Potion"):
    # Take potion
```

It's not technically too long, but to show how we can lower the line length and even make the condition in the if statement more readable, let's rewrite this snippet as follows:

```
var can_heal: bool = player_health > 0 and player_health < 100
var has_potion: bool = inventory.has("Potion")

if can_heal and has_potion:
    # Take potion
```

As you can see, there are no extra-long lines now and the if statement is way more readable.

Utilizing the documentation

Sometimes, it is hard to anticipate how the built-in classes, functions, or variables of the Godot Engine work. Luckily, the engine has great documentation that explains everything in great detail.

Accessing a class's documentation

We can always access the documentation of any internal class by simply using *Ctrl* + clicking on the name of the class. This will take you to the specific documentation page of that class.

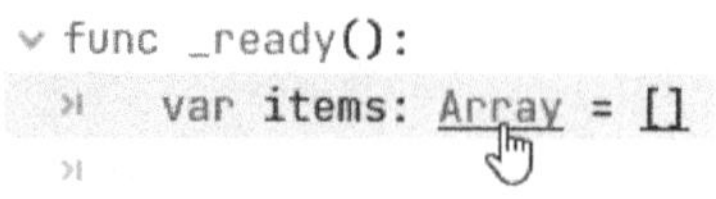

```
v func _ready():
>I      var items: Array = []
>I
```

Figure 5.2 – Ctrl + clicking on an internal class name, such as the Array class

As shown in *Figure 5.3*, the documentation page starts with a simple description of what the class is used for and sometimes this part gives usage examples.

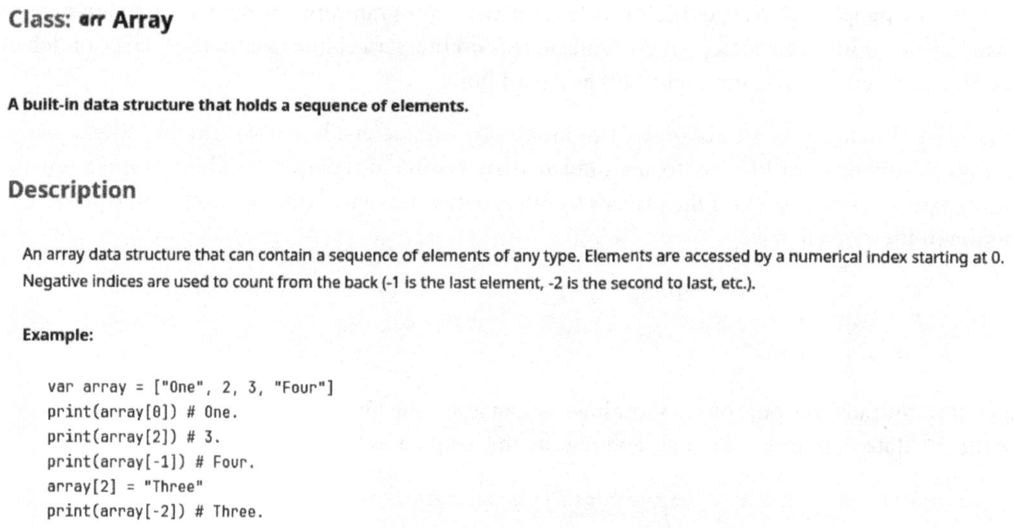

Class: ◂▸ Array

A built-in data structure that holds a sequence of elements.

Description

An array data structure that can contain a sequence of elements of any type. Elements are accessed by a numerical index starting at 0. Negative indices are used to count from the back (-1 is the last element, -2 is the second to last, etc.).

Example:

```
var array = ["One", 2, 3, "Four"]
print(array[0]) # One.
print(array[2]) # 3.
print(array[-1]) # Four.
array[2] = "Three"
print(array[-2]) # Three.
```

Figure 5.3 – The documentation page for the Array class

Then follows an overview of the class's member functions, variables, signals, and operators. We'll see more about signals in *Chapter 9*. Note that you can easily click on the function or variable names to directly go to their explanation.

> **Important note**
>
> Remember that functions can also be called methods and variables can be called properties. This is because functions bound to a class are called methods and variables bound to a class properties.

After the overview section, there is a detailed description of each function and variable. For the functions, we get an explanation of what the function does, what parameters the function takes, and what data type gets returned.

- bool is_empty() const

Returns true if the array is empty.

Figure 5.4 – The documentation section for a function

For variables, we also get a description of what this variable is used for and what data type the value should be.

- Vector2   position [default: Vector2(0, 0)]
              set_position(value) setter
              get_position() getter

Position, relative to the node's parent.

Figure 5.5 – The documentation section for a variable

This way of accessing the documentation works very well if we want to get a general feel for what a class does.

Directly accessing a function or variable's documentation

To directly go to the documentation of a function or variable, you just have to press *Ctrl* + click that function or variable and you'll go directly to the relevant section.

```
func _ready():
>I      var items: Array = []
>I      items.is_empty()
>I
```

Figure 5.6 – Holding Ctrl + clicking on a function or variable will bring
you to the right section in the documentation directly

After clicking the link, we directly get to the section from *Figure 5.4*.

Going to the definition of a function or variable

This shortcut also works with our own code: if you hold *Ctrl* + click on Windows or Linux or *option* + click on Mac a function or variable that we defined somewhere, the editor will show where this function or variable was defined in the code.

As an experiment, try using this shortcut on the different functions we defined on the Enemy classes we created in *Chapter 4*.

Searching the documentation

You can also search all the classes, functions, and variables. Simply follow these steps:

1. Press *F1* and a search bar will pop up.

2. Type in any class, function, or variable you want to search for.

3. Select the right search result.

The result is shown in *Figure 5.6*:

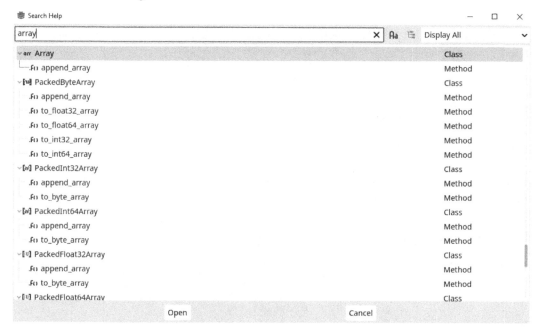

Figure 5.7 – You can also search all the documentation by pressing F11 on your keyboard

This makes it easy to find the right section in the documentation if you are not able to hold *Ctrl +
click* on Windows and Linux or press *Option + click* on Mac, on a class, function, or variable within
your code.

Accessing the online documentation

All of this documentation is also hosted online. There are some pages and tutorials on the online version
that you cannot access in the offline one. It's also easier to open up multiple pages of documentation
on the online version.

Just navigate to: https://docs.godotengine.org/.

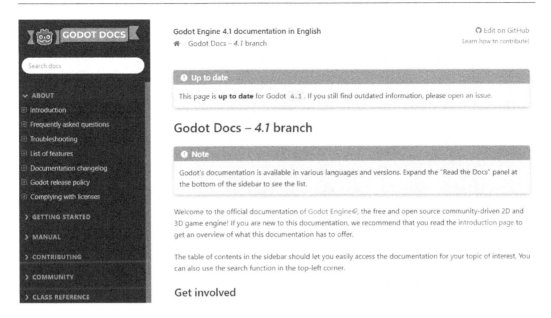

Figure 5.8 – The online documentation

In the menu bar on the left, you can see all the different articles available and navigate to sections that interest you.

Summary

There we go! Throughout *Part 1* of the book, we learned how to program and we topped it off with some extra tips on becoming a good programmer during this chapter. Remember, no tips in this chapter are chiseled in stone or enforced by the engine. So, you can break them where needed. But they are here for your own good and many programmers have adopted them as daily practices.

In the next chapter, which is also at the beginning of the next part of the book, we will finally start working on our game! I hope you are as excited as I am!

Quiz time

- What are the three naming conventions used in the Godot Engine and GDScript?
- Have the following functions been named well?
  - CalculateLifePoints()
  - stop_moving()

- `do_a_thing()`
- `drawcircles()`

- Have the following classes been named well?

    - `Player`
    - `normal_enemy`
    - `MOTORCYCLE`

- What do the acronyms DRY and KISS stand for?

Part 2: Making a Game in Godot Engine

With the fundamentals of programming under our belt, we will finally start working on our very own game from scratch. In this part, we'll learn all about Godot Engine's flexible node-based system and create a *Vampire Survivors*-like game.

By the end of this part, you will have created a whole game using different nodes and game development techniques. You will even be able to play the game with your friends, because we will end this part with a chapter on making the game multiplayer.

This part has the following chapters:

6

Creating a World of Your Own in Godot

In *Part 1* of this book, you learned the basics of programming! No small feat if you ask me. So, congrats on that milestone! Now, it's time to tie it all together and start working on our game.

In the early days of game development, everything happened through code. A computer wizard had to program everything, from systems and features to levels and asset placement. In recent times, the tooling for creating games has gotten way better, is free, and is very user-friendly.

Godot, like most modern game engines (Unity, Unreal Engine, Construct, and others), has a graphical interface that makes it easy to drag and drop elements of our game into levels or other scenes. In this chapter, we'll learn how to use this graphical interface by creating a rudimentary player character and a little world for them to inhabit.

We'll also learn some tricks to tie the code and graphical editor together with node references and variable exports.

In this chapter, we will cover the following main topics:

- The node-based system of Godot
- Creating a player character
- Referencing nodes in scripts
- Exporting variables
- Making rudimentary shapes

Technical requirements

Because we will create a game from scratch, I took the liberty of providing you with the base of a project. You can find this base project in the folder for this chapter under /start. This project supplies some assets, such as pictures and sounds. Creating these assets is outside the scope of this book. The resulting project files for this chapter can be found under /result of this chapter's folder.

In the subsequent chapters, you'll find the resulting project in the root folder of that chapter. It's assumed that you use the results from the previous chapter as a starting point.

So, get the starting project, and let's dive in: https://github.com/PacktPublishing/ Learning-GDScript-by-Developing-a-Game-with-Godot-4/tree/main/ chapter06/start.

Game design

Before mindlessly creating a game, let's plan out what kind of game we want to make. This will structure our thoughts and make sure we work toward the game we want to make without taking unnecessary detours. The best way to do this is through a **game design document** (**GDD**). Though there is no set format for this kind of document, it should eventually answer some basic questions about the game:

- Which genre is the game?
- What mechanics will be in the game?
- What is the story?

Some game design documents are hundreds of pages long. But as this is not a game design book, let's define our game regarding these three questions and then work out the details as we go.

Genre

Recently, we have witnessed the birth of a new genre known as **vampire survivor-likes**, also known as a **VS** game. In this type of game, you control a character in a 2D top-down world. The character has to defeat waves of monsters coming after them by shooting them. The player can control the character by moving them around, but shooting happens automatically. It does not require input.

This genre has a huge player base, and the base game is relatively simple to implement and yet satisfying to play. Therefore, it would be the ideal type of game to recreate throughout the following chapters.

Mechanics

The survivor-like genre has some staple mechanics that are very important to get right:

- **2D world**: The playing field is a 2D plane on which we have a top-down view. Some of them are indeed in 3D, but the mechanics still shine in 2D.

- **Movement of the character**: We need to be able to move the character around in the world.

- **Waves of enemies**: We need enemies that threaten to kill the player and we need to spawn them so that they pose a proper challenge .

- **Automatic shooting**: The player character will automatically shoot projectiles aimed at the enemies.

Now that we have sorted out the genre and staple mechanics, let's work out the story our game will be based on.

Story

Let's not burden ourselves too much with writing the whole story. In games, the story can also be told through how the game looks and feels. So, we can specify a general setting that binds the whole experience together.

How about this as our setting: You are a medieval knight fighting in the king's tournament to find the strongest soldier in the whole land. You'll have to battle multiple enemies, such as orcs and trolls, in multiple rounds, each harder than the last. The only weapon you are given is a bow, with which you can shoot arrows at your adversaries.

Now that we have an idea of the kind of game we are creating, let's get into it!

Creating a player character

We'll start by creating a rudimentary player character for our game:

1. Open the main.tscn file I provided in the project base.

2. Select the root node, called Main, and press the **Add Child Node** button:

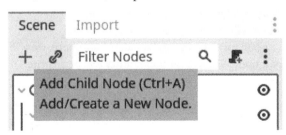

Figure 6.1 – The button to add a new child node to the selected node in the tree

3. Then, find and add a **Node2D** node. You can use the search bar at the top to make searching for the node easier. This is a node that has a position in 2D space:

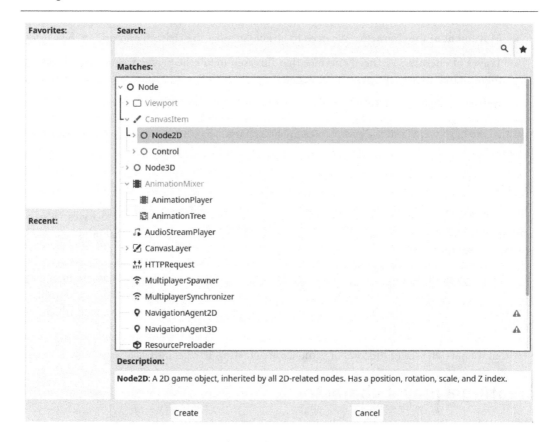

Figure 6.2 – Finding and selecting the Node2D node

4. Next, rename this Node2D as `Player` by right clicking the node and choosing **Rename**, just like we did in *Chapter 2*.

`Player` will be the base node for our player character. From here, we will add all the other nodes that comprise the `Player` node. The first of these nodes will be a sprite.

Adding a sprite

The first thing we can do to flesh out our player character is to give it a visual, something that the player can relate to as the main character. Follow *Steps 1* to *3* in the *Creating a player character* section again to add a node called `Sprite2D` to the `Player` node so that the scene tree looks like this:

Figure 6.3 – The scene tree so far

The `Sprite2D` node is a node that can display an image, also called a **sprite**. If you click on `Sprite2D`, you'll see that the **Inspector** view on the right-hand side gets populated with information about that node:

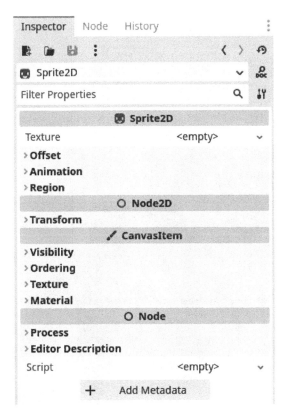

Figure 6.4 – The Inspector view of a Sprite2D node

There are settings for **Texture**, **Offset**, **Animation**, **Region**, and more. You can look through them to get an idea of all the available settings. The different tabs are **Property Groups**, while the settings themselves are called **Properties**.

We are only interested in the **Texture** property because this is where we can set the image this node displays. So, let's add a sprite for our character!

1.   In the **FileManager** area, navigate to `assets/sprites/character`.

     Here, you'll find a bunch of premade character sprites.

Kenney assets

The assets we are using in this book all come from Kenney and are free to use in any project you want. You can find more of his great assets at `https://kenney.nl/`.

---

2. Drag and drop any of them onto the **Texture** property of the `Sprite2D` node. I'm using the `character01.png` texture.

3. The **Inspector** view for the `Sprite2D` node should now look something like this:

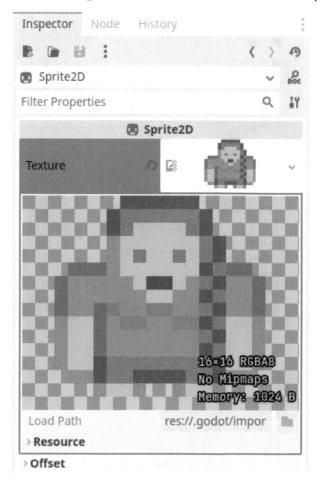

Figure 6.5 – Adding a texture to a sprite node

The sprite should also turn up in the 2D view of the editor. However, it seems to be very small. That's because the image is only 16 × 16 pixels in size. Let's scale it up a little. Under the **Transom** tab in the sprite's **Inspector** view, set **Scale** to 3. You can set the scale for the X and Y axes separately, but we want them both to be equal so that the sprite scales without stretching:

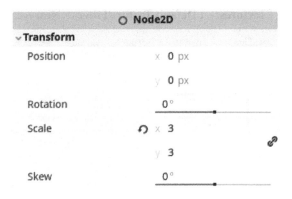

Figure 6.6 – The Transform properties of a sprite node

Oh no – what's this?

Figure 6.7 – A blurry pixel art sprite

The sprite looks blurry! This happened because we're using **pixel art** assets, a style well known for its blocky pixels. When upscaling, Godot Engine uses an algorithm that blurs out these pixels. This is great for other art styles, such as hand-drawn or vector art, but not for pixel art. Luckily, there is a solution. Follow these steps:

1. Navigate to **Project | Project Settings...**:

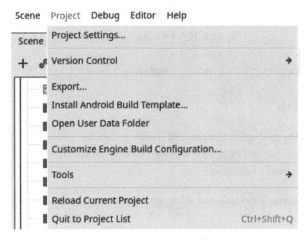

Figure 6.8 – Going to Project Settings...

2.   Under **Rendering | Textures**, set **Default Texture Filter** to **Nearest**:

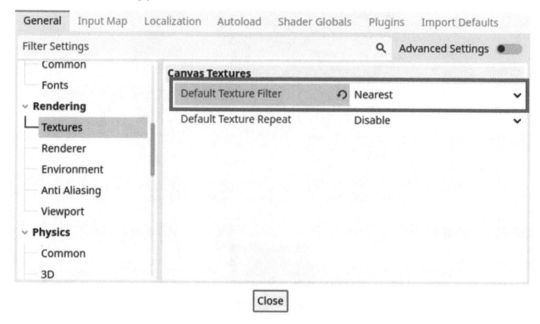

Figure 6.9 – Setting Default Texture Filter to Nearest

These settings will scale the image in a way that is better suited for pixel art. Now, our sprite looks way better!

Figure 6.10 – A crisp pixel art sprite

Now that we can see our player, let's look into displaying a health UI.

Displaying health

Next, let's add something to display the player's health above the character. Sure, we haven't created a script for the player yet that tracks health, but we can put the visuals in place. We will use a `Label` node, which can display text in the game:

1.   Find and add a `Label` node to the `Player` node.

2. Name the node `HealthLabel`:

Figure 6.11 - The scene tree with the HealthLabel node added

3. When selecting the `Label` node, the **Inspector** view will contain a **Text** property. Type `10/10` into it as if the player has 10 out of their 10 lives:

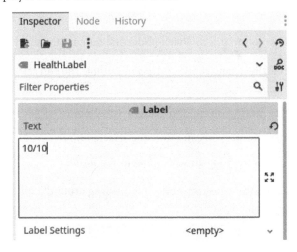

Figure 6.12 – The Inspector view of a Label node with the text set to 10/10

4. Next, drag the label on top of the player so that it's out of the way of the sprite:

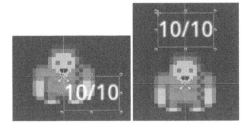

Figure 6.13 – Repositioning the HealthLabel node above the player character

Great! With the `HealthLabel` label in place, we can update it through a script later on (see the *Creating the player script* section). This is all we need to set up the nodes in the scene tree.

Now, let's see how we can manipulate the nodes we've added.

Manipulating nodes in the editor

Now that we have a small scene tree in place, let's look at what tools we have available to manipulate the nodes. If you look at the top right of the 2D editor, you'll see some of these tools:

Figure 6.14 – The toolbar in the 2D editor view

There are many interesting tools in this toolbar, but the first four are the most important ones for now:

- **Select mode**: This is the default mode and is a multitool. You can select nodes within the scene and drag them around.

- **Move mode**: In this mode, you can move the selected node.

- **Rotate mode**: In this mode, you can rotate the selected node.

- **Scale mode**: In this mode, you can scale the selected node.

Try these modes by selecting the `Player` node and messing around a bit. This could lead you to a result like this:

Figure 6.15 – The Player node after multiple transform manipulations

You'll also notice that when you move, rotate, or scale a node, its child nodes will be manipulated in the same way. This inheritance of transformation is the strength of the hierarchical node system.

If you look at the **Transform** tab in the **Inspector** view of the `Player` node, you'll see the exact modifications you made to it. If you change any of these values, you'll see them reflected in the 2D editor too:

○ **Node2D**		
⌄**Transform**		
Position	↺ x 559 px	
	y 298 px	
Rotation	↺ 160.4 °	
Scale	↺ x 0.748	
	y 2.703	
Skew	0 °	

Figure 6.16 – The Transform parameters after multiple transform manipulations

As an experiment, try changing the value for Skew from the **Inspector** view.

Before you continue with the following sections, don't forget to reset all these manipulations in the **Transform** tab of the Player node. You can do this simply by pressing the ↺ symbol next to each property. This button will set the property back to its default value. Let's also set the position of the Player node so that the player character is roughly centered on the screen:

Figure 6.17 – Positioning the player character in the middle of the screen

With that, we've finished creating the base for our player character and learned how we can manipulate nodes within the editor. Next, we'll focus on the player character's script and learn how we can manipulate nodes through code.

Creating the player script

This is the moment we have been training for. We already know how to do this! So, start by creating a new script that is attached to the Player node:

1. Right-click the Player node and select **Attach Script**:

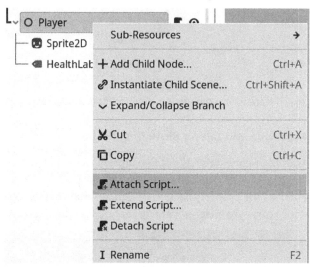

Figure 6.18 – Attaching a script to the Player node

2. In the dialogue that pops up, call the script player.gd:

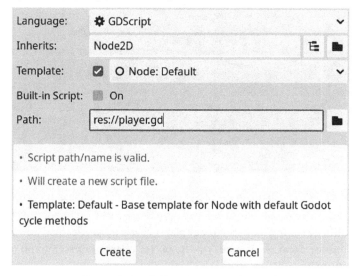

Figure 6.19 – Calling the script player.gd

3. We'll keep it simple for now and just add some code to manage the health of the player:

```
extends Node2D

const MAX_HEALTH: int = 10

var health: int = 10

func add__health_points(difference: int):
    health += difference
    health = clamp(health, 0, MAX_HEALTH)
```

The `clamp()` function we use in the `add_health_points()` function takes a numeric value as the first argument and keeps it in between the second two numeric parameters.

This way, the health is always between 0 and `MAX_HEALTH`, which is 10 at the max.

> **Important note**
>
> Remember that you can *Ctrl* and click on Windows and Linux or *Option* and click on Mac on any function to go to the documentation and have a look at what it does.

With this in place, we can change the player's health. Now, let's look at how we can update the `HealthLabel` node we created earlier to reflect this value.

Referencing nodes in a script

We want to update the `HealthLabel` node of our player character according to the amount of health the player still has left. To change nodes in our scene from within the script, we need to be able to reference them. Luckily, this is pretty easy in Godot 4.

There are multiple ways to get a node's reference, but the easiest is the dollar notation. This notation looks like this:

```
$HealthLabel
```

The notation starts with a dollar sign ($), followed by the path through the scene tree to the node we want. Here, we reference the health label we created earlier.

Note that this path is relative to the node with the script where this path is mentioned. So if the main node has a script and we want to reference the player's health label, the notation would look like this:

```
$Player/HealthLabel
```

So, now that we know how to get the reference to a node, let's create a small function that updates the player's health label and call it in the add_health_points() function:

```
func update_health_label():
    $HealthLabel.text = str(health) + "/" + str(MAX_HEALTH)
```

In this update_health_label() function, we take the HealthLabel node and directly change its text variable. This will change whatever text the label is showing on the screen.

Here, we use a new function named str() in update_health_label(). This function takes any parameter and converts it into a string. We need to do this because the + sign can only concatenate other strings together, so to concatenate the health and MAX_HEALTH values, which are integers, we'll have to convert them into a string.

Now, we can use this update_health_label() function whenever we change the health value:

```
func add_health_points(difference: int):
    health += difference
    health = clamp(health, 0, MAX_HEALTH)

    update_health_label()
```

Just like this, we can directly change what the HealthLabel node is displaying. But there is a better way of accessing or referencing nodes within the scene tree: by caching them. We'll take a look at that next.

Caching node references

Though the dollar notation is very convenient, sometimes, you will need to access a certain node often. In such cases, using the dollar notation will be slow because the engine will have to keep searching for the node within the tree and accessing it every time.

> **Caching**
>
> In computer lingo, caching means storing a certain piece of data for later so that you don't have to load it every time it is needed.

To stop searching the node each time, we can save a reference to the node in a variable. For example, we can change the player script like so:

```
extends Node2D

@onready var _health_label: Label = $HealthLabel

func update_health_label():
    _health_label.text = str(health) + "/" + str(MAX_HEALTH)
```

Here, you see that we save the reference to the `HealthLabel` node in a variable called `_health_label`. Later on, we can use this reference.

The upside is, of course, that we only have to change the path to the node at one point: the line where the reference gets stored in a variable. Another upside is that we can type-hint the variable with the type of the node. So, we are making it even safer than the previous way of referencing the node.

You'll also notice that I use the `@onready` annotation. We call commands that start with an @ annotation, like the one shown previously. This annotation executes that line of code when the node is ready and has entered the scene tree. This is right before the `_ready()` function of that node is called. In Godot, the `_ready()` function of each node gets called after each of its children are ready, meaning that their `_ready()` functions get called before the parent node's `_ready()` function. We need to wait for this moment to get any nodes in the tree because otherwise, there is a possibility for them not to exist yet!

> **Annotations**
>
> There are more annotations. We'll return to them when they are applicable. But it's already good to know that all of these annotations affect how external tools will treat the script and don't change any logic within the script itself.

I advise that you always cache variables as described here because it will keep your code clean and fast.

Trying out the player script

To try out what we have created so far, we can run a quick test by adding the `_ready()` function to the player script:

```
func _ready():
    add_health_points(-2)
```

Now, when you run the scene, you should see that the health label says **8/10**, like so:

Figure 6.20 – The player's health label has been updated to 8/10

After testing the script, remove the preceding lines again so that they don't interfere with the rest of our coding.

In this section, we learned how to reference nodes from the scene tree within our code and how to update the values of these nodes. We also set up a basic script for tracking the health of our player. In the following section, we'll learn about exporting variables.

Exporting variables to the editor

We have always defined variables within code and every time we wanted to change them, we had to change the code too. But in Godot, it is straightforward to expose variables to the editor so that we can change them without even opening the code editor. This is extremely useful when you want to test things out and tweak variables on the fly. An exported variable pops up in the **Inspector** view of that node, just like the transformation and text properties we saw in the *Manipulating nodes in the editor* section.

> **Important note**
>
> An exported variable is also useful for people who don't know how to code, such as level designers, but still want to change the behavior of specific nodes.

To export a variable to the editor, we can use the `@export` annotation. Let's change the line where we define the `health` variable, like so:

```
@export var health: int = 10
```

Make sure you save the script. Go to the 2D editor using the button at the top of the editor.

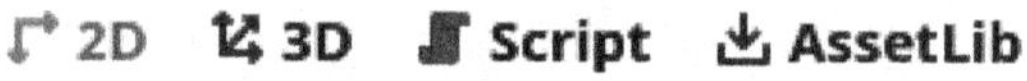

⌐ 2D   ⌾ 3D   ▰ Script   ⇩ AssetLib

Figure 6.21 – Click 2D to go back to the 2D editor

Click on our `Player` node, and see the `health` variable in the **Inspector** view. This is our exported variable. Changing it will change the variable's value at the start of the game, not directly in the script itself:

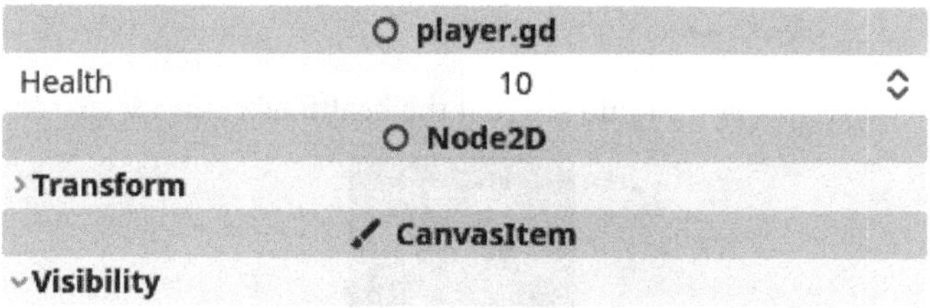

○ player.gd		
Health	10	⇕
○ Node2D		
› Transform		
✏ CanvasItem		
˅ Visibility		

Figure 6.22 – The health variable as an exported variable in the Inspector view of the Player node

Now, when you change the player's health value through the **Inspector** view and run the game, you'll see that it doesn't display the correct value. All we have to do to solve this is update the `health` label in the `_ready()` function, like so:

```
func _ready():
    update_health_label()
```

This will ensure that the health label is updated from the moment the `Player` node enters the scene tree.

> **More information**
>
> If you want to learn more about export variables, you can check out the official documentation: `https://docs.godotengine.org/en/stable/tutorials/scripting/gdscript/gdscript_exports.html`.

Now, we start the game with the correct amount of health displayed on the health label. But there is a better way of updating this health label: using setters and getters.

Setters and getters

When you change the player's health value through the **Inspector** view and run the game, you'll see that the value doesn't update. But the correct value gets printed out if you run it with a `_ready()` function, like so:

```
func _ready():
    print(health)
```

That is because the `update_health_label()` function is not being called when we change the value!

Luckily, we can fix this. In programming, **getter** and **setter** functions exist. These functions are called when you get or set the value of a variable. With these getter or setter functions, we can execute all the logic needed to handle a new value. We can define a getter and setter for our health variable like so:

```
@export var health: int = 10:
    get:
        return health
    set(new_value):
        health = clamp(new_value, 0, MAX_HEALTH)
        update_health_label()
```

So, the getter is defined by `get:`, followed by the code block that defines the getter logic, and the setter by `set(new_value):`, followed by its code block. `new_value` is the new value that is assigned to the variable. Within the setter, we get the opportunity to process this value if needed or set other processes in motion. In our case, we don't want to process the new value, but we do want to update the health label.

The getter does nothing special – it just returns the health value. On the other hand, the setter clamps the new value so that it is valid and then updates the health label.

When we get or set the `health` value, the interpreter will execute these functions first. Here's an example:

```
print(health) # Execute the getter
health = 100 # Execute the setter
```

This also simplifies the `add_health_points()` function because we no longer have to clamp the new health value as this already gets done in the setter. So, let's update the `add_health_points()` function to the following:

```
func add_health_points(difference: int):
    health += difference
```

But what is this? The project errors when we run it now!

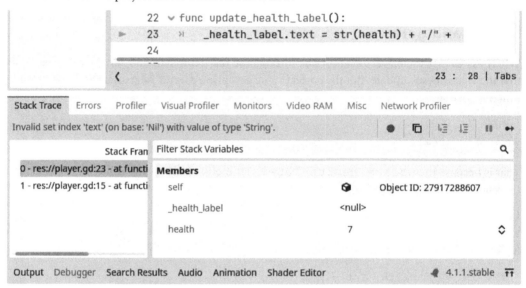

Figure 6.23 – An error showing that the health label is non-existing

The setter function gets executed before the `_health_label` reference is created. So, we must make sure that the `_health_label` is filled in before we update its text. If it isn't, we can just return from the function:

```
func update_health_label():
    if not is_instance_valid(_health_label):
        return

    _health_label.text = str(health) + "/" + str(MAX_HEALTH)
```

The `is_instance_valid()` function checks if the reference to a node is valid. It returns `true` if it is and `false` otherwise.

Checking if a node reference exists

Your first instinct might be to check if the reference to the node is not `null` by running `_health_label != null`. However, this does not guarantee that the node is available. When the node is deleted, for example, this check for `null` will still return `true` because the reference still exists within the variable. `is_instance_valid(_health_label)` will check more than just whether the variable is `null` – it will also make sure that the node still exists and is in use within the scene tree.

At this point, the code for the player should look like this:

```
extends Node2D

const MAX_HEALTH: int = 10

@onready var _health_label: Label = $HealthLabel

@export var health: int = 10:
    get:
        return health
    set(new_value):
        health = clamp(new_value, 0, MAX_HEALTH)
        update_health_label()

func _ready():
    update_health_label()

func update_health_label():
    if not is_instance_valid(_health_label):
        return
    _health_label.text = str(health) + "/" + str(MAX_HEALTH)

func add_health_points(difference: int):
    health += difference
```

Setters and getters help us encapsulate behavior related to updating variables, as we saw in *Chapter 5*. It abstracts the logic behind what needs to happen when updating this variable so that the user of the class doesn't have to worry about it.

With this code set up, the health of our player can easily be updated using the regular or special assignment operators and the health label will update accordingly.

Changing values while the game is running

Another cool thing about these exported variables, now that we have a setter and a getter defined for them, is that we can change them while the game runs! So, if you run the game and change the `health` parameter in the **Inspector** view while it is running, you will see that change reflected in the health label instantaneously.

This (mostly) works with all built-in parameters too! If you keep the game open and change the player's **Transformation** parameters, for example, you'll see them change in real time.

This will be useful later on so that we don't always have to re-launch the game when working on it.

Different types of exported variables

When exporting a variable that we type hinted, Godot will choose the right input field type for that type. It will have a numerical input field with up and down arrows for integers, while it will use a normal text input for strings, like so:

```
@export var health: int = 10
@export var damage: float = 0.0
@export var player_name: String = "Erika"
```

These three lines will each export a variable to the editor, but each with a different data type: integer, floating-point number, and string, respectively. The result is that we get a different kind of input field for each of the variables:

	O **player.gd**	
Health	↻ 7	⌄
Damage	0	
Player Name	Erika	

Figure 6.24 – Different variable types that get exported

There are also other export annotations to be even more specific. One of those is the `@export_range` annotation, which specifies a number range the value should be in, like so:

```
@export_range(0, 10) health: int = 10
```

In the preceding code excerpt, we export the `health` variable and specify that it should be a number between 0 and 10, including the outer values of 0 and 20. When you try out this ranged export, you'll see that you cannot input values that fall outside of this range.

To make it more dynamic, we can use the MAX_HEALTH variable we defined earlier within the player's script:

```
@export_range(0, MAX_HEALTH) health: int = 10
```

Exporting variables is a very important technique to keep in our toolkit for tweaking variables and values when testing out the game. Now, let's direct our attention to the arena and world the player will be walking around in.

Creating a little world

Now that we have a little player character, let's create a world for them to inhabit! In this section, we'll flesh out the arena in which the player has to battle challenging foes.

Changing the background color

Let's start simple by changing the background color for our arena. We can easily do this from the project settings:

1. Navigate to **Rendering | Environment** in the project settings:

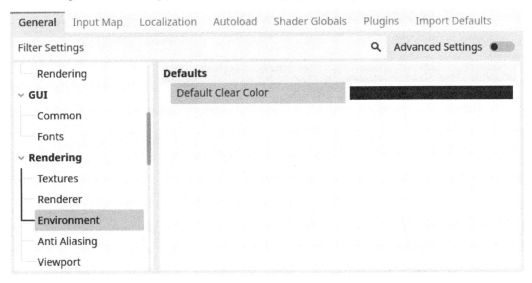

Figure 6.25 – Finding Default Clear Color under Rendering > Environment in the project settings

2. Set the **Default Clear Color** setting to an appropriate color. I chose #e0bf7b because it looks like sand or dried-up mud:

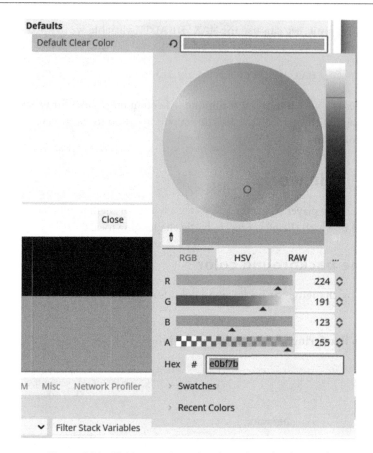

Figure 6.26 – Picking a color using the color selection tool

With this nice color in place, let's add some features, such as boulders and walls, to our arena.

Adding Polygon2D boulders

Now that we have a ground for the player character to stand on, let's add some boulders that will serve as obstacles in the arena. To do this, we will be using the Polygon2D node. This node can draw any polygon shape on the screen in any color we want:

1. Add a **Node2D** node called Arena to the root node of our Main scene.

2. Now, drag the Arena node we just created above the Player node. This will ensure everything within the Arena node will be drawn beneath the Player node. See the *Node drawing order* section to learn more about this.

3. We will put all our arena elements, such as boulders and walls, into this node. This way, we'll keep the tree structure nice and tidy.

4. Now, add a `Polygon2D` node under the `Arena` node and call it `Boulder`:

Figure 6.27 – The scene tree with the Arena node and a Boulder node

5. You can add points to the polygon by left-clicking anywhere on the screen while the `Boulder` node is selected. Right-clicking will remove a point. You can also drag earlier placed points around. Place some points and close the shape by clicking on the first point you put down:

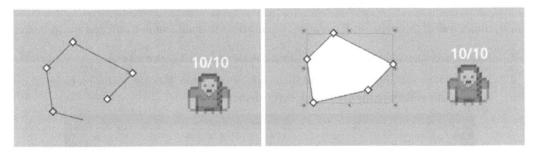

Figure 6.28 – Drawing a boulder using a Polygon2D node

6. Set the `Boulder` node's color property to something that resembles a stone. I chose `#504f51`.

These boulders might look simple, but they will serve our purpose.

Node drawing order

So, why did we drag the `Arena` node above the `Player` node? By default, the nodes get drawn in the order they're in within the tree. The nodes closest to their parents get drawn first and the ones further away from the parent node within the tree structure are drawn on top of the ones below.

There are ways to circumvent this, but that's out of the scope of this book. So, for now, we must structure our node tree correctly:

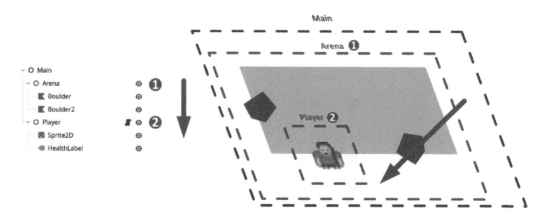

Figure 6.29 – Nodes get drawn in the order they are in within the scene tree

A well-structured tree will draw all nodes in the exact order we want them to be.

Creating an outer wall

For the outer wall of the arena, we'll use a `Polygon2D` node again, but in a different way this time:

1. Add a `Polygon2D` node under the `Arena` node and call it `OuterWall`.

2. Draw a rough rectangle that will be the inside of the arena. It's okay if this rectangle is not perfect. This will make the arena look extra medieval:

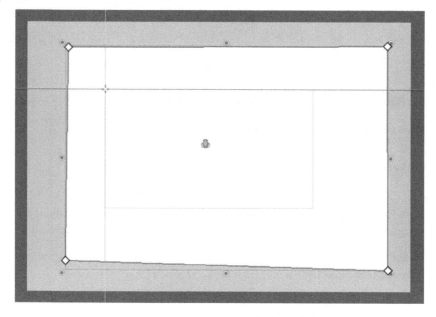

Figure 6.30 – Drawing an arena outer wall using a Polygon2D node

3. Now, with `OuterWall` selected, find and enable the **Invert** parameter in the **Inspector** view. This option inverts the shape and makes it look like the outer walls of the arena:

Figure 6.31 – Inverting the shape of a Polygon2D node

4. Set the **Border** property under the **Invert** section to a high number, such as `1000px`, so that the walls expand very far.

5. Give the wall a fitting color. I chose `#2d2c2e`, which is a little darker than the boulders, so that the player sees the difference:

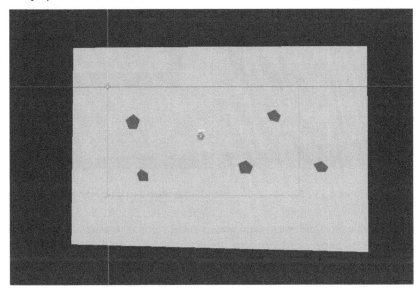

Figure 6.32 – The resulting arena

Inverting a polygon makes it very easy to create the internals of an arena or room. The natural next step is to let our imagination loose and make a visually nice arena.

Getting creative

With these simple tools, get creative and create some interesting terrain to serve as an arena.

For instance, you can add some more boulders to your arena. You can do this by creating an entirely new `Polygon2D` node or by duplicating your earlier boulder and altering them a bit by dragging points around and using the **Transform** tools we learned about.

You can also add more walls and change the outer boundaries of the arena some more.

I came up with this arena:

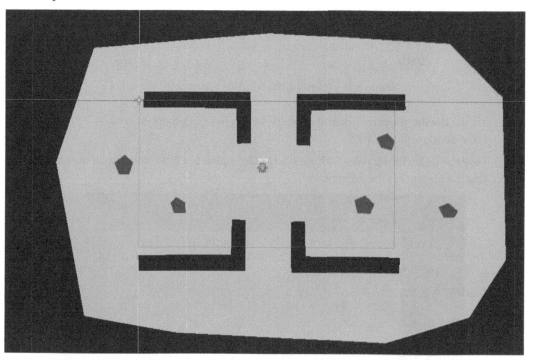

Figure 6.33 – My arena after spending some more time refining it

Now that we can create our little worlds and arenas using colored rectangles and polygons, we have everything to create the basic visual structure of our game. Next, we'll do some extra exercises and summarize this chapter.

Additional exercises – Sharpening the axe

1. Start by making more boulders and walls based on what we learned in the previous section so that you can populate your arena.

2. Based on what you learned about the `health` value of the player, add an exported variable that tracks the number of coins the player has, called `number_of_coins`, to the player script.

3. Add a setter and getter for the `number_of_coins` variable.

4. Lastly, make a label that shows the coins above the player's head. Make sure that everything gets handled and updated correctly so that we can update the variable from the editor and the code while the label always stays up to date when running the game.

Summary

In this chapter, we created our first real scene. We saw how different nodes do different things for us and we extended **Node2D** with a script that will manage the player's health. We also created the area in which all the action will take place.

In the next chapter, we'll make it possible for the player to move around and we'll also refresh our vector math. Don't worry – it won't be painful, but a bit of math will be useful.

Quiz time

*   Why did we start by making a Game Design Document (GDD) instead of jumping right into creating the game?

*   How do you reference nodes within a script?

*   What keyword can we use to make a variable, such as the amount of health, available in the **Inspector** view?

*   What are setter and getter functions used for?

7

Making the Character Move

If I say **physics engine**, you might have images flashing in front of your eyes of scientists doing all kinds of simulations of real-world phenomena trying to predict what would happen in the real world – maybe to study car crashes, the weather, or wind park optimization.

Games use a physics engine, too. However, in games, this engine has other priorities. Unlike the ones scientists use, physics in games doesn't have to be 100% accurate. It just has to give the feeling of realism or, contrarily, the lack thereof.

In this chapter, we will learn how to use the physics engine of Godot, so we don't have to deal with complex interactions such as moving characters or collisions between multiple physics objects within the world.

First, we will have to make a detour and refresh our basics in two-dimensional vector math. I promise a little bit of math won't hurt!

In this chapter, we will cover the following main topics:

- 2D vector math
- The physics engine
- Keyboard and controller input
- Debugging a live game

Technical requirements

As for every chapter, you can find the final code on the GitHub repository in the subfolder for this chapter:

```
https://github.com/PacktPublishing/Learning-GDScript-by-Developing-
a-Game-with-Godot-4/tree/main/chapter07.
```

Vector math refresher

I know math isn't the first thing people think about when talking about game development, but the truth is that it's an important part when dealing with positions, movement, and physics. It is a great tool that will serve us well along our complete game development journey.

In this section, we'll refresh our minds on vectors and how to manipulate them.

The 2D coordinate system

Let's first look at how we define positions in 2D space. Two-dimensional space is defined by two axes: a horizontal axis named *x* and a vertical axis named *y*. Each point within the space can be expressed as values over these axes:

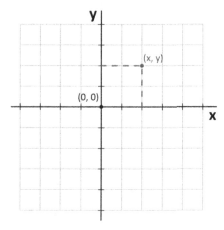

Figure 7.1 – A point in 2D space is defined by an x and a y value

Mathematically, and in this book, we write these positions as (x, y). The first value in the brackets is the *x* value and the second is the *y* value.

In school, you probably learned that the x-axis is positive to the right side and negative to the left, while the y-axis is positive when going upward and negative downward. However, this is not how they work in computer graphics! In Godot, just like in almost every other game engine and computer graphics application, the y-axis is positive when going *downward*:

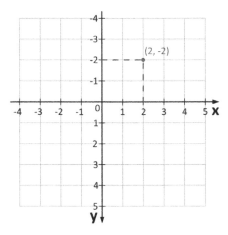

Figure 7.2 – The point (2, -2) in the Godot engine

This might be counterintuitive at first, but it will grow on you after some time.

> **Important note**
>
> The reason the y-axis points down is that computer graphics were calculated this way, with the pixel on the screen that corresponded to an x of 0 and a y of 0 being in the top left of the screen. The two prevalent explanations are:
>
> Early computers often displayed Latin-based text, which goes from left to right, top to bottom, so they used to have the (0, 0) character in the top left.
>
> Early monitors were CRT screens, which often scanned the screen with an electron beam from the top left and worked their way, line by line, downward.

What is a vector?

What if we think of a position as an offset from the (0, 0) point, i.e. the origin? Well, that is what we call a **vector**! You can think of them as an arrow going from the origin to the position we defined.

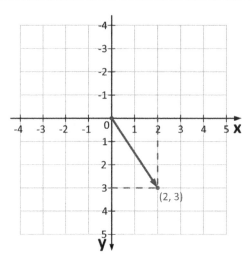

Figure 7.3 – A vector that is defined from (0, 0) to (2, 3)

Mathematically, vectors are defined by a **magnitude** (length) and a **direction** (angle). We are going to use the *offset from the origin* way of thinking because it is more intuitive in terms of game development.

The math we'll learn will apply to all kinds of vectors, positions, and forces, even when dealing with vectors in more than two dimensions. Let's constrain ourselves to two dimensions.

In Godot, a 2D vector is represented by the `Vector2` and `Vector2i` classes. To create a vector, you simply give an x and a y value to the constructor:

```
var vector: Vector2 = Vector2(2, 3)
```

Now, we can just access the x and y variables of this vector as usual:

```
vector.x = 2
if vector.y > 0:
    # Rest of the code
```

The `Vector2` class basically just holds an x and a y component for our vector and can thus represent a vector as well as a position, like we saw in the previous *The 2D coordinate system* section.

`Vector2i` is very similar to `Vector2`, the only difference is that the x and y coordinates need to be integer values, while `Vector2` uses floating point numbers. We'll stick with the `Vector2` class for the rest of the chapter and book.

Scaling vectors

To scale a vector, making it longer or shorter, we just have to multiply or divide the x and y values by the same number. The number by which we multiply the vector is called the **scalar**. For example, if we want to make a vector double in length, we just multiply its x and y values by 2:

```
(x, y) * 2 = (x * 2, y * 2)
```

Figure 7.4 shows the scaled vector:

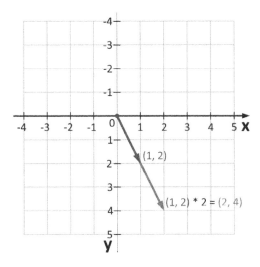

Figure 7.4 – Vector (1, 2) scaled by 2 results in vector (2, 4)

In Godot, we can directly multiply or divide vectors using normal mathematical operations and don't have to manually set the x or y value:

```
vector * 2
vector / 2
```

The interpreter will run the multiplication or division on both the x and y components for us and spit out a new vector with the result.

Adding and subtracting vectors

Next, we can also add two vectors together. We do this by adding the *x* values together and taking the result as the x value for the new vector, and doing likewise for the *y* values:

```
(x1, y1) + (x2, y2) = (x1 + x2, y1 + y2)
```

Figure 7.5 shows the result of vector addition:

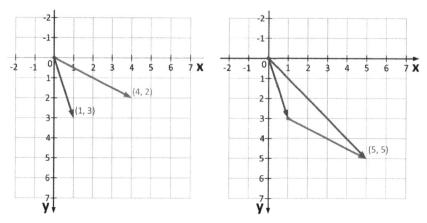

Figure 7.5 – Adding (1, 3) to (4, 2) results in vector (5, 5)

You can think of this operation as first moving to the first vector's position and then, from there, moving along the second vector. It's as if you glue the second vector to the end of the first one.

It doesn't matter in what order you add the two vectors together, the operation will always result in the same vector.

Figure 7.6 shows the operation in the other order:

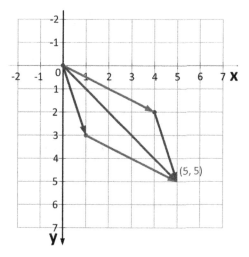

Figure 7.6 – (1, 3) + (4, 2) results in the same vector as (4, 2) + (1, 3)

Subtracting vectors works in the same way as adding them together. Just subtract the individual components. `(x1, y1) - (x2, y2)` is the same as `(x1, y1) + (-x2, -y2)`.

In Godot, you can easily add or subtract vectors by using the regular plus and minus operators:

```
var vector_a: Vector2 = Vector2(2, 3)
var vector_b: Vector2 = Vector2(4, 1)

var vector_c: Vector2 = vector_a + vector_b
var vector_d: Vector2 = vector_a - vector_b
```

You'll see that `vector_c` will contain the sum of vectors a and b, while `vector_d` contains their subtraction.

More vector operations

Now, as any mathematician will tell you, there are a lot more formulas and operations that can be done with vectors. A lot of these are very interesting for us as game developers. However, these are a bit more intricate to explain, and the truth is that most of these are already implemented in Godot. We will not have to worry about how they work but knowing that they exist is very important.

> **More information**
>
> There are more great functions than we will cover here; you can go and have a look at the documentation for `Vector2` yourself: `https://docs.godotengine.org/en/stable/classes/class_vector2.html`.

Length of a vector

The length of a vector is the distance from the origin, `(0, 0)`, to the x, y position the vector represents. We also call this length the magnitude of the vector. To get this length, we simply use the `length()` function:

```
var vector_length: float = vector.length()
```

Figure 7.7 demonstrates this function:

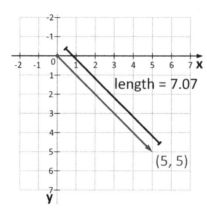

Figure 7.7 – Getting the length of a vector

In the background, this `length()` function uses the Pythagorean theorem, which, if we were to write it out manually, would look like this:

```
sqrt(x * x + y * y)
```

The `length()` function will perform all the necessary calculations for us and will even be faster than if we tried to write this math ourselves within GDScript.

Clamping a vector

Sometimes, you want the length of a vector to stay between a lower and upper bound. To do this, we use the `clamp()` function:

```
var clamped_vector: Vector2 = vector.clamp(0, 5)
```

Figure 7.8 demonstrates this function:

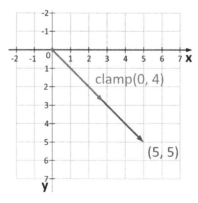

Figure 7.8 – Clamping a vector between a length of 0 and 5

Whatever the length of the vector was before, after running this statement with a `clamp()`, its length will be between `0` and `5`.

Distance between two points

Often, we will need to know the distance between two points in space. For example, when we want to know the distance between an enemy and the player to see if the enemy is within shooting range and can shoot at the player. To do this, we use the `distance_to()` function:

```
var distance: float = vector_a.distance_to(vector_b)
```

Figure 7.9 demonstrates this function:

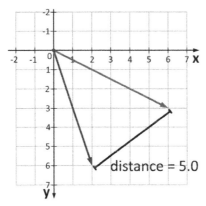

Figure 7.9 – The distance between two vectors

This `distance_to()` function will return a floating point number, telling us the exact distance between the two points in space.

Rotating a vector

Rotating a vector or position is useful when steering a vehicle, rotating the player, or adjusting a vector's direction:

```
var vector_b: Vector2 = vector_a.rotated(PI)
```

Figure 7.10 demonstrates the `rotated()` function:

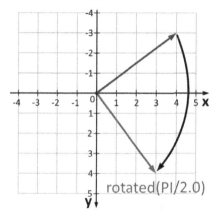

Figure 7.10 – Rotating a vector with the rotated() function

Note that, by default, angles should be in radians for Godot to be able to work with them. If calculating in radians is not your strong suit, there is also the `deg_to_rad()` function that takes a value in degrees and converts it into radians:

```
var vector_b: Vector2 = vector_a.rotated(deg_to_rad(180))
```

This `deg_to_rad()` function is very useful and fast.

> **Important note**
>
> Remember that a full circle is 360 degrees or Pi * 2, also known as Tau, radians, which means that 1 radian roughly equals 57.3 degrees.

Normalizing a vector

Normalizing a vector means that we change its length to be exactly 1. A vector that is longer than 1 will get shortened, while a vector that is shorter than 1 will get longer. We call the resulting vector a **unit vector**:

```
var unit_vector: Vector2 = vector.normalized()
```

Figure 7.11 demonstrates this function:

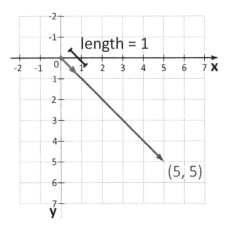

Figure 7.11 – Normalizing a vector sets its length to 1

A normalized vector is useful to work with because what we are left with is the direction of the original vector without its magnitude. In this form, we can easily use the unit vector for other math operations, such as when we want to keep the velocity of a car constant:

```
velocity = velocity.normalized() * 500.0
```

This way we keep `velocity` always at a length of 500.0. Going deeper and really learning the math behind all these functions will be beneficial for sure! However, with the understanding gained from this section and the functions described here, we can already make lots of games. I encourage you to open a math textbook or look up some instructional videos online but don't feel bad if you're not up for it yet.

> **Learning resources**
>
> Here are three great resources to learn more mathematics for game development:
>
> The official Godot documentation has a great article on vector math within the engine: `https://docs.godotengine.org/en/stable/tutorials/math/vector_math.html`.
>
> James M. Van Verth and Lars M. Bishop's book *Essential Mathematics for Games and Interactive Applications*: `https://www.sciencedirect.com/book/9780123742971/essential-mathematics-for-games-and-interactive-applications`.
>
> Freya Holmér's *Math for Game Devs* video series: `https://youtube.com/playlist?list=PLImQaTpSAdsArRFFj8bIfqMk2X7Vlf3XF&si=JZNObwqQNg3ZbGLy`.

Alright, with the theory of vector math brushed up and fresh in our minds, let's dive into making the player character move.

Moving the player character

Cool, after that detour to vector math, let's continue working on our game. The first thing we'll start out with is player movement.

Changing the current player node

Godot has a physics engine baked into it. To utilize it, we will have to use the physics nodes provided by Godot itself. The player is currently a **Node2D**, but we actually want it to be a **CharacterBody2D**.

Luckily, it is very easy to change the type of a node. To do so, follow these steps:

1. Right-click on the `Player` node.
2. Select **Change Type** as shown in the following figure:

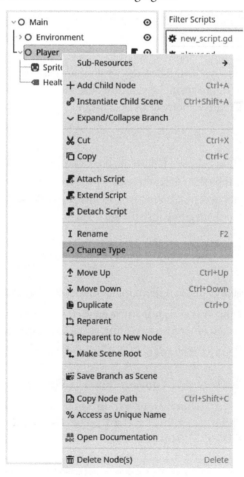

Figure 7.12 – Node type can be changed through the menu that pops up when right-clicking that node

3. Search for **CharacterBody2D** as follows:

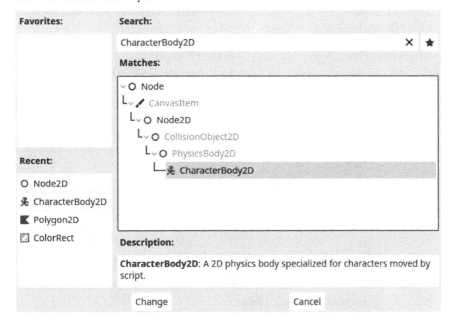

Figure 7.13 – Search for the CharacterBody2D node type

4. Select the **CharacterBody2D** node and you will see the icon for the `Player` node change to reflect our selection:

Figure 7.14 – The player node changes from Node2D to CharacterBody2D

5. You will notice that a yellow warning sign appeared. If you hover over it, you'll see it tells us that the player needs `CollisionShape2D` or `CollisionPolygon2D`.

These shapes help us to do correct collision handling. Let's ignore that for now. We will deal with collision detection in *Chapter 9*.

The script of our player will still work as before because the **CharacterBody2D** node is a child class of the Node2D class and, as we saw in *Chapter 4*, treating **CharacterBody2D** as **Node2D** works because of the principles of polymorphism.

We want to use certain functionalities of the **CharacterBody2D** node in our script, so we will have to change the class our player script extends from to **CharacterBody2D**:

```
extends CharacterBody2D
# Rest of the player script...
```

The Player node is correctly converted to a physics entity. Let's learn how to move it in the next section.

Applying forces to the player

Now that the player character is a physics body, we will be able to apply physical forces to it and make it move!

Before we implement the complete movement schema, let's first make it so the character moves toward the right. Just add this little snippet of code to the player script:

```
func _physics_process(delta: float):
    velocity = Vector2(500, 0)
    move_and_slide()
```

Moving a **CharacterBody2D** node has to be done in two steps:

1. Calculate and set the velocity variable for the body. This velocity is a member variable of **CharacterBody2D** and represents the speed and direction the body is moving in. In this example, I set it to a vector of (500, 0), which means a force to the right.

2. Call the move_and_slide() function. This function will apply the velocity we just set and handle all the collision detection for us. If a collision is detected, this function will also slide along the surface of that collision shape. This results in natural-looking movement that does not snag on things too much. *Figure 7.15* demonstrates this function:

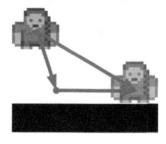

Figure 7.15 – move_and_slide() encountering a collision and sliding along the surface

The velocity sets the force we want to apply to the character. Calling `move_and_slide()` then truly applies that force and calculates all the repercussions and interactions between other physics bodies. For now, there are no other bodies to interact with; we'll implement those in *Chapter 9*.

3. Run the game and you'll see the player character slowly scroll off the screen toward the right.

As an experiment, try making the character move upward.

In the preceding code snippet, you can see that we use the `_physics_process()` function to do our movement calculations. Let's have a look at why we use this function specifically in the next section.

Process and physics process functions

We already saw the `_process()` function briefly in *Chapter 1* but didn't use it back then. This function gets executed for every frame the game runs on each node, which means that if the game runs at 120 frames per second, this function gets executed 120 times per second. In reality, the framerate of a game varies a lot, so the `_process()` function can be run more or fewer times per second.

For physics simulations, varying the frame rate is a problem. Physics calculations can quickly become very inaccurate, miss collisions, and introduce jitter if the framerate at which they get done isn't stable. This is why physics engines introduce the concept of physics frames. They get executed at a stable interval and try very hard not to fluctuate. So, the `_process()` function gets executed as many times per second as possible, while the `_physics_process()` function gets executed at a rate that is as stable as possible.

This is why we use `_physics_process()` in the previous example. This function gets called every physics frame, every time the physics calculations happen. By default, in Godot, this rate is 60 times per second.

The `delta` parameter provides us with the elapsed time since the last time the `_physics_process()` function was called, just like the `delta` parameter in the regular `_process()` function. When we have 60 physics frames per second, this time should be stable at 1.0 / 60.0 frames per second = 0.01667 seconds.

Both `_process()` and `_physics_process()` work very similarly in that they get called periodically during the execution of the game. But for physics calculations, we want to use `_physics_process()`.

Mapping input

To move the player's character in the direction the player intended to, we first need input from the player. This input is typically given through a keyboard, mouse, or controller.

The common input methods for moving a video game character are summarized in *Table 7.1*:

	Arrows	**Keys**	**Analog stick**	**D-pad**
Move left	←	A	Left on x-axis	←
Move right	→	D	Right on x-axis	→
Move up	↑	W	Up on y-axis	↑
Move down	↓	S	Down on y-axis	↓

Table 7.1 – Input methods for moving a video game character

To coordinate all these different inputs and devices into one coherent system, Godot has a built-in **input map** tool. This will manage the complexity for us, so we can just focus on using the inputs within the game.

The input map basically groups **input events** (such as the left arrow, the *A* key, the left joystick movement, and the left button on the D-pad) into one **action** (moving left). All we have to do is define each action and link all the input operations we want to support.

Let's set up our input map:

1. Open up the **Project Settings**. You'll find these in the **Project** menu item at the top of the editor.
2. Then navigate to the **Input Map** tab:

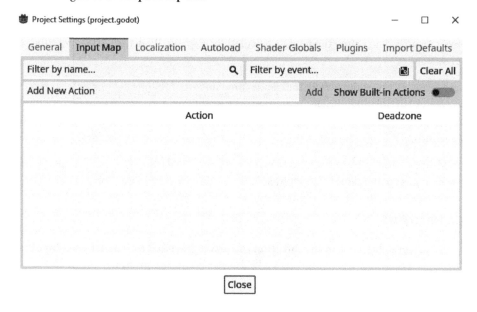

Figure 7.16 – The Input Map tab within Project Settings

3. Type move_left in the input field that says **Add New Action** and press **Add**. You'll see a new action appear in the main section of the window now:

Figure 7.17 – Adding a new action called move_left

4. Press the + sign next to the action name to add an event to our action.

5. Now, with the top input field selected, press the left-arrow key on your keyboard.

6. Make sure **Physical Keycode** is selected in the bottom dropdown menu and press **OK** to add the event to the action:

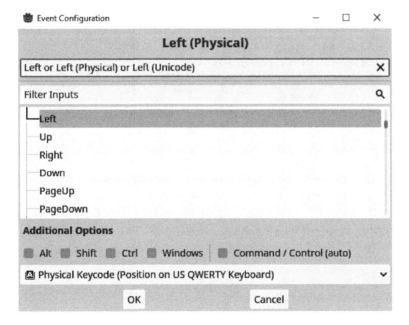

Figure 7.18 – Configuring the event to be the left arrow key

Notice that the physical keycode is selected at the bottom.

7. Repeat *steps 3 to 5* for the *A* key if you are on a QWERTY keyboard or use the equivalent key for your keyboard's layout.

8. Repeat *steps 3 to 5* for the analog stick movement and D-pad button of a controller if you have one lying around. If you don't have one to connect to your computer, you can just search for the next events in the menu:

   - **Joypad Axis 0** (left stick, joystick 0 left)

   - **Joypad Button 13** (D-pad left)

9. Now create the move_right, move_up, and move_down actions and repeat the previous steps to add all the appropriate input events to each.

Your input map should look a bit like this when you are finished:

Action	Deadzone			
⌄ move_left	0.5	⇕	+	🗑
◩ Left (Physical)			ⓘ	🗑
✖ Joypad Axis 0 - (Left Stick Left, Joystick 0 Left) - All Devices			ⓘ	🗑
✖ Joypad Button 13 (D-pad Left) - All Devices			ⓘ	🗑
⌄ move_right	0.5	⇕	+	🗑
◩ Right (Physical)			ⓘ	🗑
✖ Joypad Axis 0 + (Left Stick Right, Joystick 0 Right) - All Devices			ⓘ	🗑
✖ Joypad Button 14 (D-pad Right) - All Devices			ⓘ	🗑
⌄ move_up	0.5	⇕	+	🗑
◩ Up (Physical)			ⓘ	🗑
✖ Joypad Axis 1 - (Left Stick Up, Joystick 0 Up) - All Devices			ⓘ	🗑
✖ Joypad Button 11 (D-pad Up) - All Devices			ⓘ	🗑
⌄ move_down	0.5	⇕	+	🗑
◩ Down (Physical)			ⓘ	🗑
✖ Joypad Axis 1 + (Left Stick Down, Joystick 0 Down) - All Devices			ⓘ	🗑
✖ Joypad Button 12 (D-pad Down) - All Devices			ⓘ	🗑

Figure 7.19 – The complete input mapping to make the player character move

Physical keycode

Each key on a keyboard has a unique scancode. This is a simple number that identifies that unique key. This scancode gets interpreted by the operating system into a keycode, that is, a letter, character, or any of the other operations on the keyboard. This interpretation takes the keyboard layout into account (QWERTY, AZERT, etc.). The problem is that keys get put in different places depending on the keyboard layout and operating system you are using.

To simplify this, Godot has physical keycodes that directly use the scancode of a key instead of its underlying character or operation. This way, we make sure that the movement keys (which on a QWERTY keyboard are WASD, but on an AZERTY keyboard are ZQSD) are always in the same spot no matter the keyboard layout.

Using the input

Using the input actions we set up for the directional movement of the player character is quite easy in Godot because it has a built-in function that can take four actions and spit out a vector that represents the direction the player wants to move in.

This function is defined on the global `Input` object and is called `get_vector()`. It takes four arguments, which are the names of the action for the negative x direction, positive x direction, negative y direction, and positive y direction.

> **Singletons**
>
> Global objects are objects that are accessible from any part of the code base and are automatically instantiated. They are also called singletons or auto loads.

To make our character move, all we need to do is the following:

```
func _physics_process(delta: float):
    var input_direction: Vector2 = Input.get_vector("move_left", "move_
right", "move_up", "move_down")

    velocity = input_direction * 500.0
    move_and_slide()
```

You can see that we store the input direction in a variable called `input_direction` and then multiply this directional vector by 500. This is because the vector that comes back from `get_vector()` has a length of 1, which is very short and would make our character's movement almost indistinguishable from standing still.

When running the game, we can finally move our character using all the different input methods we set up. Success!

As an experiment, try not multiplying the input direction by 1000.

Smoothing out the movement

Now, the player movement already works fairly well, but it feels very stiff. From the moment our character starts moving, it moves at the maximum speed and when we let go of all buttons, the character instantly stops. This is not how things move in the real world. There always is a period of acceleration and deceleration before and after moving.

Let's first start off by defining some export variables so we can play around with all the different parts of the movement. This will make tweaking and polishing way easier.

At the top of the player script, add an export variable for the maximum speed, acceleration, and deceleration:

```
@export var max_speed: float = 500.0
@export var acceleration: float = 2500.0
@export var deceleration: float = 1500.0
```

Then, rewrite the _physics_process() function once more, as follows:

```
func _physics_process(delta: float):
    var input_direction: Vector2 = Input.get_vector("move_left", "move_
right", "move_up", "move_down")

    if input_direction != Vector2.ZERO:
        velocity = velocity.move_toward(input_direction * max_speed,
acceleration * delta)
    else:
        velocity = velocity.move_toward(Vector2.ZERO, deceleration *
delta)

    move_and_slide()
```

Vector2.ZERO is just a nice replacement for Vector2(0, 0). It's not shorter, but it is easier to read.

You can see that we put the input vector in a new variable. Then we checked whether it was equal to the zero vector (0, 0). In this case, the player is giving input, so we have to accelerate in the direction of the input_direction. We do this using the move_toward() function. This function will move the vector we call it on, which in this case is the velocity variable, to match up with another vector, which in this case is the input_direction scaled by max_speed; the scaled input_direction is the first parameter for the distance over which we move, which is the second parameter. The great thing about move_toward() is that it doesn't overshoot the target vector, so we don't have to do any additional calculations. *Figure 7.20* demonstrates this:

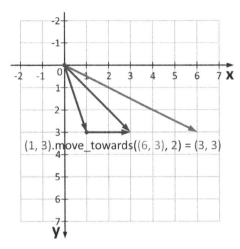

Figure 7.20 – move_towards demonstrates that moving from (1, 3) to (6, 3) over 2 units results in (3, 3)

The vector we want to move toward is input_direction multiplied by max_speed, which is basically the vector we had in the last section, *Using the input*.

The amount with which we try to move towards the new vector is acceleration times delta that comes into the _physics_process() function. This makes sure that the acceleration and deceleration always get applied at the same rate and are independent of framerate. We don't need to multiply velocity itself by delta because move_and_slide() already incorporates delta between physics frames by default.

In the case where the input_direction is equal to the zero vector, we want to decelerate. We do this in exactly the same way as accelerating, moving the velocity toward the zero vector using deceleration as the amount of this movement.

When you run the game now, you'll see that the movement feels way better. You can play around with the exported variables a bit to finetune everything to your liking.

> **Important note**
> Remember that you change these variables while the game is running because we exported the variables!

In this section, we have learned how to set up a physics object to move around and how to process directional input and we have done a deeper dive into smooth movement. Next, let's learn how to debug a game while it is running.

Debugging a running game

Until now, we have been able to debug our game by printing values to the output console. This is a very quick and effective way of debugging, but there are actually more options available that can shed way more clarity on what is happening during our game's execution.

Let's look at these ways in detail.

Breakpoints

The first, and most classic way of debugging is by using **breakpoints**. A breakpoint literally breaks, or halts, the program at the line of code in which the breakpoint was put. To place a breakpoint, click next to the line number of a line of code within the code editor.

```
 37  v  func _physics_process(delta: float):
 38     >|     var input_direction: Vector2 = Input
 39
 40  v >|     if input_direction != Vector2.ZERO:
 41     >|     >|    velocity = velocity.move_toward(
 42  v >|     else:
 43     >|     >|    velocity = velocity.move_toward(
 44
 45     >|     move_and_slide()
```

Figure 7.21 – Adding a breakpoint in the code

When the interpreter comes over this line, and thus this breakpoint, it will stop everything and show you where the execution of the code is.

Try it out by placing a breakpoint in the _physics_process() function of the player. Once the program halts, the **Debug** panel will unfold from the bottom. In this panel, you can examine a bunch of different things:

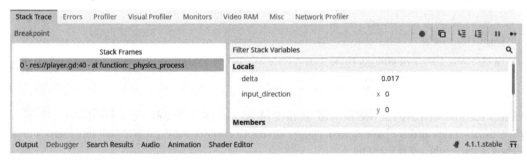

Figure 7.22 – The Debug panel shows context about the breakpoint

On the right, you can see all the variables that are currently in scope along with their values. This is incredibly useful as we can see the state of all variables at one quick glance. With printing, you could only see the values we put into the print statement, but now we see all current values in scope:

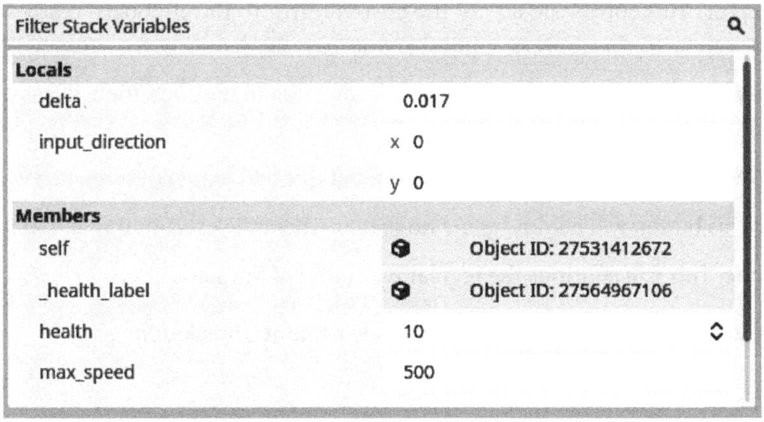

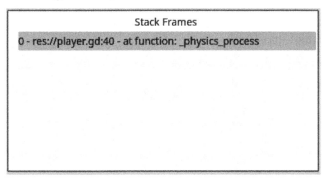

Figure 7.23 – All the values of the variables currently in scope shown in the Debug panel

On the left side of the panel, you can see the current stack, which means the different functions the program went through to end up here. For now, this is just the `_physics_process()` function because it is the only function being executed. Later on, this panel will show us the succession of functions that were called to get to this point in the code:

Stack Frames

0 - res://player.gd:40 - at function: _physics_process

Figure 7.24 – The stack frame shows all the functions executed to get to the breakpoint

In the top right of the panel, we have some debug controls:

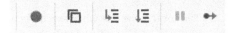

Figure 7.25 – All the debug controls

These controls allow us to decide what happens next now that we are at the breakpoint:

- **Skip breakpoints**: This toggles whether the interpreter should halt at breakpoints or not.

- **Copy error**: This copies the text of the current error to the clipboard ready to paste it in a Google search. This is not very applicable now but very handy when running into an error.

- **Step into**: This will make the interpreter take one step in the code and will step into any user-defined functions it comes by.

- **Step over**: This is the same as `Step Into`, but this will not go into functions.

- **Break**: This button will halt the game no matter where the execution is at that moment.

- **Continue**: This will continue the regular execution of the game.

These buttons will help us navigate through the code while at a breakpoint.

> **Important note**
>
> Breakpoints exist in mostly all programming languages, such as JavaScript and Python, and code editors, such as Jetbrains' Rider, in one way or another. It is good to get acquainted with them.

Remote tree

The second way of debugging is very Godot-specific. As each scene is built out of a scene tree and this tree is constructed and directly altered during the game's execution, you would expect that we could take a look at what the tree and its nodes look like at each point in the game. And you are right, that is exactly what the **remote tree** is!

First, start the game. In the editor, two new buttons will appear right above the scene tree: **Remote** and **Local**. Currently, we are in the **Local** scene tree, which is the scene tree of the scene we are editing:

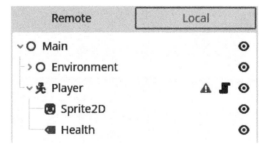

Figure 7.26 – The Local scene tree while executing our game

If we switch to **Remote**, we switch to the tree as it is in the running game:

Figure 7.27 – Switching over to the Remote tree using the Remote button

You can search through the remote tree for the `Player` node. If you click it, the inspector will show you the values of this node as they are in the game. If you scroll down to the node's position and move the player in the game a bit, you will see that the values in the inspector change according to the position of the player character:

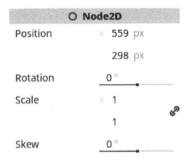

Figure 7.28 – Changing the position of a node in the Remote tree

If you ever don't know what is happening, remember printing, breakpoints, and the remote tree and you will surely figure the bug out!

Additional exercises – Sharpening the axe

Here are some other exercises you can do in Godot:

1. Tweak the movement variables of the player character so it feels like you are ice skating.

2. Rewrite the `_physics_process()` function of the player by replacing the `move_toward()` function with raw vector operations. You'll need to add a vector to the `velocity` variable in the direction of the `input_direction` that has the length of the `acceleration` variable. You'll then have to make sure that the `velocity` variable doesn't exceed the `max_speed` variable.

Summary

This chapter was all about physics and moving the player. We even refreshed our vector math a bit. Now the player character can move off the screen! Furthermore, they can run through walls.

In *Chapter 9*, we'll fix these problems in collision detection, even creating collectibles, such as money.

First, we'll need to learn how to separate parts of our scene tree into their own scene files and use those. Come along for a little detour in the next chapter.

Quiz time

- With what class are vectors represented in GDScript?
- Solve the following vector math equations:

  - (2, 4) + (-4, 3)

  - (-1, 2) - (6, 6)

  - (3, 1) * 2

- If we want to move the player using the physics engine, do we do that in the `_process()` or `_physics_process()` Function?

  - How many times per second gets the `_process()` function called?

  - How many times per second gets the `_physics_process()` function called?

- Why did we use the Physical Keycode to register keyboard buttons in our project's input map?

8
Splitting and Reusing Scenes

It is possible to create the whole game within one Godot scene, but this can get quite unwieldy. Not only do we have to recreate every part over and over again, such as every boulder or enemy, but if we want to change something about the rocks, we have to go and find every rock to change them.

This is not scalable for any kind of game. Luckily, in Godot, there are such things as *scenes*. In *Chapter 2*, we saw how to create new scenes from scratch, but in this chapter, we will learn how we can create a scene for each element so that we can easily reuse it throughout the game. This way, we can make one scene for the rocks and use that to populate the arena instead of having multiple unique rocks.

Next to reusing components, it's also way easier to work on certain parts of the game in isolation instead of having a big scene. Saving parts of the game like this will keep us focused on what we are working on.

Other game engines have very similar systems. Unity has Prefabs, Unreal Engine has Blueprint Classes, and so on. The great thing about Godot scenes is that they behave just like any other node once they are instanced in the scene tree.

In this chapter, we will cover the following main topics:

- Saving a branch as a new scene
- Using saved scenes
- Organizing scenes in a project

Technical requirements

As for every chapter, you can find the final code in this book's GitHub repository in the subfolder for this chapter: `https://github.com/PacktPublishing/Learning-GDScript-by-Developing-a-Game-with-Godot-4/tree/main/chapter08`.

Saving a branch as a new scene

In the *Creating new scenes* section of *Chapter 2*, we learned how to create new scenes for different code experiments. This process can be followed to create any scene at all. But another way to do this is to save part of an existing scene tree. We'll be splitting a branch of the scene tree into its separate sub-scene that we can reuse anywhere.

Creating a separate player scene

Let's save the Player node as a separate scene so that we can work on it in isolation. Go to our Main scene and follow these steps:

1. Right-click the Player node.
2. From the pop-up menu, select **Save Branch as Scene**:

Figure 8.1 – Selecting Save Branch as Scene to save the node as a separate scene

3. Now, we have to select a location and name for the new scene. Leaving everything as-is should do the trick:

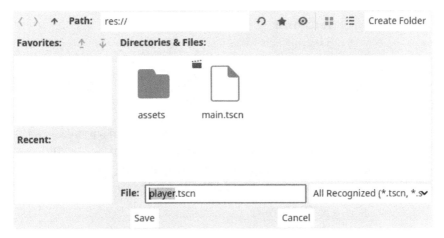

Figure 8.2 – Saving the scene under an appropriate name

4. The new scene will now open and only contain the Player node and its child:

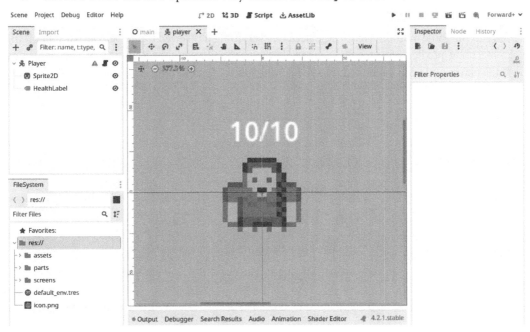

Figure 8.3 – The player.tscn scene, which only contains the Player node and its children

5. Reset the `Player` node's position so that it is positioned at (0, 0) within the scene:

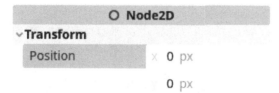

Figure 8.4 – Resetting the position of the root Player node to (0, 0)

If you go back to the main scene, as shown in *Figure 8.3*, you'll see that the `Player` node, which first had some child nodes underneath it, is replaced by one node called `Player`. This one node now represents everything that is within the **Player** scene. Visually, nothing changed in the 2D editor; the player is still there complete, with its **Sprite2D** and **Health** labels:

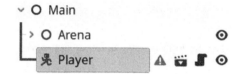

Figure 8.5 – The Player node and its children are replaced with a single node

If you run the game, nothing will change because everything has stayed the same. We just split off the `Player` node into its own scene file. You can check this by going into the **Remote** tree and confirming that the player node gets expanded into all its parts when the game starts to run:

Figure 8.6 – The Player node expands to have all its child nodes in the Remote tree when running the game

There is also a new button available in the `Player` node. Pressing this button will bring us straight to the `Player` scene. This is very convenient for when we'll be working with lots of different scenes and nodes later on:

Figure 8.7 - The new button that will bring us directly to the Player scene

Now, the player has their own scene that we can work in without having to deal with everything in the whole game.

The root node of a scene

You'll also see that the root node of the player scene is the `CharacterBody2D` node called `Player`, which we chose for it in *Chapter 7*. Scenes can have any type of node as their root. You can choose this type when creating the scene, as we did in *Chapter 2*, or later on, by changing the node type, as we did in *Chapter 7* for the `Player` node.

Having a separate scene file allows us to create multiple instances of that scene within another scene. We'll see how we can do that in the next section.

Using saved scenes

Because we will use only one player in the game, we are not going to reuse the player scene multiple times. However, we will want to reuse the rocks and walls within the arena. Follow the steps in the *Saving a branch as a new scene* section to separate one boulder into a new scene:

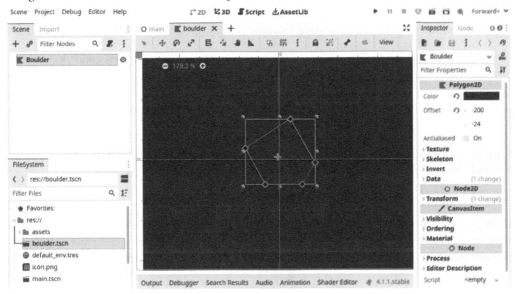

Figure 8.8 – The boulder.tscn scene

Now, let's reuse this new scene in our arena as the default rock:

1. Go back to the main scene. Remove all the rocks from the scene; we don't need them anymore.

2. Select the `Arena` node. By doing so, everything we add will be added as a child of this node.

3. Now, drag and drop the boulder scene from **FileSystem** into the 2D editor. You will see the visual of the boulder pop up while you're still dragging it around:

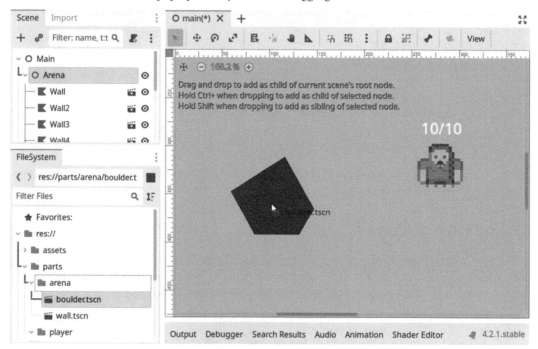

Figure 8.9 – Dragging and dropping the boulder.tscn scene into the main scene tree

Now, you can do the same for the inner walls in the scene and repopulate the arena with rocks and walls so that it looks less barren. However, don't do the same for `OuterWalls` – we aren't going to reuse it, so this one can stay the same.

When placing the boulder and wall scenes, you can use the transform parameters, such as rotation, scale, and skew, to give variety to the instances so that they don't all look too similar.

The cool thing is that we can use any scene within any other scene!

Having many smaller scene files has lots of upsides, with the maintainability of the code and easy reuse being just two of them, but it will also complexify the file structure of the project. Because of this, we'll have to think about how we'll organize all the files within the project. We'll do that in the next section.

Organizing scene files

Now that we have more files to worry about, we'll have to start being smart regarding how we organize them. Let's separate scenes into different folders that make sense for our project. This way, we'll always know where to find something or save a new scene.

Add the following folders in the root folder of our project:

- `parts`:
  - `environment`
  - `player`
- `screens`:
  - `game`

The `parts` folder will contain all the scenes that are part of a different scene, such as the player, walls, enemies, collectibles, UI buttons, and so forth.

`screens`, on the other hand, will contain all scenes that can stand on their own, such as the game screen, full-screen menus such as the main menu or pause menu, and so forth. These scenes are made up of scenes from the `parts` folder.

At the beginning of the project, I gave you an `assets` folder. This folder is used to hold all the art assets, from sprites to animations and sounds.

Now, move all scenes and scripts to the appropriate folders, like so:

Figure 8.10 – Our project with better file management

Once you look at other game projects made in Godot, or other game engines, you'll see that everyone has their own way of organizing different files within their project. I like to keep scenes and scripts together within the same folder, for example, because most of the time, you will use and edit them very closely together. However, I will keep assets, such as pictures and sounds, separate because these are easier to reuse over different scenes.

Over time, you will probably develop an organizational structure for projects and that's fine. Whatever makes the most sense to you is what you should use, so long as you are consistent.

Additional exercises – Sharepening the axe

1. Using what we learned about splitting off scenes, try making a second boulder scene with a different shape than the first one. Call the first boulder scene `boulder01.tscn` and the second one `boulder02.tscn`.

Summary

Reusing parts of your work is almost always a good idea. In this chapter, we learned how to reuse whole branches of the scene tree as separate scenes. This will come in handy in the following chapters as we are now able to work on the player's camera movement separately and create collisions in all rocks and walls simultaneously. But that's for the next chapter.

Quiz time

- How can you save a branch within the scene tree as a separate scene?
- Is it important to organize our scenes, scripts, and assets in the **FileSystem** area? Why?

Cameras, Collisions, and Collectibles

While playing a game, the player doesn't want to have to think about the camera and its placement. The camera should always follow the player's character and anticipate what the player wants to achieve so it doesn't obstruct the player's vision.

In bigger games, full teams are tasked with producing the smoothest camera possible. In this chapter, we will attempt to do the same with some Godot Engine nodes.

After that, we'll stop the player from walking through walls and have a look at sprinkling collectibles, such as health and money, around our arena.

In this chapter, we will cover the following main topics:

- Making a camera that follows the player

- Collisions with boulders and walls

- Collision masks

- Creating inherited scenes

- Connecting to signals

Technical requirements

As for every chapter, you can find the final code on the GitHub repository in the subfolder for this chapter at `https://github.com/PacktPublishing/Learning-GDScript-by-Developing-a-Game-with-Godot-4/tree/main/chapter9`.

Making a camera that follows the player

At the moment, our character can run around, but at some point, it will run off the screen and get lost forever. Our in-game camera should follow them around so the player knows where they are.

Luckily, the Godot Engine has a pretty nice camera system that we can use. It can be a bit basic, but it is all we need, and with some extra nodes, we'll be able to achieve a very smooth-moving camera.

Setting up a basic camera

For 2D games, Godot provides the **Camera2D** node.

Open up the `player.tscn` scene and add a **Camera2D** node to the `Player` node. This is all we need to make a basic camera that follows the player:

Figure 9.1 – The player scene with an added Camera2D node

But this basic camera feels a bit stiff; it starts and stops moving at exactly the moment the character does. This doesn't feel very natural. Let's see how to solve this.

Adding drag margins

To make the camera movement appear natural, we will use **drag margins**. Find and enable **Horizontal** and **Vertical** drag in the camera's inspector:

Drag		
Horizontal Enabled	↺ ☑	On
Vertical Enabled	↺ ☑	On
Horizontal Offset		0
Vertical Offset		0
Left Margin	↺	0.1
Top Margin	↺	0.1
Right Margin	↺	0.1
Bottom Margin	↺	0.1

Figure 9.2 – The drag margin settings for the Camera2D node in the inspector.

Now, the camera only moves when the player exits a certain area in the middle of the screen. This is the margin within which nothing happens. If you enable **Draw Drag Margin** in the camera's inspector, you can see the drag margins visualized:

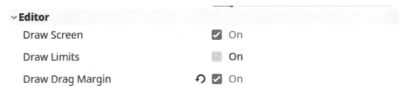

Figure 9.3 – Showing the drag margins in the editor by enabling them in the Camera2D inspector

With **Draw Drag Margin** enabled, you should be able to see the blue rectangles indicating when the camera will start moving:

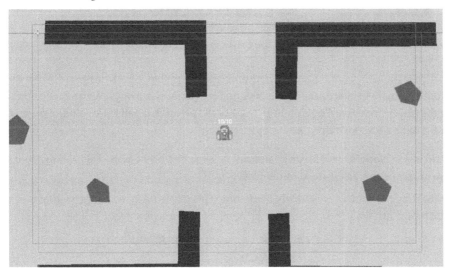

Figure 9.4 – The editor now shows the drag margins in light blue

You can play a bit with the left, top, right, and bottom margins in the inspector. I chose to set them all to 0.1, as seen in *Figure 9.2* earlier.

Great, the drag margins already feel great. But the camera still starts and stops moving very abruptly and seems to lag behind the player. Let's fix that next.

Making the camera look ahead

The movement of the camera feels pretty great now. But there is something wrong; we need something more fundamental than nice, smooth movement. When the player moves, the camera drags behind, showing where the player has been and not where the player is going.

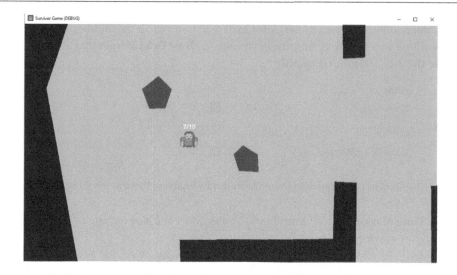

Figure 9.5 – The camera lags behind the player and does not show where the player is going

This is not great; imagine running somewhere and only being able to look backward. What we actually want is for the camera to look ahead in the direction the player is moving. We can do this by, instead of tracking the player itself, tracking a point in front of the player. Basically, it is as if the player character is holding a selfie stick. So, follow these steps:

1. Add a new **Node2D** to Player and call it CameraPosition. This will become the point we are going to track instead of the player itself.

2. Now drag the camera we already made onto this CameraPosition so that it is a child of the new node:

Figure 9.6 – Put the Camera2D node under a separate node called CameraPosition

3. Make sure that the position of the **Camera2D** and CameraPosition is set to (0, 0) in the inspector:

Figure 9.7 – Make sure the Camera2D and CameraPosition nodes are at position (0, 0)

4. Add a script to the `CameraPosition` called `camera_position.gd`.

This script will keep the position in front of the camera. We can do this based on the `velocity` that the player character has.

The complete script looks like this:

```
extends Node2D

@export var camera_distance: float = 200

@onready var _player: CharacterBody2D = get_parent()

func _process(_delta):
    var move_direction: Vector2 = _player.velocity.normalized()

    position = move_direction * camera_distance
```

First, we define an export variable that we can play with called `camera_distance`. This will be the distance in front of the player at which we will keep the camera while the player is moving.

With `_physics_process()`, which gets executed for each physics frame of the game, we calculate the position of the camera point. Remember that this position is relative to the `Player` node, so a position of `(0, 0)` is right where the player is. The idea is to take the direction in which the player is moving and multiply that by the `camera_distance`. The direction the player is moving in can be derived from the `velocity` of the player. So first, we get the player node using the `get_parent` function and cache it in the `_player` variable. This function returns the parent of a node, in this case, the `Player` node because the `CameraPosition` is a direct child of that node.

Then, to get the direction the player is moving in, we normalize this `velocity` vector. Normalizing a vector, as we saw in *Chapter 7*, means that you take the whole vector and make it of length `1`. So, the whole vector is `1` pixel long. This will leave us with the direction of the `velocity` without its length. Now we can easily scale this direction to whatever length we want by multiplying it with the `camera_distance` to define the `position` of the `CameraPosition`. If you run the game now, you'll see that `CameraPosition` does what you want it to and makes the camera look ahead in the direction the character is moving. But it is still a bit janky, so let's smooth that out one last time.

Smoothing out the look ahead

The problem now is that the camera starts moving very suddenly and abruptly stops. This happens because the `CameraPosition` we created jumps around quite quickly. To fix this problem, we should make the movement of the `CameraPosition` itself smooth.

First, add a new exported variable, like so:

```
@export var position_interpolation_speed: float = 1.0
```

Now, let's change the `_process()` function of the `camera_position.gd` script as follows:

```
func _physics_process(delta):
    var move_direction: Vector2 = _player.velocity.normalized()
    var target_position: Vector2 = move_direction * camera_distance

    position = position.lerp(target_position, position_interpolation_
speed * delta)
```

We do largely the same things as in the preceding section, but this time, we save the position we want the `CameraPosition` to have as a `target_position`. Then, in the next line, we calculate the actual `position`.

To calculate the position, we use a new function, `lerp()`. This is short for **linear interpolation**. This function works very much the same as `move_towards()`, which we used in *Chapter 7*. However, while `move_towards()` moves the position a certain number of pixels toward the target position, `lerp` moves the position toward the `target_position` according to a percentage between the two, which is the last argument in the function. This percentage is expressed in a value from `0.0` to `1.0`, where `0.0` is `0%` and `1.0` is `100%`.

So, let's say we want to move `50%` between the position and its target, then the resulting position will be right in the middle between the two points.

This process is called **linear interpolation** because we interpolate between two values linearly. The way we use linear interpolation in our camera position script is to move toward the target position a little bit every frame.

The percentage of the linear interpolation that I chose was `5.0 * delta`. I put this value in an exported variable so we can easily tweak it from the editor. Because delta is the time between two frames, the result of this product is very small and should result in an interpolation of around `10%` per frame. We multiply by `delta` because, just like for the movement speed of the player, we want the speed of the camera not to change on faster or slower computers that run at a higher or lower framerate. We talked about frame rate independent calculations in *Chapter 7* too when making the character move.

You can play around with the speed of the interpolation by changing the `position_interpolation_speed` to anything else through the inspector.

In this section, we learned a great deal about creating a smooth and useful camera that frames where the player is moving toward. As mentioned in the introduction of this chapter, big-budget games have whole teams that work on nothing else but the camera. But using some smart tricks, we achieved a fairly nice camera for our little game. Now, we'll shift gears and make sure the player stops running through walls by adding collision detection.

Collisions

With our brand-new camera in place, let's take a look at collisions. For now, we have the visuals of a nice arena, including walls and rocks, but they don't really act like them. The player character is able to just run through them as if they were made out of air instead of solid matter.

Just like with the movement of the player, we can solve this using the built-in physics engine. Let's start by taking a look at the different physics bodies at our disposal.

The different physics bodies

For the player character, we used the **CharacterBody2D** physics body. But this is not the only kind that comes with the physics engine Godot. There are a few other ones:

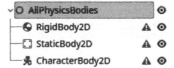

Figure 9.8 – The three different physics bodies as displayed in the scene tree

For 2D games, there are three different kinds of physics bodies available. Each has its own uses within a game or physics simulation. Let's take a look at each.

RigidBody2D

A rigid body is a physics object that is fully simulated. Rigid bodies are completely dependent on outside physical forces and collisions. You are not supposed to control them directly.

> **Important note**
>
> These bodies are called rigid because the body itself does not deform. So, it gets used for simulating solid objects from cars to bones to walls. The **StaticBody2D** and **CharacterBody2D** can also not deform and are therefore also rigid bodies, but more in the mathematical sense of the word and not in how they are implemented within the engine.

We cannot directly control a rigid body; they are fully managed by the physics engine, which resolves how it moves and how the velocities and forces get applied. The only way to control a rigid body is by applying external forces to it. This is like hitting a golf ball with a stick. With enough practice and fine-tuning, you can get the ball in the general direction of the hole, but picking it up and dropping it in there, though easier, is not an option.

Simulating non-rigid, bodies, also known as soft bodies, is generally harder to do mathematically and performantly within a game. Soft bodies could be sponges, rubber objects that deform, jelly, and so on. There are ways to simulate these within a rigid body simulation, but it's not advised to do this. In 3D, there is a **Softbody3D** node, but it is not for 2D.

StaticBody2D

A static body is a physics body that stays static, meaning it does not move around and also cannot be pushed by external forces. This is the simplest of physics bodies to deal with and will be ideal for making our walls and rocks out of.

CharacterBody2D

A character body is a physics body that we are able to control through code. A **RigidBody2D**, as we saw earlier, is fully managed by the physics engine. This makes it hard to control to get it to do what you want it to.

A character body, on the other hand, gives us a good middle ground. Like in the `player.gd` script, we have to calculate the `velocity` ourselves and call `move_and_slide()`. But the physics engine still helps us out with collisions and calculating where the body is supposed to move based on the velocity.

> **More information**
>
> The Godot documentation also has a great write-up of the different physics bodies and how they can be used: `https://docs.godotengine.org/en/stable/tutorials/physics/physics_introduction.html#collision-objects`.

These were the three types of physics bodies available in Godot. But there is actually a fourth physics object, which is not a body. Let's take a look at the **Area2D** node.

The Area2D node

The three physics bodies we just saw all collide with each other and react to this collision or make other bodies react to it. In essence, their movements get processed by the physics engine.

The last physics object, **Area2D**, only detects and influences other physics objects. It is not subjected to physics calculation, like for movement. But it can detect if another physics object is overlapping it and throws a signal when these other physics objects enter or leave.

We will use this functionality near the end of this chapter to make the player pick up health potions when they come near them.

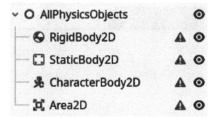

Figure 9.9 – The four different physics objects as they are displayed in the scene tree

Now that you know about the three types of physics bodies currently available, we can start utilizing them to create proper collisions.

Adding a collision shape to the player node

Since we created the player node all the way back in *Chapter 6*, there has been this little orange triangle next to it. When we hover over it, the tool tip explains to us that this node is missing a shape. This makes sense, how can the physics engine detect collisions if it doesn't know what shape a physics body is?

Let's solve this little warning:

1. Find and add the **CollisionShape2D** node as a child of the `Player` node:

Figure 9.10 – Add a CollisionShape2D to the player scene

2. Select this newly created **CollisionShape2D** node and click on the empty **Shape** field to reveal a drop-down menu with different shapes.

3.   Select the **CapsuleShape2D** option.

☐ CollisionShape2D		
Shape	⟳ ◌	CapsuleShape2D ⌄
Radius	10 px	
Height	30 px	
Custom Solver Bias	0	
› **Resource**		(1 change)

Figure 9.11 – Select a CapsuleShape2D as the CollisionShape2D's shape

4.   A capsule-like blue shape will appear on the screen. This is the shape of the physics body. Use the orange circles on the periphery of the shape to change its size and try to cover most of the player sprite:

Figure 9.12 – Make sure the CapsuleShape2D covers the player sprite

The **CollisionShape2D** node in itself does not have a shape, but it will hold one for us. That is why we had to add one to the **Shape** property.

Other shapes that are interesting as collision shapes are **RectangleShape2D** and **CircleShape2D**. The others are used in specialized situations, such as for very thin or disjointed objects, so don't worry too much about them just yet.

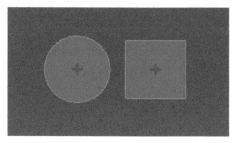

Figure 9.13 – The CircleShape2D and RectangleShape2D

Running the game now will not result in the player colliding with the boulders or walls, simply because first, we'll also need to add physics bodies and shapes to the scenes of these two.

Creating static bodies for the boulders

In the *The different physics bodies* section, we learned that **StaticBody2D** nodes don't move; that sounds ideal for a boulder. So, let's make them solid:

1.   Go into our `boulder.tscn` scene.

2.   Add a **StaticBody2D** node under the root node:

Figure 9.14 – Adding a StaticBody2D with a CollisionPolygon2D as a child of the boulder scene

3.   Add a `CollisionPolygon2D` node under this newly created static body.

4.   Now add points to the collision polygon by clicking within the 2D editor. Try to cover the boulder completely:

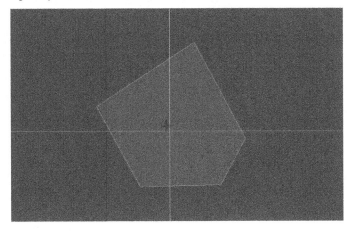

Figure 9.15 – Cover the boulder with the PolygonShape2D

Note that we use a different kind of collision shape. Now we use `CollisionPolygon2D`. This shape lets us define our own arbitrary shape. The advantage is that we can create any shape we like. The disadvantage is that arbitrary polygons are a bit slower for the physics engine to handle. But this should not be a big problem in our game because we will not have thousands of objects that require complex physics calculations.

Now that we know how to create static bodies, we can do the same for other static objects in our game, such as walls.

Creating static bodies for the walls

Let's do something similar by adding collision to the walls within the game:

1. Open up `wall.tscn`.

2. Add a **StaticBody2D** node.

Figure 9.16 – The wall's StaticBody2D has two CollisioniShape2D children

3. Instead of using a **CollisionPolygon2D**, add two **CollisionShape2D** nodes.

4. Give them each a **RectangleShape2D** in their **Shape** property.

5. Now make sure that the combination of these two shapes covers the wall:

Figure 9.17 – Covering the wall using the two RectangleShape2Ds

From this example, you can see that a single physics body can actually contain multiple collision shapes. This is very useful when constructing complex shapes without having to resort to a **CollisionPolygon2D**. Although we used two rectangle shapes, we could have used two different shapes if we wanted to, even combining regular shapes and polygons. We can add as many shapes under one physics body as we desire.

In this section, we learned how to use different physics bodies to do collision detection and make sure the player doesn't walk through walls and boulders. In the next section, we'll extend this knowledge to also use the physics engine to detect whether the player is within a certain region or not.

Creating collectibles

Now, let's create some collectibles for our hero to pick up. We'll create two different collectibles:

- A health potion, which will replenish the health of the character
- A coin, which will add one gold to the player's money

We'll start off by creating a base collectible, from which we can easily implement the two different behaviors we want the two collectibles to have.

Creating the base collectible scene

The base scene and class that we will build to inherit each specific collectible is very important; it should cover the use case of all other collectibles that we want to create. So let's start:

1. Create a new scene called `collectible.tscn` in a new folder, `parts/collectibles`.

2. Set up the scene as shown in *Figure 9.18*:

   I.   Make the root node a **Node2D** and call it `Collectible`.

   II. Add an **Area2D** node and a **Sprite2D** as direct children.

   III. Add a **CollisionShape2D** to the area.

Figure 9.18 – The base scene structure for our collectibles

3. Fill the **Shape** property of the **CollisionShape2D** with a **CircleShape2D**.

4. Update the radius of the circle shape to be 25 pixels.

We use a new node type, **Area2D**. An **Area2D** node can detect collisions when another physics body or area enters its shape. As we are using this physics object, the **Area2D** node will not act out any physics, nor will it influence the physics of the other physics body. **Area2D** nodes are used to detect whether other bodies or areas overlap their collision shape. We will use this functionality to detect if the player character overlaps the collectible because when this happens, we have to execute the code associated with the collectible.

With the base collectible scene ready, we can easily inherit from it in the next section.

Inheriting from a base scene

If you were wondering why we didn't add a texture to the collectible scene yet, that's because we want to do that for specific collectibles, such as the health potion and coin, and not for the base.

So let's create a specific collectible:

1. Right-click on the `collectible.tscn` scene in the file manager and select **New Inherited Scene**.

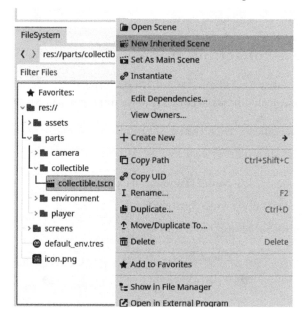

Figure 9.19 - Right-clicking the collectible.tscn file and choosing New Inherited Scene

2. A new scene will open up. Rename the root node to `HealthPotion`:

Figure 9.20 – The inherited nodes are greyed out

3. Save the inherited scene as `health_potion.tscn` in the same folder as the `collectible.tscn`, which is `parts/collectibles`.

4. Now add the `HealthPotion.png`, from `assets/visual/collectibles`, as a texture to the **Sprite2D** node.

5. The sprite is a little small, so set the scale to `(2, 2)`, as we did for the player's sprite in *Chapter 6*:

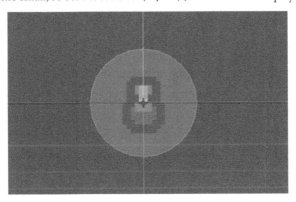

Figure 9.21 – This is how our health potion collectible should look in the editor

You can see that all the nodes, except for the root node, are greyed out, as in *Figure 9.22*. That is because these nodes are managed by the scene we are inheriting from, the `collectible.tscn` scene in this case.

Figure 9.22 – When inheriting a scene, the inherited nodes are greyed out

---

Try it yourself

Just as an experiment, go back to the `collectible.tscn` scene, put the sprite node in a different location, and save. If you have a look in the `health_potion.tscn` scene, you'll see that the sprite moved to the same location too!

With the technique of inheriting scenes, we can easily build out the functionality of collectibles without having to alter each collectible's scene separately or copy-pasting. We can just define the base structure and functionality once.

With our base health potion scene done, we can now add its logic. First, we need to know when the player is actually close enough to pick up the collectible. We'll learn how to do this in the next section.

Connecting to a signal

In the *Creating the base collectible scene* section, I told you that we were going to use an **Area2D** node to detect when the player's physics shape enters and thus when we know the collectible should be collected.

To do this, we'll learn about a new concept in Godot Engine: **signals**. All nodes can throw signals; a signal could be something such as *"a physics body entered my shape"*. We could listen, or connect, to this signal and run a piece of code whenever it happens.

We will now do this for the signal that the **Area2D** node throws when a physics body enters its collision shape:

1.   Go to the collectible.tscn scene.

2.   Add an empty script to the root node. To connect to a signal, we first need a script. Make sure to delete all the code within the script except for the first one that says it extends the **Node2D**. Save the script as collectible.gb.

3.   Now select the **Area2D** node. In the right panel, where we normally see the Inspector for a node, there is also a tab called **Node**. Click it.

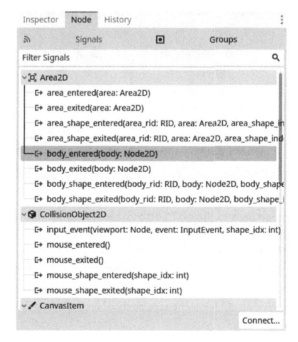

Figure 9.23 – The list of signals an Area2D node can throw; body_entered is the one we need

4. This tab shows us the different signals a node can throw. The one we want to connect to is called `body_entered` because it gets thrown from the moment a physics body enters the **Area2D** node. Select this signal and press the **Connect** button in the bottom right.

5. A modal pops up asking us to which node in the current scene we want to connect this signal. The root `Collectible` node should already be selected, so just press the **Connect** button.

Figure 9.24 – Selecting the node we want to connect the signal with, the Collectible node in our case

6. We will now directly be taken to the `collectible.gb` script and you can see that a new function, `_on_area_2d_body_entered`, got added for us:

```
1    extends Node2D
2
3
4  v func _on_area_2d_body_entered(body):
5    >|    pass # Replace with function body.
6
```

Figure 9.25 – A new function will automatically be created for us after connecting the signal

The connection of the signal is done; now, every time the `body_entered` signal is thrown by the **Area2D** node, the `_on_area_2d_body_entered` function of that collectible will be executed.

Also notice that the generated function has a parameter called `body`. This is the body object that overlapped the **Area2D**; for example, the player. Signals can give some context when they are being throw in the form of these parameters. Different signals have different parameters, and most have no parameters at all.

Writing the code for collectibles

Now we'll finally write some real code to give the player some new health points when picking up the health potion, though it will not be that much, to be honest. Let's write the code necessary to make our health potion functional:

1. First, go back to the `collectible.gd` script. We'll make this script a named class by adding a line defining the class name at the top:

    ```
    class_name Collectible
    ```

> **Important note**
>
> Creating a named class with `class_name` is not 100% necessary here, but it is good practice to name classes that you are going to inherit from.

2. Now in the `health_potion.tscn` scene, right-click on the root node, and select **Extend Script**.

3. Save the new script as `health_potion.gd` in the same folder as `health_potion.tscn`. This will create a script that inherits from the `Collectible` class and assigns it to the **HealthPotion** node for us.

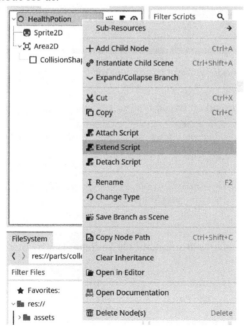

Figure 9.26 – Right-clicking the HealthPotion node and selecting Extend Script

4. Next, override the `_on_area_2d_body_entered()` function by defining a new one, like so:

```
func _on_area_2d_body_entered(body):
    body.health += 5
    queue_free()
```

This function is used in the `Collectible` class to connect to the `body_entered` signal. By overriding it here, we effectively replace the function that will be executed.

You can see that we take the body that is provided as an argument and simply update its health value by adding 5.

The last line introduces a new function that we can call on nodes: `queue_free()`. This function will queue the node for deletion so that the engine knows it can be removed from the scene tree. The engine will delete the node at the end of the current frame.

Let's try this out! Go back to the main scene and add a health potion somewhere by dragging and dropping the scene anywhere in the arena:

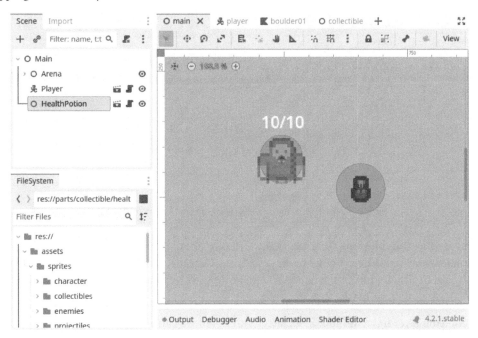

Figure 9.27 – Adding a HealthPotion in the main scene

If you put the health potion somewhere without boulders or walls, you will be able to walk over there with the player character and pick it up. But if you put the health potion too close to a boulder or wall, you'll get an error! Oh no! Let's learn how to solve this next.

Using collision layers and masks

There is one problem! The signal will now be thrown for every physics body that enters the **Area2D** of the collectible, so even for boulders and walls. But we only want to trigger the functionality when our player enters the area.

Luckily, we can only trigger the overlap detection for certain bodies using collision layers and masks.

Introducing collision layers and masks

If you select the **Area2D** node within the `collectible.tscn` scene, you'll see the **Collision Layer** and **Collision Mask** properties in the inspector. These two dictate what other physics bodies and areas can interact with the area.

- **Collision Layers** dictates what layer the physics object is in and can be detected by other physics objects.

- **Collision Mask** dictates what layers this physics object is looking at for collision detection.

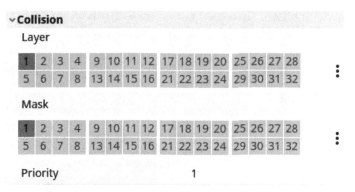

Figure 9.28 – There are 32 separate collision layers and masks

This means that the collision layers are used to tell other bodies and areas that you exist, while the collision mask is used to detect other bodies and areas. Note that these don't need to be the same. The layers could be different from the mask, and that one body or area can be active in multiple layers and can look at multiple masks.

Each collision layer has a number associated with it, but we can actually give them a name that is easier to read for humans. We'll do that in the next section.

Naming collision layers

What we are going to do is use one layer, `layer number 1`, as the layer for wall collisions and another layer, `layer number 2`, for collectible detection. Because it is difficult and non-descriptive to talk about `layer number 1` and `layer number 2`, we can name layers within the Godot Editor. This will help us in the long run:

1. Open up the **Project Settings**.

2. Navigate to **Layer Names | 2D Physics**:

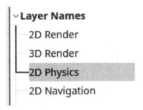

Figure 9.29 – Naming collision layers under the 2D Physics category

Here, you can see the different collision layers and their names. None of them have a name yet.

3. Give **Layer 1** the name `Collision` and **Layer 2** the name `Collectible`:

Figure 9.30 – Naming two of the layers

4. If we now select the **Area2D** node from the collectible scene again and hover over the layer numbers, we'll see the name pop up:

Figure 9.31 – Hovering over a collision layer number shows us its name

5. We can also click on the ellipses next to the layers for easier layer selection to see our names there.

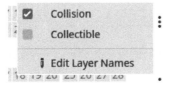

Figure 9.32 – Pressing the ellipses makes it easy to select named collision layers

With these collision layers having a name, it will be easier to assign them in the future. So let's do that in the next section.

Assigning the right layers

Now that we understand collision layers and masks and know how to name them, let's use them so that only the player can trigger collectibles.

We'll have to adjust the collision layers and masks of all physics bodies in the game. Luckily, we made separate scenes for all of them, so this will go fast and, in the future, we can take these layers into account while making the scenes.

For the `player.tscn` root node, configure the layers and mask as follows:

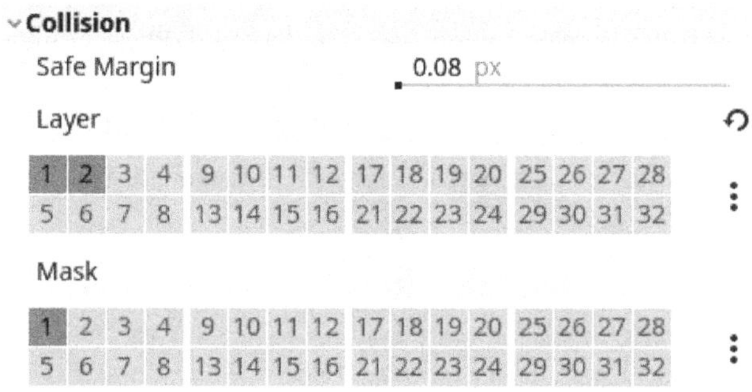

Figure 9.33 – The collision layer and mask configuration for the player

For the `boulder.tscn` and `wall.tscn`, we want the following configuration:

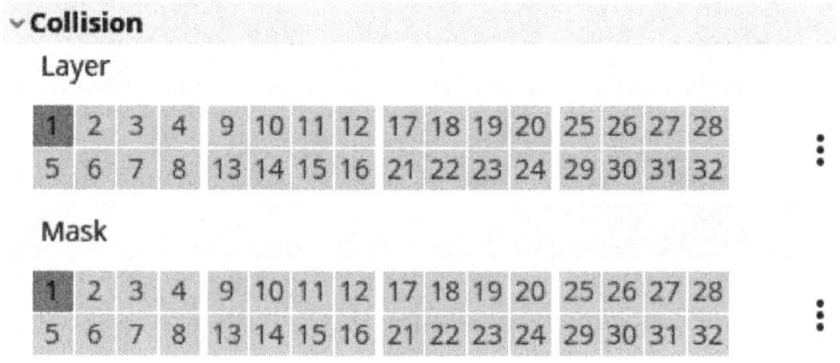

Figure 9.34 – The collision layer and mask configuration for boulders and walls

Lastly, for the `collectible.tscn` scene, set the configuration as follows:

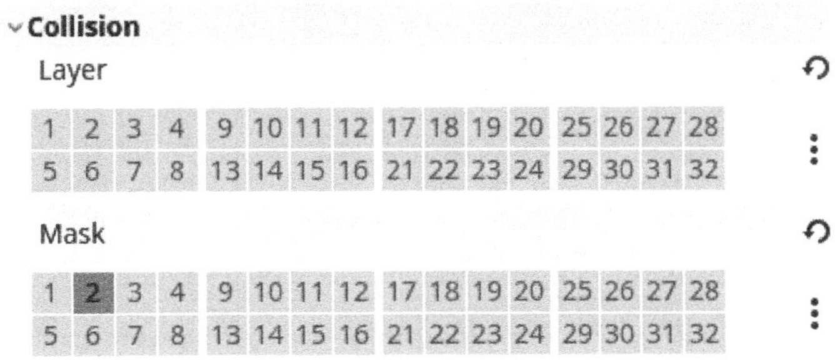

Figure 9.35 – The collision layer and mask configuration for collectibles

You can see that the player, boulders, and wall are in both the collision layer and collision mask. This is because they need to be able to interact with each other. On the other hand, the player is in the collectible layer and not the collectible mask, while the collectible scene does the opposite. We define the layer and mask for collectibles this way because the player doesn't directly need to interact with collectibles and doesn't need to detect them; the collectible scene does all the work for us.

Your turn!

Great, we created our health potion! Now you can implement the coin so the player can collect gold. Here are some of the steps you could take:

1. Make a new inherited scene from the `collectible.tscn` scene as we saw in the *Inheriting from a base scene* section.

2. Extend the collectible script, as we did in the *Writing the collectible code* section.

3. Track the amount of gold the player owns using a variable.

4. Show how many coins the player owns on the screen using a label.

I'll leave a possible implementation of all this in the repository of the project.

We learned a lot in this section. We discovered what **Area2D** nodes are, and collision layers and masks are no longer a mystery but a useful tool for defining what bodies and areas we want to interact with. Let's do some last exercises before summarizing and ending the chapter.

Additional exercises – Sharpening the axe

1. Oh no! We added collisions to the boulders and inner walls of the arena, but not to the outer walls. Add a **StaticBody2D** that stops the player from escaping the arena.

2. Create a base scene for the boulders, inherit two boulders from that, and make their shapes different. Also, make sure you update the collision shape so that the player collides correctly with them.

Summary

We started this chapter learning all about the **Camera2D** node and making it smooth and usable for the player so that they don't have to think about it while navigating around the playing field.

After, we added colliders to the player and all solid objects within the game. We even used collision shapes to create little collectible items, such as a health potion.

Along the way, we saw what signals are and how we can connect them to functions in a node's script.

In the next chapter, we'll flesh out our game with enemies and menus so that we have a full game loop.

Quiz time

- Why did we use a point in front of the player to position the camera?

- What does the last parameter of a `Vector2`'s `lerp` function represent? Here is an example:

```
var position: Vector2 = Vector2(1, 1)
var target_position: Vector2 = Vector2(3, 5)
position.lerp(target_position, 0.5)
```

- Why did we use a **CharacterBody2D** for the player character and not a **RigidBody2D**?

- What are **Area2D** nodes used for?

- We have two objects: an **Area2D** node and a **CharacterBody2D** node. We want to be able to detect the **CharacterBody2D** with the **Area2D** node. How do we need to configure their collision layers and masks?

- The **Area2D** and **CharacterBody2D** nodes should be in the same collision layer.

- The **Area2D** node should be in the same collision mask as the **CharacterBody2D** node's collision layer.

- The **Area2D** and the **CharacterBody2D** nodes should be in the same collision mask.

- Signals notify us of certain actions that happen in a node. To what signal did we connect to detect if a player entered the **Area2D** node of a collectible?

10

Creating Menus, Making Enemies, and Using Autoloads

Although it was a lot of fun setting up all the current systems, the game is still kind of boring. There is no real adversary, nothing to stop the player from just picking up all the gold coins they desire. Let's bring some challenge into the mix by creating enemies that attack the player and try to stop their road to glory and fame!

Next to that, we'll also create a little menu to start our game from. We'll do this with Godot's **user interface** (**UI**) system, which makes use of **Control** nodes. In this chapter, we will discuss the following topics:

- Creating a menu
- Making enemies
- Shooting projectiles
- Scoring highscores in autoloads

Technical requirements

As for every chapter, you can find the final code on the GitHub repository in the subfolder for this chapter: `https://github.com/PacktPublishing/Learning-GDScript-by-Developing-a-Game-with-Godot-4/tree/main/chapter10`.

Creating a menu

The most exciting part of developing a game is, of course, making the game itself! Making things move, fight, jump, shoot, interact, and so forth. But there is another part that is just as important: the UI. A UI binds everything together. It informs the player of what is happening and lets them navigate from menu to menu with ease and without having to think about how to get from one interface to the other.

Good user experience, UI, or human-computer interaction design is hard! But it all starts with learning how to make the UI in the first place. So, let's have a look at how we can create menus and interfaces.

Control nodes

The Godot engine comes with an extensive library of interface nodes. We already made use of one, the **Label** node, in *Chapter 6*. These nodes are called **Control nodes** and get labeled by the color green:

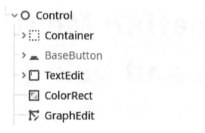

Figure 10.1 – Some Control nodes can be recognized by their green color

If you go and open the **Create New Node** menu, you'll see there are a lot of these **Control** nodes. We could categorize these into three different groups. Let's go over some of the nodes and what they can do for us in each group.

Nodes showing information

The first group of nodes shows information. In this group, you would find the **Label** node we used in *Chapter 6*, but also the **ColorRect** and **TextureRect** nodes:

- **Label**: Shows a short string of text.

- **RichTextLabel**: Shows a longer piece of text that can be formatted in specific ways.

- **ColorRect**: Shows a solid rectangle in one color.

- **TextureRect**: Shows a texture in a rectangle. This node is similar to the **Sprite2D** node in that they are both used to show a texture but in different contexts.

In the following figure, you can see what these nodes look like in the editor:

Figure 10.2 – Examples of Control nodes that show information

These nodes all show something to the user.

Nodes taking input

Any good UI can also take input, with – for example – buttons. Here are some of the input nodes that the Godot engine UI nodes provide:

- **Button**: A simple button that can be clicked.
- **CheckBox**: A checkbox that can be turned on and off.
- **CheckButton**: The same as a checkbox, but just with a different aesthetic.
- **LineEdit**: A simple node that can take a single line of text input and provide it as a string.
- **HSlider** and **VSlider**: Sliders that are used to input a number. **HSlider** slides horizontally while **VSlider** slides vertically.

In the following figure, you can see what these nodes look like in the editor:

Figure 10.3 – Examples of Control nodes that take input

These nodes all take input in one way or another.

Nodes containing other nodes

Lastly, there are the nodes that you don't see but that are very important because they make sure all the other UI elements are placed correctly. These nodes form the skeleton in which the other **Control** nodes can find their place.

Container nodes help us to lay out the UI as we want. This type of node can display elements nicely next to each other, add some spacing between nodes, and so forth.

These containers can also help keep the interface usable and beautiful when we resize the screen. This does not happen often, but games can be played on so many different screen sizes and aspect ratios these days. Just think about the difference between a computer screen and a phone screen.

Some interesting container nodes are the following:

- **VBoxContainer** and **HBoxContainer**: Organize all their child nodes nicely, vertically or horizontally

- **CenterContainer**: Centers its child nodes

- **GridContainer**: Organizes all its child nodes in a tidy grid

- **MarginContainer**: Adds spacing around its child nodes so that they have some room to breathe

- **Panel**: Provides a background that shows this part of the UI logically belongs together

In the following figure, you can see what these nodes look like in the editor:

Figure 10.4 – Examples of Control nodes that can contain other nodes

Container nodes all contain and place their child nodes in a specific way.

The lists of nodes in this section are not exhaustive; a quick glance in the **Control** node category while adding a node makes this pretty obvious. But these are the most important nodes that you will likely use first. The others are more specialized.

The cool thing is that the complete Godot editor itself is constructed out of these Control nodes, just to show how flexible and powerful they are for building out UIs.

Now that we have a basic knowledge of the different **Control** nodes, we can start making a menu with them.

Creating a basic start menu

Let's create a start menu that displays when we start up the game. This menu should simply display the game's name, a button to start playing, a button to exit the game, and lastly, we could add some information on who created the game:

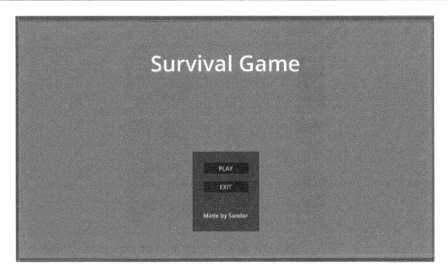

Figure 10.5 – This is what our start menu will look like

Let's go over the steps to create a start menu, as shown in *Figure 10.5*:

1. Create a new scene called `menu.tscn` under a new `screens/ui` folder.

2. Select **User Interface** as the root node's type:

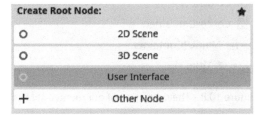

Figure 10.6 – Choosing User Interface as the root node for our menu

3. Rename the root node `Menu`.

4. Let's start by adding a **ColorRect** node to the menu; this will be our background color.

5. Now, to stretch the **ColorRect** node to cover the whole screen, **Control** nodes have a handy dandy little menu in the top bar. Select the **ColorRect** node in the scene tree and select **Full Rect** from the **Anchor preset** list:

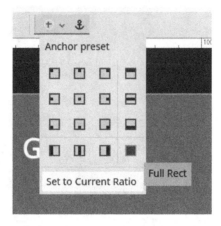

Figure 10.7 – Choosing Full Rect to make the ColorRect node cover the full screen

6. Now, add a **CenterContainer** node to the root node, give it a **VBoxContainer** node as a child, and call it `MainUIContainer`.

7. Now, add a **Label** node as the first child under the **MainUIContainer** node. Rename this `TitleLabel`. This label will show the title of our game:

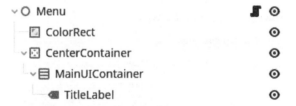

Figure 10.8 – The scene tree of our menu until now

8. Think of a good title for the game and put it in the text field of the **TitleLabel** node.

9. Now, go to **Theme Overrides** and set the **Font Size** option to something more appropriate for the game's title, such as 60 px:

Figure 10.9 – You can change the font size of a label in Theme Overrides

This was just to create a title label for our game UI. It might seem like a lot of steps, but some of the nodes we used will make it easy to extend the UI in the next few steps.

Let's add a panel with buttons and a credit line:

1.   Add a **PanelContainer** node to the **MainUIContainer** node.

2.   Now, create the following structure in this panel container:

Figure 10.10 – The scene tree structure from the PanelContainer node

3.   Rename the first button **PlayButton** and change its text to PLAY.

4.   Rename the second button **ExitButton** and change its text to EXIT.

5.   Rename the label **CreditLabel** and change its text to whatever you would like it to say!

6.   Now, go into the first **VBocContainer** node and change the **Separation** constant to 50 px.

7.   Change the **Separation** constant of the second **VBoxContainer** node to 20 px.

8.   Lastly, set the **Separation** constant of the **MainUIContainer** node to 200 px.

Great work – the UI layout is finished. The complete scene tree should look like this:

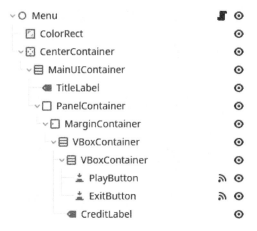

Figure 10.11 – The complete scene tree of our menu

The only thing left to do is to make the buttons functional! Let us do that real quick:

1. Add an empty script to the root **Menu** node called `menu.gd`.

2. Now, connect the pressed signal of the **PlayButton** node to this node.

    The body of the connected function is quite simple:

    ```
    func _on_play_button_pressed():
        get_tree().change_scene_to_file("res://screens/game/main.
    tscn")
    ```

3. Also, connect the pressed signal of the **ExitButton** node.

    The body of this function is even simpler:

    ```
    func _on_exit_button_pressed():
        get_tree().quit()
    ```

In the preceding code snippets, we reached out to the root of the scene tree with `get_tree()`. This function returns `SceneTree`, the object that manages the whole hierarchy of nodes while the game is running.

In the function that is connected to the **Play** button, we call the `change_scene_to_file()` function on this object, which switches out the current running scene to the one that is specified by the path we provide to the function. So, to start the main game scene, we just give it the path, starting from the root of the project, to the `main.tscn` scene.

> **Important note**
>
> It's good to note that from the moment it is called, `change_scene_to file()` will also load the scene file it is supposed to switch to. This means that the game will block or freeze for this loading duration. This is not great when we are switching to a big scene, which we luckily are not doing in our case.

In the function that is connected to the **Exit** button, we call the `quit()` function, which simply shuts down the runtime.

You can now try out the menu by running it!

Setting the main scene

To make sure our menu is the main scene that boots up the game, we'll quickly need to step into the project settings to declare this. In the project settings, under **Application | Run**, specify that `menu.tscn` is the main scene:

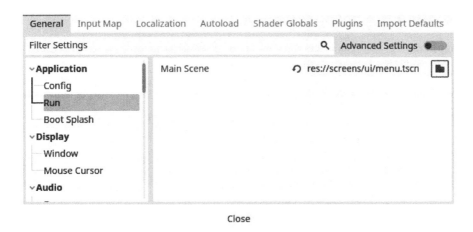

Figure 10.12 – Setting the main scene in the project settings

This will make sure that when we run the game, using the **Play** button at the top or using the *F5* shortcut, the menu.tscn scene is the scene that gets launched by default.

> **Important note**
>
> Remember that when there is no main scene set and we run the game through the aforementioned methods, Godot will ask us if we want to use the currently opened scene as the main scene.

We learned a lot about **Control** nodes and how to use them to quickly construct UIs. Let's go and make some enemies.

Making enemies

In real life, making enemies is never a good idea. But in the context of video game development, it is often a great way to challenge the player and put them against some opposition.

The enemy that we will be creating is fairly simple and straightforward. But we will still learn a lot along the way – for example, how to let enemies navigate toward the player to attack them.

Like I said, we'll keep the enemy simple. We'll be making an enemy that spawns at a random time in a random spot of the arena and starts charging toward the player. From the moment the enemy touches the player, we'll deduct one health point from the player's life and remove the enemy from the game. This way, the player has some adversaries but should not get overwhelmed by a horde of enemies.

In the following section, *Shooting projectiles*, we'll develop a way for the player to defend themselves. But for now, we'll solely focus on the enemy and its behavior.

Constructing the base scene

As with any new part of our game, let's start by creating the base structure in a scene tree for the enemy and add code and other interesting things later in the section:

1. Create a `parts/enemy` folder, and within it, create a new scene called `enemy.tscn`.

2. Recreate the following scene tree. Note that the root is a **CharacterBody** node:

Figure 10.13 – The scene tree of our Enemy scene

3. Choose a sprite from the `assets/sprites/enemies` folder as the texture for the **Sprite2D** node:

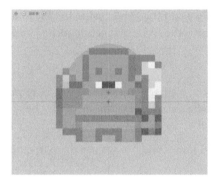

Figure 10.14 – The Enemy scene in the 2D editor

4. Make sure you set the scale of the sprite node to `(3, 3)`.

For the moment, the `Enemy` scene is very simple. Let's look into how we could do navigation to complexify it a little bit.

Navigating enemies

We can easily make enemies move directly toward the player. The problem with this is that they will get stuck behind walls and bump into boulders, which doesn't feel very natural and makes them look quite dumb.

Luckily, the Godot engine comes with a **NavigationServer** property that calculates a path around all these obstacles and makes enemy movement more natural and fluent.

To accomplish this, we will look at two new nodes: `NavigationRegion2D` and `NavigationAgent2D`.

Creating a NavigationRegion2D node

Firstly, we need to define in what region of the level our enemy can move around, then we want to cut out spots where a wall or boulder is situated from this region. This is exactly what the `NavigationRegion2D` node does! Let's define one:

1. Go to the `main.tscn` game scene.

2. In the root node called `Main`, add a `NavigationRegion2D` node.

3. Click on the empty **Navigation Polygon** property and select **New NavigationPolygon**:

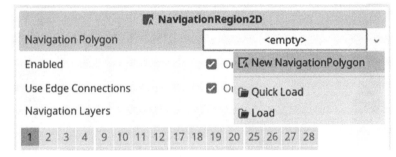

Figure 10.15 – Clicking on New NavigationPolygon

4. Now, we'll first define the outer bounds of where enemies will be able to move. Draw a polygon shape by clicking in the editor. Try to trace the outside of the arena closely. Don't forget to close the shape by clicking the first point you placed:

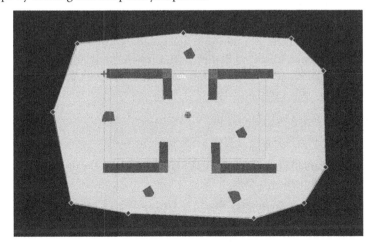

Figure 10.16 – Creating the outer bounds of the NavigationRegion2D node

5. Press **Bake NavigationPolygon** at the top of the window to create a navigation polygon:

Figure 10.17 – Pressing Bake NavigationPolygon

After following these steps, the `NavigationRegion2D` node should look like this:

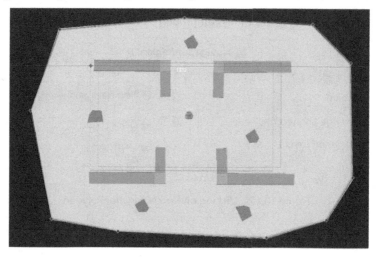

Figure 10.18 – The NavigationRegion2D node after baking the polygon for the first time

The blue/greenish area is where enemies will be able to navigate and move in. But you can already see a problem – this region also spans over our walls and boulders. We don't want enemies to think that they can walk through them because, well, they can't; they are static physics bodies. Luckily, Godot has the functionality to automatically detect these and bake the `NavigationPolygon` property in such a way that it takes them into account.

Unfold the **Navigation Polygon** property of the `NavigationRegion2D` node by clicking on it and configure it as follows:

1. Set **Geometry | Parsed Geometry Type** to **Static Colliders**. We do this to only consider static colliders in the automatic generation.

2. Set **Geometry | Source Geometry Mode** to **Group With Children**. This way, the automatic generation will scan through the children of nodes to find the static colliders.

3. Set **Agents | Radius** to 40 px. With this, we define the radius of the agents we want to use in the `NavigationRegion2D` node, and the automatic generation can take this into account so that agents don't bump into obstacles they should be able to avoid:

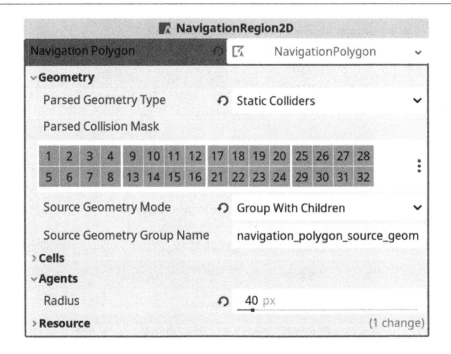

Figure 10.19 – Configuring the NavigationPolygon property

4. Select the Arena node and switch to the **Node** tab, next to the **Inspector** tab:

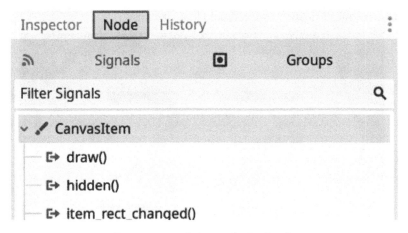

Figure 10.20 – Going to the Node tab

5. Switch to the **Groups** tab, which is next to the **Signals** tab:

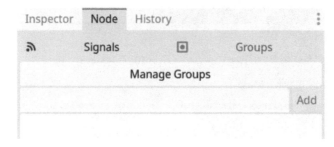

Figure 10.21 – Switching to the Groups tab

6. Paste `navigation_polygon_source_geometry_group` into the text field and press **Add**:

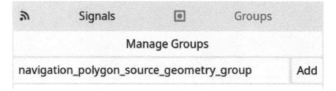

Figure 10.22 – Adding the navigation_polygon_source_geometry_group group

7. Now, select the `NavigationRegion2D` node again and press **Bake NavigationPolygon** again.

When you are done, the navigation region should look like this:

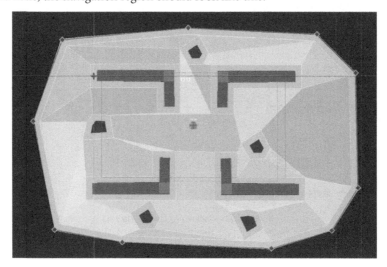

Figure 10.23 – The resulting NavigationRegion2D node

The blue/greenish region now nicely avoids walls and boulders. You can also see that there is some margin between obstacles and where the region begins. This is what we set up when defining the **Radius** property of the agents. This margin makes sure the pathfinding doesn't come too close to obstacles, making enemies avoid colliding with them.

In *steps 2* to *4*, we added the `Arena` node to a **node group**. We did this because, when baking the **NavigationPolygon** property, it will look for all nodes in the `navigation_polygon_source_geometry_group` node group and consider the static bodies within them. Let's take a small detour to talk about node groups.

What are node groups?

Groups or **node groups** in the Godot engine are like tags in other pieces of software. You can add any number of groups to a node. We can simply do this through the **Groups** tab, just like we did in the steps of the last section.

Groups are extremely useful because you can, for example, do the following:

- Check if a node is part of a group.
- Get all nodes within a group from the tree.
- Call methods on all nodes within a group.

We'll use groups some more later on.

The `NavigationRegion2D` node is ready, so now, let's take a look at the process of adding a `NavigationAgent2D` node to the Enemy scene.

Adding a NavigationAgent2D node to the Enemy scene

The last thing we need to add to the `enemy.tscn` scene from within the editor before starting to write code is a `NavigationAgent2D` node. This node handles pathfinding and navigation within the `NavigationRegion2D` node that we created in the previous section.

Just add a `NavigationAgent2D` node in the root Enemy node. We don't have to do any other setup:

Figure 10.24 – Adding a NavigationAgent2D node to the Enemy scene

Now, we can start writing the code for our enemy!

Writing the enemy script

The code for our enemy is going to be very similar to the code for our player. They both walk around based on the physics of an accelerating velocity. The only difference is that for the enemy, the position where it wants to move is defined by the `NavigationServer` property. This server looks at the `NavigationRegion2D` node and the current position of the `NavigationAgent2D` node to calculate the best route with the point on the map we choose to go to.

Let's start out by writing some boilerplate code that defines some of our enemy's movement:

```
class_name Enemy extends CharacterBody2D

@onready var _navigation_agent_2d: NavigationAgent2D =
$NavigationAgent2D

@export var max_speed: float = 400.0
@export var acceleration: float = 1500.0
@export var deceleration: float = 1500.0

var player: Player

func _physics_process(delta: float):
    _navigation_agent_2d.target_position = player.global_position

    if _navigation_agent_2d.is_navigation_finished():
        velocity = velocity.move_toward(Vector2.ZERO, deceleration *
delta)
    else:
        var next_position: Vector2 = _navigation_agent_2d.get_next_path_
position()
        var direction_to_next_position: Vector2 = global_position.
direction_to(next_position)
        velocity = velocity.move_toward(direction_to_next_position *
max_speed, acceleration * delta)

    move_and_slide()
```

In general, this code is very similar to the movement code that we wrote for the `player.gd` script. The only difference is that we now use the `NavigationAgent2D` node to say where we need to go:

```
_navigation_agent_2d.target_position = target.global_position
```

As you can see, we are going toward the global position of the `player` variable. We'll define this `player` variable in a bit.

> **Position and global_position**
>
> The `position` variable of a **Node2D** node is always the position relative to its parent node. The `global_position` variable, on the other hand, is the position of the node in world space, relative to the root of the scene tree. Both get automatically updated when the node moves in 2D space; it is basically the same data but with a different point of reference.
>
> We need to use the `global_position` variable here because the target position of a `NavigationAgent2D` node has to be a global position.

Then, we need to check whether we need to move or not:

```
if _navigation_agent_2d.is_navigation_finished():
```

If we need to move, we ask the `NavigationAgent2D` node what the next position we should move to is:

```
var next_position: Vector2 = _navigation_agent_2d.get_next_path_
position()
```

Then, all we need to do is calculate the direction from our current position to this next position, and the rest of the code is exactly the same as for the `Player` scene from *Chapter 7*.

To select the `Player` node, we are going to use node groups by adding this `_ready()` function:

```
func _ready():
    var player_nodes: Array = get_tree().get_nodes_in_group("player")
    if not player_nodes.is_empty():
        target = player_nodes[0]
```

To get the player from within the scene tree, we do something new. We ask the current scene tree for all nodes that are in the `player` group. This function will return an array with nodes that belong to this group. So, we'll have to take the first element, if there is any.

> **Important note**
>
> It might look weird to ask for all the player nodes in the scene while there is only one. We do this so that we can use roughly the same code to target more players when we deal with multiple players in the next chapter.

These node groups are a useful feature of the Godot engine because the engine will keep track of all nodes within a group so that we can easily query them or check if a node belongs to a certain group.

Now, this code will not work yet because, well, the player is actually not yet in the `player` group! To add them to this group, we need to alter the `Player` scene a little:

1. Go to the `player.tscn` scene.

2. Select the root node.

3. In the window that contains the node's signals, there is a button called **Groups**. Press it, and you will see the **Groups** window:

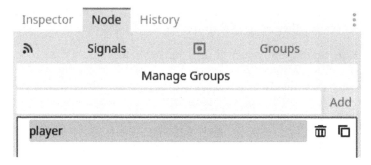

Figure 10.25 – Adding the player's root node to the node group called player

4. Here, type `player` into the line input and press **Add**.

Put an enemy in the main scene, and you will see that it starts moving toward the player! This is great. But enemies should be able to damage the player, so let's work on that next.

Damaging the player in a collision

To detect if an enemy is close enough to the player to deal damage, we are going to use an **Area2D** node, as we did for collectibles in *Chapter 9*:

1. Let's start by adding a `get_hit()` function to the `player.gd` script. This function will get called when the player is hit by an enemy and lower the health of the player:

    ```
    func hit():
        health -= 1
    ```

2. Add an **Area2D** node to the `enemy.tscn` scene and call it `PlayerDetectionArea`.

3. Under this area, add a **CollisionShape2D** node:

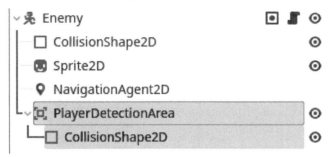

Figure 10.26 – Adding an Area2D node to the Enemy scene

4. Make this collision shape a **CircleShape2D** node that is a little bigger than the enemy's sprite:

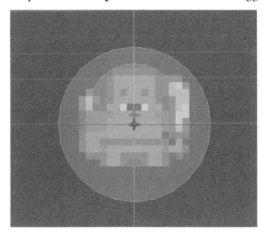

Figure 10.27 – Covering the whole enemy with some margin with the CollisionShape2D node

5. Connect the `body_entered` signal to the root node of the enemy.

6. Now, use the next snippet of code as the body of the connected function in the enemy's script:

```
func _on_player_detection_area_body_entered(body: Node2D):
    if not body.is_in_group("player"):
        return

    body.get_hit()
    queue_free()
```

The code of this function is straightforward. First, we check if the body that entered the area actually is the player. We can do this simply with the following check:

```
body.is_in_group("player")
```

This way, we can check whether a certain node is in a certain group. If this body is not in the `player` group, we return out of the function.

But if the body is a player node, then we remove one point from its health and free the enemy that made contact.

Great – our enemy can now damage the player when it comes close enough. There is only one more problem: there are only as many enemies as we can drag and drop into the scene. Enemies should be able to spawn automatically and constantly! Otherwise, the game would be over very quickly. Let's make an automatic spawner that spawns enemies but also health potions.

Spawning enemies and collectibles

To automatically spawn enemies or collectibles in our playfield is actually harder than it looks at first sight. We can randomly pick a location and spawn something there. Doing this, however, could spawn an enemy or a collectible within a wall or boulder. Even worse, the enemy or collectible could spawn miles away from the arena and the navigation region, rendering them useless.

We could solve this in many smart and abstract ways, but often, the simplest way is the best to start out with. That is why we'll construct our own entity spawner that can spawn different kinds of entities, enemies, collectibles, or anything else.

Creating the scene structure

An easier way of solving the problem of the location of enemy spawning is by defining certain points within the arena at which we are sure the enemy can safely spawn. So, that is what we are going to do in the following steps:

1. Create a new scene that derives from the **Node2D** node called `EntitySpawner`.

2. Save this scene as `entity_spawner.tscn` under `parts/entity_spawner`.

3. Under `EntitySpawner`, add another **Node2D** node called `Positions`. Here we'll later define all positions where we can spawn something:

Figure 10.28 – The structure for our EntitySpawner scene

4. Drag and drop an instance of `EntitySpawner` into the `main.tscn` scene and rename it `EnemySpawner`.

5. Now, right-click `EnemySpawner` and select **Editable Children**:

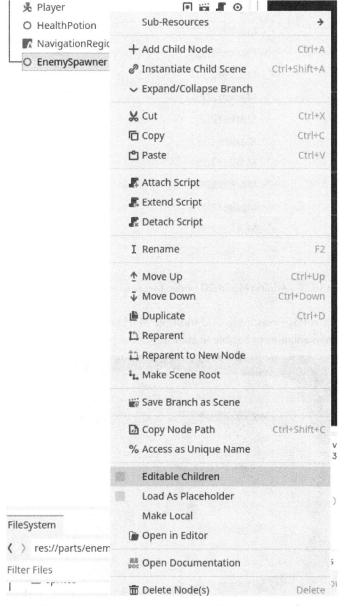

Figure 10.29 – Enabling Editable Children to directly edit the children of an instanced scene

You will see the **Positions** node that is a child of the EnemySpawner scene:

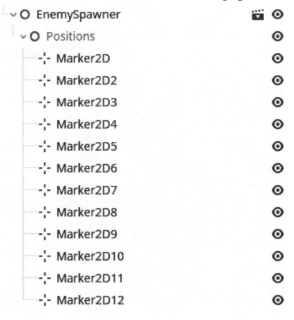

Figure 10.30 – Adding Marker2D nodes that will be used to position enemies

6. Now, under this **Positions** node, add multiple **Marker2D** nodes and place them at locations where you want enemies to be able to spawn:

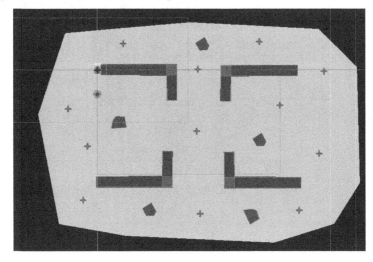

Figure 10.31 – The different positions at which I wanted enemies to spawn

The EnemySpawner node was pretty simple to set up until now, but we did use some new things. Firstly, we enabled **Editable Children** on a node that is a complete scene. This exposes that whole scene's structure to us and makes it easy for us to edit the individual nodes within. This is very useful for reusing scenes very directly.

Note that the nodes under the EnemySpawner node are grayed out. This means that we can edit them, move them around, and such, just like when we inherited from the collectible scene to make the health potion, but we cannot delete these grayed-out nodes.

Next to editing the children, we used a new node type: **Marker2D**. This is a node that actually does nothing special during the game, but in the editor, it will display a little cross to mark the location it is positioned at. This node gets used if you need to mark a position like we are doing here.

Writing the base code

For the code, we'll do something pretty simple and provide a spawn_entity() function that spawns a new entity, be it an enemy or a health potion, at one of the defined positions:

```
extends Node2D

@export var entity_scene: PackedScene

@onready var _positions: Node2D = $Positions

func spawn_entity():
    var random_position: Marker2D = _positions.get_children().pick_
random()

    var new_entity: Node2D = entity_scene.instantiate()
    new_entity.position = random_position.position
    add_child(new_entity)
```

The first new thing that we encounter is an exported variable of the PackedScene type. This PackedScene variable is basically the definition of any scene – a scene file. Any scene file can fill this variable.

Difference between a PackedScene variable and a Node variable

A PackedScene variable represents a scene file, such as the enemy.tscn file. It is a template that we can use to create new nodes from.

A Node variable, on the other hand, is a building block of the scene tree and can be an instance of a PackedScene variable.

You could see a PackedScene variable as a class, while a Node variable is an instanced object of that class.

Then, later, we can use this packed scene to instantiate a new entity:

```
var new_entity: Node2D = entity_scene.instantiate()
```

The last thing we need to do to make this new instanced entity a part of the scene tree is to add it to an existing node within the tree because if we don't add it somewhere within the scene tree, it is not used within the game or its execution.

We can add a new node as a child to another node by calling the `add_child()` function on any node within the tree with this new entity node as the parameter. The entity will then get added as a child to that node. Here, we add the entity node to `EntitySpawner`:

```
add_child(new_entity)
```

Now, the entity is truly put into the tree and thus within the game.

To select a random position, we also do something new. First, we get an array of children from the **Positions** node with `get_children()`, which is an array of position markers. Then, to pick a random element from this array, we can make use of the `pick_random()` function to easily select one random position marker:

```
var random_position: Marker2D = _positions.get_children().pick_
random()
```

This will provide us with a **Marker2D** node at random that we can use to spawn the enemy.

To make our `EnemySpawner` node that is in the `main.tscn` scene spawn enemies, we just need to drag and drop the `enemy.tscn` scene on top of the **Entity Scene** property in the **Inspector** tab for the `EnemySpawner` node:

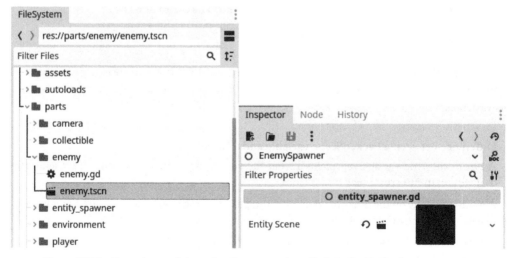

Figure 10.32 – Dragging and dropping the enemy.tscn file into the Entity Scene property

With this set up, we can start spawning entities at a fixed time interval.

Automatically spawning entities

Now that we have a function that can spawn an entity, we still need to trigger it at some point. To do this, we are going to make use of the **Timer** node. This node counts down a certain amount of time and throws a timeout signal when the timer runs out.

Let's add a **Timer** node to the EntitySpawner scene:

1. Add a **Timer** node to the entity_spawner.tscn scene file and call it SpawnTimer.

2. Now, connect the timeout signal to the EntitySpawner root node.

3. In the connected function, just call the spawn_entity() function:

    ```
    func _on_spawn_timer_timeout():
        spawn_entity()
    ```

4. Add a reference to the SpawnTimer node and an export variable that will represent the interval at which we'll spawn entities at the top of the script:

    ```
    @onready var _spawn_timer: Timer = $SpawnTimer
    @export var spawn_interval: float = 1.5
    ```

5. Now, we can add two extra functions that help us start and stop the timer:

    ```
    func start_timer():
        _spawn_timer.start(spawn_interval)

    func stop_timer():
        _spawn_timer.stop()
    ```

6. Lastly, to autostart the timer at the start of the game, add this _ready() function to the EntitySpawner script:

    ```
    func _ready():
        start_timer()
    ```

> **Important note**
> Remember – when we talk about a scene, we talk about a whole scene file, such as the entity_spawner.tscn file. When we talk about a node, we are talking about a specific node within the scene file, such as the EntitySpawner node.

The start and stop functions will help when we want to stop enemies from spawning when the player dies, for example. In the body, they just start and stop _spawn_timer directly. You can see that when starting a timer, we can give a time in seconds that will be used as the amount of time before the timer runs out.

Running the game now, we'll get a new enemy every 1.5 seconds. Great! Now that we have a stream of enemies coming in, let's spawn some potions so that the player can heal themselves.

Spawning health potions

To spawn health potion collectibles, we can easily use the same `EntitySpawner` node that we just constructed! Here's how:

1. Add a new `EntitySpawner` node to the `main.tscn` scene and call it `HealthPotionSpawner`.

2. Make this spawner's children editable and add **Marker2D** nodes to the **Positions** node at which you want to spawn health potions:

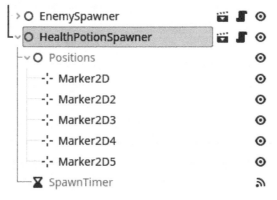

Figure 10.33 – Adding Marker2D nodes where I would like to spawn health potions

3. Drag and drop the `health_potion.tscn` scene into the `Entity Scene` property of the spawner.

4. Set the **Spawn Interval** value of the spawner to a bigger number, such as 20, so that we don't spawn too many health potions:

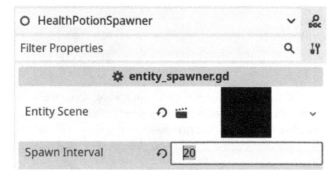

Figure 10.34 – Setting the Spawn Interval value to 20 seconds

That is it! Spawning new things is easy if we create a scene, `EntitySpawner`, that is easily reusable for it, isn't it?

Making a Game Over screen

Now that enemies can damage the player and the player's health goes down, we need to account for the scenario where the player's health reaches 0. This would mean the end of the game. We'll add a little Game Over screen that gives the player the option to retry or go back to the main menu after dying.

Creating the base scene

As always, we'll start off by creating the scene structure:

1. Create a new scene that has a **CenterContainer** node as root, call this node GameOverMenu, and save the scene as game_over_menu.tscn in parts/game_over_scene.

2. Recreate the following scene structure:

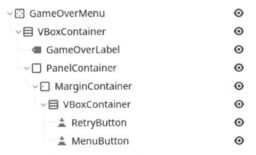

Figure 10.35 – The scene tree for the Game Over menu

3. Fill each element with the right text, enlarge the **Font Size** value of the GameOverLabel node, and add some separation to the **VBoxContainer** node that holds the two buttons. Make it so that the UI looks like this:

Figure 10.36 – What the Game Over menu will look like

4. Now, select the `GameOverMenu` root node and set its **Anchor preset** type to **Full Rect**:

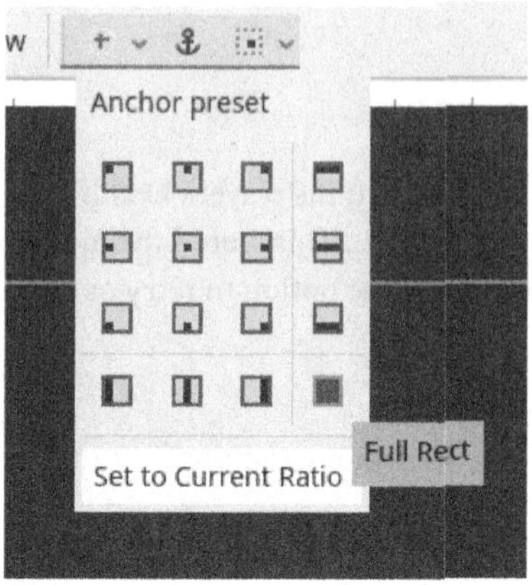

Figure 10.37 – Choosing Full Rect from the Anchor presets list

Now that we have a little menu, let's add it to the `main.tscn` scene:

1. In the `main.tscn` scene, add a `CanvasLayer` node.

2. Under this `CanvasLayer` node, add our freshly created `GameOverMenu` node:

Figure 10.38 – The GameOverMenu node added to the scene tree

3. Now, hide the `GameOverMenu` node by clicking the eye symbol next to the name of the node. We only want to show this menu when the player is dead:

Figure 10.39 – Hiding the GameOverMenu node by clicking the eye symbol next to its name

We use a `CanvasLayer` node to display our menu here because this node makes sure that all its children are displayed on top of everything else. The `CanvasLayer` node does not adhere to the display order that is determined by the scene tree order of the nodes. Within the `CanvasLayer` node, its children do again adhere to this order. This makes the `CanvasLayer` node very suitable for UIs within the game itself.

That was it for the base scene structure; now, we should add some logic to the menu.

Adding logic to the Game Over menu

The script for the GameOverMenu node is very simple. All we want to do is add functionality when the buttons are pressed. When the **Play** button is pressed, we reload the main game scene, and when the menu button is pressed, we go back to the main menu.

So, connect both buttons and load the right scene in each of their connected functions:

```
extends CenterContainer

func _on_retry_button_pressed() -> void:
    get_tree().reload_current_scene()

func _on_menu_button_pressed() -> void:
    get_tree().change_scene_to_file("res://screens/ui/menu.tscn")
```

> **Important note**
>
> Note that we used a new function, reload_current_scene(), on the tree. This function is very similar to change_scene_to_file(), except it will just change to the same scene as we are currently in, and we don't have to load the scene file as it is obviously already loaded.

The **Game Over** menu is ready; now, we just need to make use of it within the game.

Showing the Game Over menu when the player dies

We have seen how we can connect to signals that nodes throw. But we can also make and throw our own signals! We'll make use of this to detect when the player dies:

1. In the player.gd script, right under the line that carries the extends keyword, add our new signal:

    ```
    class_name Player extends CharacterBody2D

    signal died
    ```

2. Let's emit this signal and stop the player from moving in the health setter when health equals 0:

    ```
    set(new_value):
        var new_health: int = clamp(new_value, 0, MAX_HEALTH)

        if health > 0 and new_health == 0:
            died.emit()
            set_physics_process(false)
    ```

```
health = new_health
update_health_label()
```

You can see that to define a new signal, we just need to use the `signal` keyword, followed by the name of the signal.

Then, later on, we can just emit this signal by calling the `emit()` function on it. In a way, a signal is also a variable.

To check whether the player died, we check whether the current `health` value is greater than 0 and the `new_health` value is 0. This way, we are sure that we only trigger the `died` signal once, when the player goes from a living to a dead state. We don't want this signal thrown multiple times because that would signal the game that the player died more than once and create unwanted side effects.

Then, we also use the `set_physics_process()` function and give it `false` as the only parameter. This tells the node if it should stop executing the `_physics_process()` function and will effectively stop the player from moving because that is where all our movement code lives.

Now that the `Player` node throws a signal when it dies, we can hook into this with the `main.tscn` scene:

1. In the `main.tscn` scene, select the `Player` node. You'll see that a new signal has appeared – the `died` signal that we defined in the `player.gd` script:

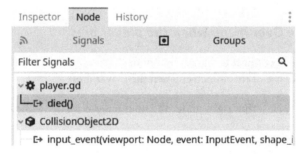

Figure 10.40 – The signal we defined in the player's script also turns up in the signal menu

2. Add an empty script to the `Main` node of the `main.tscn` scene and connect the `died` signal to it.

3. In the connected function, we should show the `GameOverMenu` node and stop the `EnemySpawner` node and `HealthPotionSpawner`:

```
extends Node2D

@onready var _game_over_menu: CenterContainer = $CanvasLayer/
GameOverMenu
@onready var _enemy_spawner: Node2D = $EnemySpawner
```

```
@onready var _health_potion_spawner: Node2D =
$HealthPotionSpawner

func _on_player_died() -> void:
    _game_over_menu.show()

    _enemy_spawner.stop()
    _health_potion_spawner.stop()
```

This script is pretty simple because it just needs to handle the menu and stop some spawners.

We covered a lot of ground in this section. We learned about how we can use the NavigationRegion2D and NavigationAgent2D nodes to make enemies navigate toward the player character. We used PackedScene variables to instance scenes from within the code. We used the **Timer** node to spawn enemies and collectibles after a certain amount of time. We used the CanvasLayer node to show a **Game Over** menu on top of the game. We created a custom signal and hooked into it. We had a lot of fun, and now it is time for the player to learn how to defend themselves!

Shooting projectiles

We've sent enough enemies at the player without them being able to defend themselves. Let's change that in this section! We'll be creating projectiles the player character automatically shoots at enemies to kill them off. To keep it simple, we'll make the projectile hone in on the target we are trying to hit; this way, it never misses.

Creating the base scene

Before we can shoot the projectiles, we'll have to construct the base scene we'll work from. Let's do that right now with the following steps:

1. Create a new scene that has a **Node2D** node as the root node and call it Projectile.

2. Create a scene structure as shown next:

Figure 10.41 – The scene tree of the projectile scene

3. Use one of the textures from `assets/sprites/projectils/` as the texture for the sprite. Remember to set the scale of the sprite to `(3, 3)`:

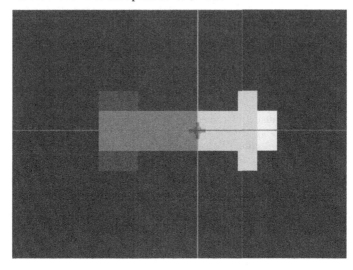

Figure 10.42 – The projectile

4. Now, use a `CapsuleShape2D` node for the `CollisionShape2D` node's shape and make sure it covers the sprite:

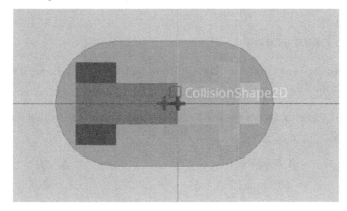

Figure 10.43 – Covering the projectile's sprite with the CollisionShape2D node

5. We'll use the **Area2D** node to detect whether the projectile hit an enemy, so rename this area node `EnemyDetectionArea`.

6. To detect the Enemy node entering the `EnemyDetectionArea` area node, name the third **2D Physics** layer **Projectile**.

7. Set the `EnemyDetectionArea` area node's **Collision Mask** property to detect the **Projectile** layer:

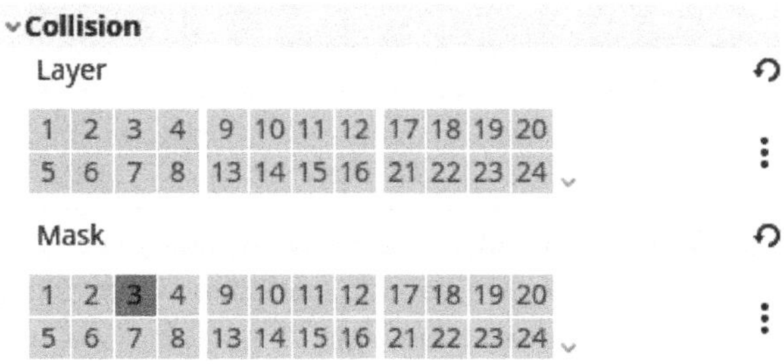

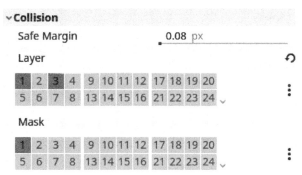

Figure 10.44 – The Collision layer configuration for the EnemyDetectionArea area node

8. In the `enemy.tscn` scene, set the `Enemy` node's **Collision Layer** property to be on the **Projectile** layer too:

Figure 10.45 – The Collision layer configuration for the enemy

This is all we need in terms of the scene structure, so let's get to writing the behavior of the projectile.

Writing the logic of the projectile

Next up is the code that steers the projectile toward a target, destroys it on impact, and notifies the enemy it has been hit. We'll make the projectile always go straight toward its target; this makes it easy for us code-wise:

1. Attach a script called `projectile.gd` to the `Projectile` root node and fill it with the following code to move it:

```
class_name Projectile
extends Node2D

@export var speed: float = 600.0
```

```
var target: Node2D

func _physics_process(delta: float):
   global_position = global_position.move_toward(target.global_
position, speed * delta)
   look_at(target.global_position)
```

We've seen most of this code already, except for the `look_at()` function. This function rotates a node to orient itself toward a point in space that we provide it. So, here, it rotates the projectile node toward the position of the target.

2. Now, connect the `body_entered` signal from the `EnemyDetectionArea` node to the projectile's script. All we need to do in the connected function is to notify the enemy that it got hit and destroy the projectile itself:

```
func _on_enemy_detection_area_body_entered(body: Node2D):
   body.get_hit()
   queue_free()
```

3. Lastly, in the `enemy.gd` script, add this `get_hit()` function that we want to use when the projectile hits the enemy:

```
func get_hit():
   queue_free()
```

This is all we need code-wise on the side of the projectile itself.

Spawning projectiles

We want the projectile to be shot automatically every so often. To achieve this, we'll need to make some changes in the `Player` and Enemy scenes:

1. Add a `Timer` node to the `Player` scene and call this new node `ShootTimer`.

2. Set the time of this `ShootTimer` node to `0.5` and enable **Autostart**:

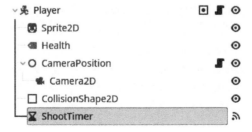

Figure 10.46 – Adding a Timer node called ShootTimer to the Player scene

3. Next, in the player's script, preload the projectile scene at the top:

```
@export var projectile_scene: PackedScene = preload("res://
parts/projectile/projectile.tscn")
```

4. While the `Player` node is selected, drag and drop the `projectile.tscn` file into the **Projectile Scene** property in the **Inspector** tab.

Just like with the `EntitySpawner` node, we export a variable of the `PackedScene` type that we can fill from the editor and instantiate later on when we need it. This time, though, we directly fill it with the `projectile.tscn` scene. The `preload()` function loads this scene and puts it in the `projectile_scene` variable, ready to be used. But this variable is also exported, which means that if, someday, we want the player to shoot a different kind of projectile, we can drag and drop this scene in the **Inspector** tab of the player.

We'll now add the logic that actually spawns the projectile:

1. In the `enemy.tscn` scene, add the root node to the `enemy` group as we did for the player. This will make sure we can access all enemy nodes later:

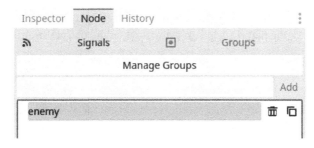

Figure 10.47 – Adding the enemy node to the enemy group

2. Add a new `export` variable to the top of the `player.gd` script. This variable will represent how far the player can shoot in pixels:

```
@export var shoot_distance: float = 400.0
```

3. Now, connect the timeout signal of the `ShootTimer` node to the `Player` node's script.

This should be the body for the connected signal:

```
func _on_shoot_timer_timeout():
    var closest_enemy: Enemy
    var smallest_distance: float = INF

    var all_enemies: Array = get_tree().get_nodes_in_
group("enemy")
```

```
    for enemy in all_enemies:
        var distance_to_enemy: float = global_position.distance_
to(enemy.global_position)
        if distance_to_enemy < smallest_distance:
            closest_enemy = enemy
            smallest_distance = distance_to_enemy

    if not closest_enemy:
        return

    if smallest_distance > shoot_distance:
        return

    var new_projectile: Projectile = ProjectileScene.
instantiate()
    new_projectile.target = closest_enemy
    get_parent().add_child(new_projectile)
    new_projectile.global_position = global_position
```

4. We should also stop the ShootTimer node when the player dies, cache the ShootTimer node at the top of the player script, and stop it when the player's health reaches 0:

    ```
    @onready var _shoot_timer = $ShootTimer

    @export_range(0, MAX_HEALTH) var health: int = 10:
        set(new_value):
            # Code to update the health

            if health > 0 and new_health == 0:
                # Code when player dies
                shoot_timer.stop()
    ```

The high-level explanation of this function's body is that we first get a list of all enemies, using the group functionality. Then, we go over every single one of them to see how far away they are from the player. While doing this loop, we always keep the enemy that is the closest along with that distance. This way, we know that we'll end up with the enemy that is nearest to the player character.

The result of this algorithm can result in no enemy being selected. That is why we need to make sure closest_enemy is not accidentally empty and need to return from the function if it is.

After all this, we create a new projectile, set its target, add it to the scene tree, and put its position to the position of the player.

That was it for creating projectiles! You can now run the game and start trying to survive as long as possible. We also saw some more intricate code with an algorithm to find the closest node from any other node and how to preload a scene within a script.

Storing highscores in autoloads

Now that the player can fight back and survive, we might need to give the player a goal to attain – something that will make them play again and again. We could add a highscore – for example, the amount of time the player was able to survive. The player can then try to better their own time or compare times with their friends.

To achieve this, we will be using an autoload. This is a node that gets initialized at the start of the game and will exist throughout the complete execution of the game.

Using an autoload

The survival time should be stored somewhere so that it is easily accessible from anywhere within the game. This way, we can change it after the player dies but also display the score on the main menu, for example.

Normal nodes and scenes have to be managed by us, the programmer. But there is another kind of node that we could use: autoloads. An autoload is a scene or script that is always loaded. The Godot engine initiates this scene for us anytime we run the game.

A node or script that is autoloaded will exist as long as the game is running. Earlier, when using `get_tree().change_scene_to_file()` to change scenes, everything of the current scene gets removed from the scene tree and switched out for the new scene. However, autoloads do not share the same faith; they stay put and retain the values of all their variables.

> **Important note**
> Although autoloads are great, they should not be misused or overused. They should only be used for systems that are truly global, such as the `HighscoreManager` autoload we are going to create in this section.

We are not going to store the highscore autoload in a file just yet; we'll do this in *Chapter 15*. For now, we just want to save and load the highscore autoload while the game is running.

Creating a HighscoreManager autoload

To create an autoload, we first need to create a normal scene or script. Because we don't really need a whole scene to keep track of a highscore, which is basically just a number, we are going to write a script. When the Godot engine initiates our game, it will create a node and attach our script to it. The following steps illustrate the process of creating an autoload:

1. Create a new `autoloads/` folder in the root of the project.

2. Add a new script in this folder called `highscore_manager.gd`.

    The `HighscoreManager` script is going to be pretty simple and straightforward:

    ```
    extends Node

    var highscore: int = 0

    func set_new_highscore(value: int):
        if value > highscore:
            highscore = value
    ```

The preceding code defined a `highscore` variable and a `set_new_highscore()`. function. This function checks if the new score is bigger than the current highscore. If it is, we save this new, higher score; otherwise, we don't need to bother.

Now, let's set this script up as an autoload:

1. Open the project settings and navigate to the **Autoload** tab.

2. Select the file icon button to search for a file:

Figure 10.48 – Pressing the folder icon to select a file that you want to load as an autoload

3. Navigate to the `autoloads/highscore_manager.gd` script.

4. Select it and press **Open**.

5. Now, back in on the **Autoload** panel within the project settings, press the **Add** button.

That is all for setting up our autoload. You'll see that the **Highscore** autoload is now displayed within the list of autoloads:

Figure 10.49 – The highscore_manager.gd script is loaded as an autoload

Next to seeing the script in the list of autoloads, there is another way we can check whether the autoload is there.

> **Using a scene as an autoload**
>
> Both scripts and full scenes can be autoloads. To use a scene, load the scene just like we did for the script just now.

Autoloads in the remote tree

As said earlier, autoloads get instantiated by the Godot engine when the game starts running. So, we can't see them present in separate scenes, but they should be there in the remote tree when we run the game.

Run the game using the **Run Project** button or any scene of the game using the **Run Current Scene** button. Open the remote tree, and you will see a node called **HighscoreManager**. This is our **HighscoreManager** autoload!

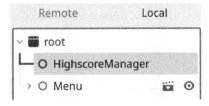

Figure 10.50 – We can see the HighscoreManager node in the remote tree

Now that we set up our **HighscoreManager** autoload, let's use it within the game and keep some highscores!

Adding a UI in the main menu and game scene

First, we'll need to make sure the player knows what their score is while playing the game. Because we said that the score would be the amount of time the player is able to survive, we'll show this score by adding a timer on the screen:

1. In the `main.tscn` scene, under the existing `CanvasLayer` node, add a **CenterContainer** node and call it `TimerUI`.

2. For the `TimerUI` node, select the **Top Wide** anchor so that it stays on the top of the screen:

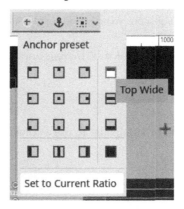

Figure 10.51 – Selecting Top Wide from the Anchor preset list

3. Add a **Label** node to `TimerUI` and call it `TimeLabel`:

Figure 10.52 – The scene structure for our timer

4. Let's fill this label with a fake time of `"123"` so that we can see how the score will look when it is filled.

5. Change the font size of this label to something larger, such as `30` px.

Now, we'll need to account for the timer in the `main.gd` game script:

1. First cache a reference to the `TimeLabel` node at the top of the script and add a variable in which we'll keep the current elapsed time:

    ```
    @onready var _time_label: Label = $ CanvasLayer/TimerUI/
    TimeLabel
    var _time: float = 0.0:
    ```

```
set(value):
    _time = value
    _time_label.text = str(floor(_time))
```

2. Now, all we need to do is update the value of this `_time` variable. We'll do this in the `_process()` function by adding the delta to the current time:

```
func _process(delta: float):
    _time += delta
```

3. Lastly, we'll need to submit this time whenever the player dies and stop the game from counting more time. So, change the function that is connected to the `died` signal from the player to include the following two lines:

```
func _on_player_died() -> void:
    _game_over_menu.show()

    _enemy_spawner.stop()
    _health_potion_spawner.stop()

    set_process(false)
    HighscoreManager.set_new_highscore(_time)
```

That's it to get the highscore linked within the game itself. Now, we'll tackle showing the highscore in the main menu too.

Using the highscore in the main menu

Now that we can make new highscores, let's display the highest score within the menu:

1. Open the `menu.tscn` scene.

2. Add a new **Label** node to the **VBoxContainer** node that contains the **Play** and **Exit** buttons and call it `HighscoreLabel`.

3. Now, in the `menu.gd` script, add the following code:

```
@onready var highscore_label: Label = $CenterContainer/
VBoxContainer/PanelContainer/MarginContainer/VBoxContainer/
VBoxContainer/HighscoreLabel

func _ready():
    highscore_label.text = "Highscore: " + str(HighscoreManager.
highscore)
```

The result is that the menu will now show the current highscore:

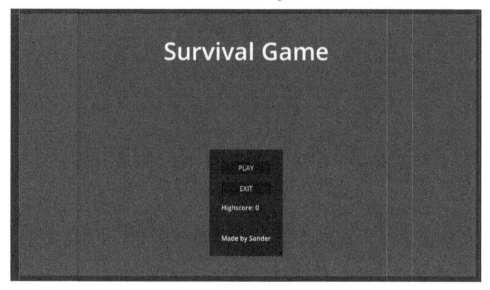

Figure 10.53 – The main menu with an added Highscore label

None of this code is new to us. First, we save the **HighscoreLabel** node in a variable called highscore_ label. Next, when the menu scene is ready, we populate the **HighscoreLabel** with a string that contains the current highest score.

That was our venture into autoloads. We saw how easy it is to add a script or scene as a node that is always loaded at the start of our game without having to manage this node ourselves. Then, we made use of this autoload through its global variable to save information between different scenes.

Additional exercises – Sharpening the axe

1. Enemies get spawned at a slow, fixed rate. This can get a little boring because the difficulty never really increases. Make it so that enemies get spawned faster and faster after every round. For a simple way of doing this, you could follow the next steps:

    I.   Add start_interval, end_interval, and time_delta as export variables to the EntitySpawner node. The start_interval variable will be the time we use between spawning entities at the start of the game, end_interval will be the final value, and time_delta is the increment at which we will go from the start_interval variable to the end_interval variable:

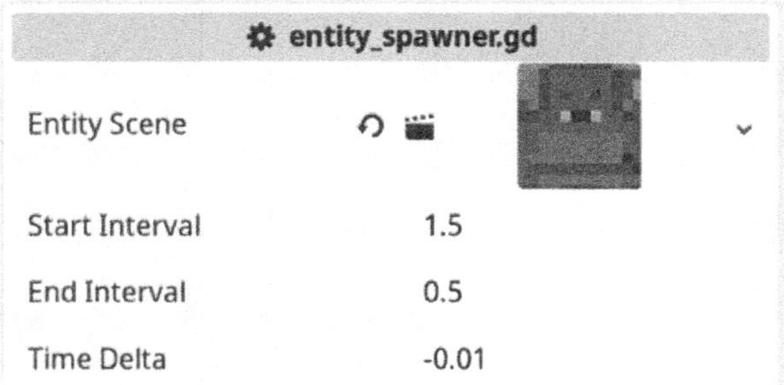

Figure 10.54 – The new exported variables for the EntitySpawner node

II.   Now, track in a separate variable, _current_spawn_interval, the time for the next enemy to spawn. Set _current_spawn_interval equal to the start_interval variable at the start of the game. This variable replaces the old spawn_interval variable.

III.   Every time we spawn an entity in the spawn_entity function, add the time_delta variable to the _current_spawn_interval variable. Make sure to not go past the end_interval variable, though.

IV.   Then, still in the spawn_entity() function, start _spawn_timer again but with the new _current_spawn_interval variable: by calling start_timer() again. For the HealthPotionSpawner node, you'll have to set time_delta to 0.0.

V.   The menu that shows up when the player dies is quite lacking in information. Add a nice label to show the score the player just achieved.

Summary

We learned and created so many different things within this chapter. First, we learned all about **Control** nodes and how to use them to construct a main menu for our game. Then we created some challenges in the game with enemies that try to stop the player. We even made these enemies navigate smartly over the playing field using the NavigationServer property. To let the player have a chance to defend themselves, we created projectiles that get shot automatically on a timer. Lastly, we added a small high-score system that stores the current highscore within an autoload so that the player is incentivized to replay the game and try to beat their own best time.

In the next chapter, we'll do something very interesting: make our game multiplayer!

Quiz time

- **Control** nodes are used to create UIs such as menus. For each of the following scenarios, give a **Control** node that could do the job:

- Showing a long piece of text

- Grouping other **Control** nodes to the center of the screen

- Showing a button to start the game

- Which node did we add to the Enemy scene to make it find a path to the player?

- Let's say that we have this piece of code where we define a signal called shot to indicate that we shot a projectile:

  ```
  signal shot
  ```

  Write the line of code that is needed to emit this signal.

- How do you load a scene from within the code into a variable?

- How can we make a script globally accessible?

11

Playing Together with Multiplayer

Playing games on your own is lots of fun. I've spent many hours exploring exotic worlds, acquiring new skills, and experiencing deep storylines on my own. But where games really shine, compared to other forms of media, is the ability for the player to create their own stories. Nothing lets players create their own story like letting them play with another real person. From cooperation and tense moments trying to help each other in games like World of Warcraft or Rocket League, to rivalry and intimidating each other in games like Call of Duty or Gran Turismo. Human behavior is still something that invokes more emotions than interacting with a complete fictional world.

In this chapter, we will cover the following main topics:

- A crash course in computer networking

- Using the `MultiplayerSynchronizer` and `MultiplayerSpawner`

- Running the game on multiple computers

In this chapter, we are going to implement networked multiplayer. This means that two people will be able to play together over the internet. Now, because of how networks work, and we still want to be safe, we'll only be able to play over a **local area network** (**LAN**). This means that people who are connected to the same Wi-Fi network, for example, will be able to play together.

The reason why you don't want to run a globally accessible server from your personal computer is quite simple: you don't want the risk of people hacking your computer. Though there are ways to do this in a safe way, this is beyond the scope of this book.

Technical requirements

As for every chapter, you can find the final code on the GitHub repository in the subfolder for this chapter: `https://github.com/PacktPublishing/Learning-GDScript-by-Developing-a-Game-with-Godot-4/tree/main/chapter11`.

A crash course in computer networking

In this section, I would like to give you a brief crash course on computer networking. Because Godot does a lot out of the box, we don't have to be complete networking wizards to implement simple multiplayer games. This means that you could skip this section and directly start with the actual implementation of the multiplayer nodes and code. However, I recommend reading on if you want at least some high-level explanation of why we do things the way we are going to do them.

Computers in networks talk to each other through a layered model. On the top level, there is the eventual application, the game. Our game needs to send information from one instance of the game, running on one computer, to another instance of the game, running on another computer, also called **another machine**. This top layer is called the **Application Layer**. In between these computers could be a vast network of interconnected servers, routers, and other networking infrastructure. This network is the lowest layer, called the **Physical Layer**.

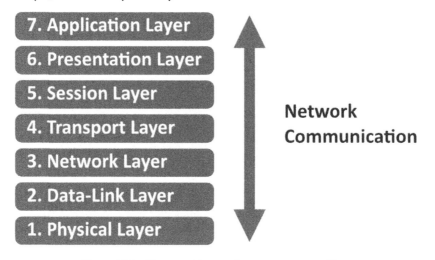

Figure 11.1 – The seven layers of computer networking

Between the Application Layer and the Physical Layer, there are multiple other layers. These layers make sure that data is sent and received between all links in the chain that need to be taken to transmit this packet of data from Computer A to Computer B and each serves a different purpose.

Though Godot provides us with a great deal of flexibility, not every layer is equally important to us at the moment. Let's take a closer look at two network layers: the Transport and Application Layers.

What is a Transport Layer?

The first layer we'll look at is the **Transport Layer**, the fourth layer of computer networking. This layer is, among other things, responsible for deciding how to cut the data we want to send in smaller packages of data, making sure that packages of data are received from one end to the other, uncorrupted.

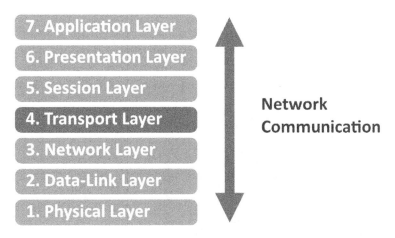

Figure 11.2 – The Transport Layer is the fourth layer in computer networking

To meet these responsibilities, different protocols have been invented that are able to take care of them with varying degrees of reliability. A **protocol** is basically a set of rules by which computers can communicate with each other.

For example, if we send out a package of data from Computer A to Computer B, we could just send it off and hope for the best. However, our package of data could accidentally get dropped somewhere within the vast internet. A server forgets to send it from one link to the other, a cable gets unplugged, or any other error could happen.

Now, how do we make sure that the data we send actually arrives? Well, we could ask for confirmation from the receiving computer. But what if that confirmation gets lost somewhere? Well, we could do a double confirmation, one from each participant in the communication.

All these rules just solve the problem of making sure a package of data gets sent and received, but there are many other problems that we need to overcome as well. You can see that these protocols quickly become complex. Luckily, smart people already thought about all of this for us.

In gaming, there are two main protocols that are used:

- **Transmission Control Protocol (TCP)**: The TCP is a Transport Layer protocol that makes sure that every package that is sent will be received. But to achieve this, the protocol takes more time, sending confirmations back and forth.

- **User Datagram Protocol (UDP)**: The UDP is a Transport Layer protocol that does not care whether packages arrive or not. It just sends them over a connection in the hopes that they make it, which most of them should do. This is way faster than the TCP but less reliable.

Godot Engine can operate using either TCP or UDP and can even switch between the two for different kinds of data, depending on how important guaranteed delivery is. For our game, we will use both the UDP and TCP for different kinds of data.

What is an Application Layer?

The Application Layer is the highest layer in the networking layers. This is when we actually use the data that we received within the game. Additionally, here, we have a choice to make; even though we have the data, how are we going to organize the computers that we are connected with?

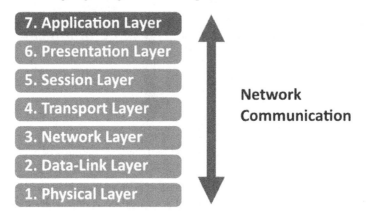

Figure 11.3 – The Application Layer is the seventh layer in computer networking

For games, there are two network architectures that prevail: peer-to-peer or client-server.

Peer-to-peer network

In a peer-to-peer network, every computer can talk to any other computer and ask it things. They are all equals and peers. For example, Computer A could ask Computer B to tell at what location its player character is located. Computer B will then send over this data so that Computer A can show its user where the player character of Computer B is situated in the game world.

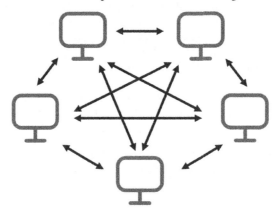

Figure 11.4 – In a peer-to-peer network, each computer can talk to the other computers

This solution is pretty elegant because every computer is equal and has the same number of rights. However, we'll also need to be vigilant because what if Computer B is used by a hacker and lies to the other computers? Instead of reporting the position of the player according to the game's rules, Computer B gives positions that are impossible to reach; maybe they teleport its player character around. This is quite a problem. The next network architecture tries to tackle this problem.

Client-server network

Instead of treating every computer as equal, we could have one of the computers as the center for all communication. Every time any of the computers in the network want information, such as the location of another computer's player character, they'll have to ask this central computer. The central computer will then answer for the other computer.

In this situation, we call the central computer the server, and the connected computers the clients.

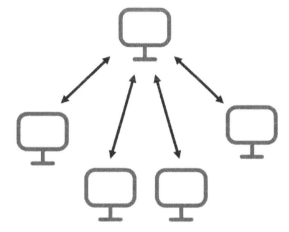

Figure 11.5 – In a client-server, network each computer talks to the server

With this architecture, the server can check up on all clients and make sure none of them are cheating.

Networking in Godot Engine

Again, Godot Engine supports both peer-to-peer and client-server network architectures. To make it easier on ourselves, we'll go with a client-server approach. This way, we can make sure that important parts of the game get run only on the server and our clients don't have to worry about them. For example, considering counting the score – clients can easily lie about this, while now the server will be the only computer keeping score.

Alright, after this short introduction to computer networking, although there is still so much to learn, we have enough knowledge of the underlying structure that we can start implementing multiplayer in our game.

Learning about IP addresses

In real life, to send mail to another person, you need to know the address of their house. For computer networks, this is pretty much the same. To send messages between computers, we need to know their **IP address**. This is a unique address that makes sure you can find any computer connected to the internet.

Currently, there are two versions of IP addresses in use: **IPv4** and **IPv6**. An IPv4 address is comprised of 4 numbers ranging from 0 to 255 separated by a period, like so:

```
166.58.155.136
```

This version is supposed to be able to have a unique address for 4.3 billion devices. But it turns out that humans have been so productive that 4.3 billion devices will probably not be enough! These days, almost any electrical device can be connected to the internet, even fridges, toasters, and watches. That is why we are slowly transitioning to IPv6 addresses, which support 340 undecillion devices. That is 340 trillion devices.

An IPv6 address looks like this:

```
e9fd:da7d:474d:dedb:d152:dce2:1294:2560
```

Depending on how your computer is connected to the internet, this IP address changes from time to time, so don't depend on it being the same.

An IP address is a postal address we can send a letter to, but then, we still need to know to whom in the household the letter is addressed. In a computer network, a **port** is used to address the exact application within the computer. Let's talk about ports next.

Using port numbers

An IP address, be it IPv4 or IPv6, only indicates where to send the data to. But computers have many applications that each need their own connection. So, from the moment the data is received, to which application do we send it? Well, each application can use different ports, which are like the different platforms in a train station. Although each train arrives at the same station, they arrive at different platforms.

Each application can choose a port, which is just a number from 0 to 65535. However, the first 1,024 are reserved for standard computer functionality and we will not be able to pick these.

To specify which port to send data to, we can add the port number at the end of the IP address, behind a colon:

```
166.58.155.136:5904
e9fd:da7d:474d:dedb:d152:dce2:1294:2560:5904
```

Here, we have an IPv4 and IPv6 address that directs to the port with the number 5904.

Now that we know about the basic mechanisms of computer networking, such as the different layers and how IP addresses work, we are able to start implementing multiplayer into our game. So, let's give that a shot!

Setting up the base networking code

In the *A crash course in computer networking* section, we saw that we wanted to set up a client-server network architecture and that we could use IP addresses and ports to find computers over the internet. In this section, we'll start implementing this.

We're going to make our multiplayer game work like this: every time you start playing, it spins up a server in the background. This way, anyone can join after one person starts the match.

Creating the client-server connection

If we want to connect our players through a client-server model, we need to be able to set up one computer as a server and the others as clients that connect to this server. Let's start by writing some code.

1. In the menu.gd script, add a constant at the top that indicates which port we want to use:

    ```
    const PORT: int = 7890
    ```

2. Now add these two functions to the bottom of the script:

    ```
    func host_game():
        var peer = ENetMultiplayerPeer.new()
        peer.create_server(PORT)
        if peer.get_connection_status() == MultiplayerPeer.
    CONNECTION_DISCONNECTED:
            return
        multiplayer.multiplayer_peer = peer

    func connect_to_game(ip_address: String):
        var peer = ENetMultiplayerPeer.new()
        peer.create_client(ip_address, PORT)
        if peer.get_connection_status() == MultiplayerPeer.
    CONNECTION_DISCONNECTED:
            return
        multiplayer.multiplayer_peer = peer
    ```

    The host_game() function will use the ENetMultiplayerPeer class to create a new server using the create_server() function that is defined on it. To create this server, we only have to specify on which port we want to receive the data. Once this is done, we check whether the connection status is disconnected; if we are not connected, then we need to return from the function. We can check the connection status using the get_connection_status() function on the peer object.

3. Lastly, we set this peer as `multiplayer_peer`, which is defined on the multiplayer global variable.

    The `connect_to_game()` function does largely the same but creates a client using the `create_client()` function on the `ENetMultiplayerPeer` peer object. The `create_client()` function takes an IP address and port. These will, of course, be the IP address and port of the server.

With these two functions in place, we can add some more UI to connect to the right server.

Adding UI

Now, for the menu, we want to be able to start a game that will set up a server or input an IP address to join an already hosted game. We won't have to let the player choose a port, both because it's less of a hassle for the player and because we don't want them to accidentally choose an invalid port number. We, the programmers, decide we are going to use port `7890`.

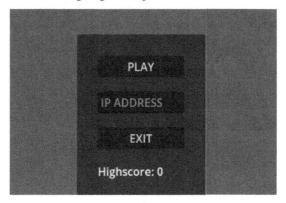

Figure 11.6 – The main menu with an input field to specify an IP address

1. Open up the `menu.tscn` scene.

2. Add a `LineEdit` node in `VBoxContainer`, which holds the play and exit buttons, and rename it `IpAddressLineEdit`.

3. Place `IpAddressLineEdit` under the `PlayButton` node, but not as a child.

Figure 11.7 – The main menu scene tree with the added IpAddressLineEdit

4. Select the `IpAddressLineEdit` node and set **Placeholder Text** to IP ADDRESS. This will show some placeholder text that will get replaced the moment the user puts anything into the line edit.

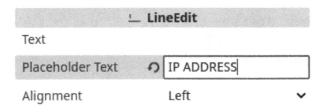

Figure 11.8 – Setting Placeholder Text in a LineEdit node

5. Now, in the `menu.gd` script, cache the `IpAddressLineEdit` at the top:

```
@onready var _ip_address_line_edit = $CenterContainer/
MainUIContainer/PanelContainer/MarginContainer/VBoxContainer/
VBoxContainer/IpAddressLineEdit
```

6. Lastly, we need to change the `_on_play_button_pressed()` function to host or connect to a game:

```
func _on_play_button_pressed():
    if _ip_address_line_edit.text.is_empty():
        host_game()
    else:
        connect_to_game(_ip_address_line_edit.text)

    get_tree().change_scene_to_file("res://screens/game/main.
tscn")
```

With all this in place, we have all that is needed to set up the client-server architecture. One computer will be the server and the others, the clients. Before we dive into the things we have to change in the code of the game itself, such as spawning playable characters for every person joining and then making sure the position of each player is synchronized between each computer, we can try out what we have already created.

Running multiple debug instances at the same time

To debug a multiplayer game, we need to be able to run our game multiple times in debug mode. Luckily, Godot Engine has a handy feature that allows us to run as many instances of our game as we want at the same time.

1. Click **Debug** in the top menu bar.

2. Under the **Run Multiple Instances** menu, choose **Run 2 Instances**.

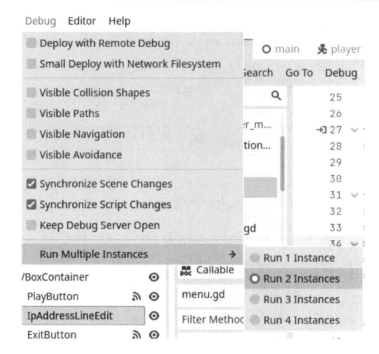

Figure 11.9 – In the Debug dropdown menu, we set the number of instances we want to run

3. Run the project. This will make two instances of the game pop up at the same time.

4. In one instance, just press **Play**. The game should start up normally.

5. In the other instance, type `::1` in the IP address input field and then press **Play**.

Figure 11.10 – Specifying the ::1 IP address will loop back to the same computer

Unfortunately, you won't see anything special happen. We still need to account for multiple players in our game code, but normally, there should be no errors in the bottom **Debug** panel.

> **Local host IP address**
>
> There is a special IP address that does not go to another computer but rather loops back to the same computer again. In the IPv6 format, this address is `::1`, and for IPv4, it is `127.0.0.1`.

You'll also see that there are now multiple tabs in the **Debug** panel, one for each instance of the game. This way, we will be able to debug each separately.

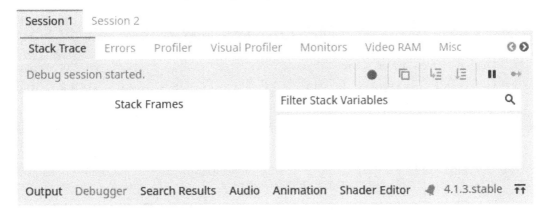

Figure 11.11 – When running multiple instances, we'll also have multiple Debug tabs

Now that we are able to create a server and connect clients, let's start by making our game multiplayer compatible and synchronizing spawned scenes between both games.

Synchronizing different clients

Until now, we learned about computer networking and set up a connection between multiple instances of our game. The next step is to change the scenes and code within our game to account for multiple players. We want to accomplish two things:

- Firstly, if the server instances a new scene, such as a new projectile, we want that scene to be instanced on every client

- Secondly, we want to synchronize values, such as the position of each player character, between all clients

We'll first look at which Godot Engine nodes can help us achieve these two goals while updating the player character to be used in multiplayer. After that, we'll update the entity spawner, enemy, collectible, and projectile scenes, too. Most of these changes will be quite small.

Updating the player scene for multiplayer

Because the player is the most important entity in the game, let's start by updating them for multiplayer. This way, we can quickly make sure everything is working correctly, too.

Using MultiplayerSpawner to spawn player scenes

To synchronize instanced scenes between the server and the clients, Godot Engine has a node called MultiplayerSpawner. It will listen to the scenes that are getting added to the scene tree and will replicate them on each of the other clients, too. Let's add one to the main game scene:

1. Open the main.tscn scene.

2. Under the root **Main** node, add a MultiplayerSpawner node, and call it PlayerMultiplayerSpawner, because it will be spawning new player characters.

Figure 11.12 – The main.tscn scene tree with an added PlayerMultiplayerSpawner

3. Now, in the inspector window for PlayerMultiplayerSpawner, press **Add Element** in **Auto Spawn List** and drag the player.tscn scene into that element.

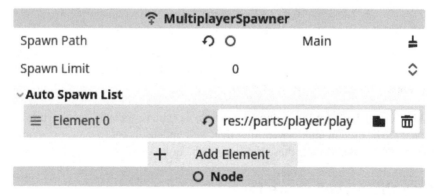

Figure 11.13 – Add the player.tscn scene as an element in PlayerMultiplayerSpawner

4. Now, to specify positions at which our players can spawn, add Node2D, called PlayerStartPositions, under the Main node with different Marker2D nodes where we can spawn players. Place each marker at a good spot to start a player from.

Figure 11.14 – The PlayerStartPositions node with Marker2D to spawn players at

5. In the `main.gd` script, we'll cache the player scene in an export variable. So, add the following line of code at the top and drag the `player.tscn` scene into this export variable in the inspector, too:

    ```
    @export var player_scene: PackedScene
    ```

6. Also, cache the `PlayerMultiplayerSpawner` node in a variable called `_player_multiplayer_spawner` and `PlayerStartPositions` in a variable called `_player_start_positions`:

    ```
    @onready var _player_multiplayer_spawner: MultiplayerSpawner =
    $PlayerMultiplayerSpawner
    @onready var _player_start_positions: Node2D =
    $PlayerStartPositions
    ```

7. We'll also add a variable at the top of the script that specifies what position we will spawn the next player at. With this variable, we will select which `Marker2D` to use as to location to spawn each player at:

    ```
    var _player_spawn_index: int = 0
    ```

8. Now, we'll add two functions to spawn new players in the `main.gd` script:

    ```
    func add_player(id: int):
        _player_multiplayer_spawner.spawn(id)


    func spawn_player(id: int):
        var player: Player = player_scene.instantiate()
        player.multiplayer_id = id
        player.died.connect(_on_player_died)

        var spawn_marker: Marker2D = _player_start_positions.get_
    childr(_player_spawn_index)
        player.position = spawn_marker.position
    ```

```
_player_spawn_index = (_player_spawn_index + 1) % _player_
start_positions.get_child_count()

return player
```

9. To use these functions, we'll add a _ready() function to the main.gd script:

```
func _ready():
    _player_multiplayer_spawner.spawn_function = spawn_player

    if multiplayer.is_server():
        multiplayer.peer_connected.connect(add_player)
        add_player(1)
```

10. Lastly, but very importantly, delete the Player node that is already in the main.tscn scene. We do this because we'll spawn each player character from code and so they don't need the node to be in there already.

In the add_player() function, we simply ask _player_multiplayer_spawner to spawn a new instance of the player scene.

Then, in the spawn_player() function, which will be used by the PlayerMultiplayerSpawner to spawn new Player scenes, we instantiate a new player scene and set its multiplayer_id property to the ID that we received as a parameter. This ID is used to determine which client owns that particular player node. We'll use it in the next section. Afterward, we must return the new player instance so that the PlayerMultiplayerSpawner can handle the rest for us.

We use the _player_spawn_index variable to select which Marker2D to select in PlayerStartPositions. After each player spawned, we increment this variable with 1 and make sure it loops back around with the % operator. This makes sure that we don't spawn players on top of each other.

In the _ready() function, first, we set spawn_function for _player_multiplayer_spawner to be the spawn_player() function that we defined. This way, the multiplayer spawner knows how to create new instances of the player scene.

Then, you see that we check the multiplayer object if this code is being run on the server, using multiplayer.is_server(). This is_server() function returns true if the code is run on the server.

If we are running on the server, we do the following:

```
multiplayer.peer_connected.connect(add_player)
```

`peer_connected` is a signal that is thrown by the `multiplayer` object when a new peer (a new client) connects to the server. Instead of connecting through the editor, like we used to do for detecting whether the player is close to the collectibles, we directly call the `connect()` function on this signal and pass along the function that we want to execute when a player connects to the server, which is the `add_player()` function.

After connecting to the `peer_connected` signal, we call the `add_player()` function with 1 as `id`, which is the default ID for the server.

We will not yet be able to run the game for now, first, we need to update the player scene.

Updating the player code for multiplayer

When you try running the game with multiple instances at the end of the last section, you will notice that there are some things off, mainly that, on each client separately, you control both players at the same time.

This behavior happens because, although we spawn a player per client, all code gets run all the time on each client separately. We have to specify that the movement code for each player character should only be run on the client associated with that player character, not all at once on all clients. Afterward, we should synchronize the position to the server.

We'll do this by setting the **multiplayer authority** of the player character node. This authority "owns" this node and decides how it behaves.

So, let's alter our code so the players work properly:

1. Firstly, add the `multiplayer_id` variable that we used in the last section somewhere at the top of the `player.gd` script:

    ```
    var multiplayer_id: int
    ```

2. Add an `_enter_tree()` function; this function is a life cycle function that gets called when the node enters the tree, right before the `_ready()` function. In this function, we set the multiplayer authority to the client that has the same ID as `multiplayer_id` of this player node:

    ```
    func _enter_tree():
        set_multiplayer_authority(multiplayer_id)
    ```

3. Cache the `CameraPosition` node at the top of the script:

    ```
    @onready var _camera_position: Node2D = $CameraPosition
    ```

4. Now, update the `_ready()` function like this:

    ```
    func _ready():
        update_health_label()
    ```

```
        if not multiplayer.is_server():
            _shoot_timer.stop()

        if not is_multiplayer_authority():
            _camera_position.queue_free()
            set_physics_process(false))
```

In *step 2*, we set the multiplayer authority for a node, which means that we determine which client is the owner of this node. For most nodes in multiplayer, the server should be the owner. But the player character is so important to each client that we give the authority of each to their respective client.

After that, we use `multiplayer.is_server()` to stop `_shoot_timer` when we are not running on the server. This way, we make sure that projectiles only get spawned on the server side and replicated to all clients from there.

Next, we use `is_multiplayer_authority()` to check whether we are the authority of this specific player node. If we are not, we free `_camera_position`. We don't need multiple cameras, only the one that is used to track the player we want to see, and we also disable the `_physics_process()` function. Only the client that owns this node will have to calculate this player's position and then report back to the server where the player is.

> **Disabling the _process() and _physics_process() functions**
>
> By default, the `_process()` and `_physics_process()` functions get called on each frame and physics frames, respectively. However, we can choose to enable or disable them manually by calling `set_process()` and `set_physics_process()` along with a Boolean that says whether they should run or not.

After all this, you can run the game with multiple instances, like we saw in the *Running multiple debug instances at the same time* section, and you should see a second player spawn! Each player is able to move properly, but their positions are unfortunately not synchronized. We'll do that next.

Synchronizing the players' positions and health

We can spawn scenes across clients and determine on which client certain pieces of code should run. The last piece of the puzzle is to synchronize certain variables, like the position and health of our players. Luckily, this is actually very easy to do using the `MultiplayerSynchronizer` node. We are going to use two of these, one for the position and one for the health. Although one synchronizer can synchronize multiple variables, we want the position to be managed by each client individually and the health to be managed by the server:

1. In the `player.tscn` scene, add two `MultiplayerSynchronizer` nodes under the root `Player` node. Call on `PositionMultiplayerSynchronizer` and the other `HealthMultiplayerSynchronizer`.

Figure 11.15 – The player.tscn scene tree after adding two MultiplayerSynchronizer nodes

2. Select `PositionMultiplayerSynchronizer` and a new panel should appear at the bottom of the editor.

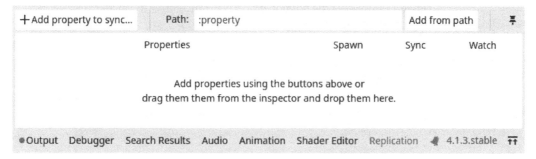

Figure 11.16 – The Replication panel that opens up when selecting MultiplayerSynchronizer

3. Here, press **+ Add property to synchronize**.

4. Select the `Player` node and press **OK**.

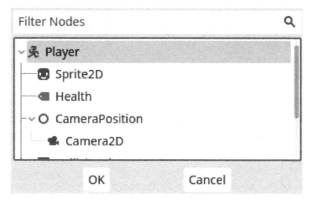

Figure 11.17 – Select the Player node to synchronize one of its values

5. Now, search for the `position` property and press **Open**.

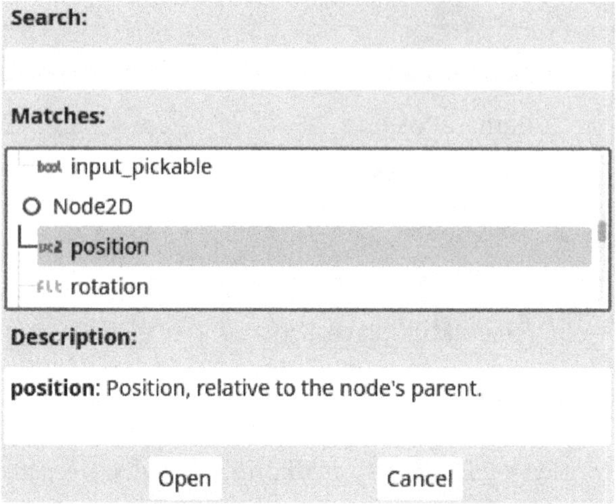

Search:

Matches:

bool input_pickable

O Node2D

└─ vc2 position

flt rotation

Description:

position: Position, relative to the node's parent.

Open   Cancel

Figure 11.18 – Select the position property to synchronize its value

6. Do *steps 2* to *5* again but add the `health` property to `HealthMultiplayerSynchronizer` this time.

Figure 11.19 – The Replication panel tracking the position value of the Player node

7. Now, update the `_enter_tree()` function of the player so that we give the multiplayer authority of `HealthMultiplayerSpawner` to the server:

```
func _enter_tree() -> void:
    set_multiplayer_authority(multiplayer_id)
    $HealthMultiplayerSynchronizer.set_multiplayer_authority(1)
```

Remember that the multiplayer ID of the server is always 1. So, to give the authority to the server, we set the multiplayer authority of `HealthMultiplayerSynchronizer` to 1.

That is all we need to do to synchronize values between different clients. `MultiplayerSynchronizer` simply tracks them for us.

Running two instances of the game and connecting them finally shows that if we move one player character in one client, it also moves that player character in the other client.

Now that we updated the hardest scene to multiplayer, the player scene, we have all the knowledge to do the same for the remaining scenes. Let's dive in so that we have a complete multiplayer game at the end!

Synchronizing EntitySpawner

To make sure the enemy and health potion scenes are spawned on each client when the entity spawner wants to, we'll have to make a few little adjustments to the `EnitySpawner` scene:

1. In the `entity_spawner.tscn` scene, add a `MultiplayerSpawner` node.

Figure 11.20 – The EntitySpawner scene tree after adding MultiplayerSpawner

2. In the `entity_spawner.gd` script, cache the `MultiplayerSpawner` node:

    ```
    @onready var _multiplayer_spawner = $MultiplayerSpawner
    ```

3. Then, in the `_ready()` function, let's add the scene this spawner uses to this `MultiplayerSpawner` node and only start the timer if we are running on the server. This ensures that not every client is spawning new entities, only the server:

    ```
    func _ready():
        _multiplayer_spawner.add_spawnable_scene(entity_scene.
    resource_path)

        if multiplayer.is_server():
            start_timer()
    ```

4. One last thing we need to do is change the exact way we add the `new_entity` to the scene. So, change the line with `add_child(new_entity)` to the following:

    ```
    add_child(new_entity, true)
    ```

In *step 3*, we add a spawnable scene to the `MultiplayerSpawner` node. This is very convenient as now we can add any scene on the fly.

In *step 4*, we supply the Boolean `true` as a second parameter to the `add_child()` function, next to the node that we want to add to the scene tree. This indicates that we want to use human-readable names for each node, names that are easy for humans to read. When we don't set this Boolean to `true`, the engine will pick a name for the node. These names look like @Node2D@2. These are reserved names that cannot be synchronized using a `MultiplayerSpawner` node. When we do set this Boolean to `true`, each new instance gets nicely named, for example, Enemy2, Enemy3, and so on. In a multiplayer scenario, this is important for the server to properly synchronize scenes and values between them.

Now that we can synchronize the spawned entities of enemies and collectibles between clients, let's synchronize their behavior, too.

Synchronizing the enemy and collectibles

For both the enemy and all collectibles, making them work with multiplayer is quite easy and straightforward:

1. Add `MultiplayerSynchronizer` to the `enemy.tscn` and `collectible.tscn`.

Figure 11.21 – The scene tree of the Collectible after adding MultiplayerSynchronizer

2. Now, add the `position` property of the root node in the **Replication** menu at the bottom.

Figure 11.22 – The Replication panel tracking the position of the Collectible node

That is about it for `Collectible`, while for Enemy, we need to do some last things in the code:

1. Cache `PlayerDetectionArea` at the top of the `enemy.gd` script:

```
@onready var _player_detection_area: Area2D =
$PlayerDetectionArea
```

2. Now, update the _ready() function like this:

```
func _ready():
    if not multiplayer.is_server():
        set_physics_process(false)
        _player_detection_area.monitoring = false
        return

    var player_nodes: Array = get_tree().get_nodes_in_
group("player")
    if not player_nodes.is_empty():
        target = player_nodes.pick_random()
```

The first thing we do in the _ready() function of the enemy is disable the _physics_process() function and _player_detection_area if we are not running them from the server. This makes sure that enemies are fully controlled by the server.

The Area2D nodes have a property, monitoring, that stops looking for collisions with other areas or bodies when set to false. This is what we are using here to disable _player_detection_area on other clients than the server.

Lastly, we want to be able to target any of the players in the game, so we change how to target a player. The pick_random() function on an array will pick any element within that array at random and return it. This is ideal for picking a random player within the scene!

Let's now look at how we can synchronize the projectiles.

Synchronizing the projectile

The last scene we need to synchronize between the multiple clients is the one of the projectiles. So, let's do that with the following steps:

1. In the projectile.tscn scene, add MultiplayerSynchronizer.

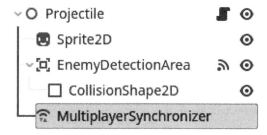

Figure 11.23 – The scene tree of Projectile after adding MultiplayerSynchronizer

2. This time, synchronize both the position and rotation properties.

Properties	Spawn	Sync	Watch	
○ Projectile:position	☑	☑		🗑
○ Projectile:rotation	☑	☑		🗑

+Add property to sync... **Path:** :property **Add from path**

Figure 11.24 – The Replication panel tracking the position and rotation of the Projectile node

Cache EnemyDetectionArea at the top of the projectile.gd script:

```
@onready var _enemy_detection_area: Area2D = $EnemyDetectionArea
```

3. Now, add a _ready() function as follows:

```
func _ready():
    if not multiplayer.is_server():
        set_physics_process(false)
        _enemy_detection_area.monitoring = false
```

4. We need to change the way the projectile is added to the scene within the player.gd script from get_parent().add_child(new_projectile) to the following:

```
get_parent().add_child(new_projectile, true)
```

> **Important note**
>
> Remember that the last parameter of the add_child() function is a Boolean that determines that the name of the new node should be human readable.

5. Lastly, we need to make sure that the projectile.tscn scene is replicated in the main scene, just like we did for the player.tscn scene. Add a MultiplayerSpawner node in the main.tscn, call it ProjectileMultiplayerSpawner, and add projectile.tscn in **Auto Spawn List**.

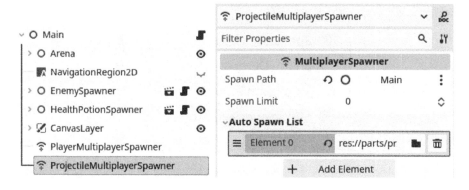

Figure 11.25 – Main scene with ProjectilMultiplayerSpawner with the projectile.tscn scene

That is it for the Projectile scene and thereby all the scenes important to playing the game itself! You can now run multiple instances of the game and everything within the game should be synchronized. The last thing we'll need to look at is synchronizing the timers within the game and the game-over menu for both players.

Fixing the timer and end game

The last thing we need to adjust for multiplayer is the timer that times our run and the end of the game, stopping the entity spawners and showing the game-over menu. So, let's get started on this last effort.

Synchronizing the timer

To synchronize the score timer, we simply have to do the following three things:

1.   Add MultiplayerSynchronizer to the main.tscn scene.

Figure 11.26 – The Main scene tree after adding MultiplayerSynchronizer

2.   Synchronize the _time property of the Main node.

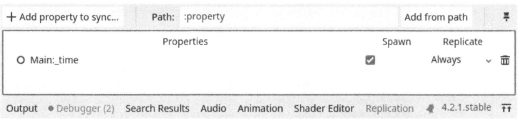

Figure 11.27 – The Replication panel tracking the _time property of the Main node

3. Now, disable the _process() function from within _ready() if we are not running on the server:

```
func _ready():
    # Other code

    if not multiplayer.is_server():
        set_process(false)
```

That is all we need to do synchronize the timer across all clients.

Synchronizing the end of the game

To make sure that when the game ends, it ends for all clients, let's do the following:

1. In the main.gd script, let's connect to each player character's died signal in the add_player() function:

```
func add_player(id: int):
    var player: Player = player_scene.instantiate()
    player.name = str(id)
    add_child(player)

    player.died.connect(_on_player_died)
```

2. Now, change the _on_player_died() function and add a new end_game() function:

```
func _on_player_died() -> void:
    end_game.rpc()

@rpc("authority", "reliable", "call_local")
func end_game():
    _game_over_menu.show()

    _enemy_spawner.stop_timer()
    _health_potion_spawner.stop_timer()

    set_process(false)
    Highscore.set_new_highscore(_time)
```

3. Then, in the menu.gd script, change the _ready() function to the following:

```
func _ready():
    _highscore_label.text = "Highscore: " + str(Highscore.
highscore)
```

```
if multiplayer.has_multiplayer_peer():
    multiplayer.multiplayer_peer.close()
```

In the first step, we simply connect to each player's `died` signal through code.

> **Important note**
> Note that only the server connects to the `died` signal because it is the server that manages the game loop.

In the second step, we do something very interesting. We call the `end_game()` function through **RPC**, which means that we call it on every client at the same time!

> **Important note**
> **Remote procedure call** (**RPC**) is a protocol that makes functions directly callable over different clients. This makes it easy to execute the same code on all connected instances of the game at the same time.

You can see that we use the `@rpc` annotation right before the `end_game()` function. This is to indicate how we would like this function to be handled when calling on every client at once. The strings we pass it along mean the following:

- `"authority"`: Only the one with authority, the server, in this case, can call this function.

- `"reliable"`: We want this command to be sent reliably over the network, using TCP.

- `"call_local"`: This function, when called, should be executed on all clients, including the one that called it.

This means that the game-over menu will be shown on every client from the moment one of the players dies.

In the third step, we simply close the multiplayer connection, when there is one, and we open up the main menu. This way, we make sure we don't stay connected while we are not playing anymore.

Now that the whole game is ready to be played in multiplayer, let's get started on actually running it on multiple machines at the same time!

Running the game on multiple computers

Until this point, we've been running multiple instances of our game on the same machine. But the strength of multiplayer comes from playing with multiple people over multiple machines.

In this section, we'll start off by showing the server's IP address on screen and then look into how we can run a debug instance on multiple computers at the same time so they can connect.

Showing the IP address of the server

We have been using ::1 as the IP address that loops back to the same computer so that we can debug our game. However, before we can connect to another computer over a network, we need to know their real IP address. To do this, we'll show the server's IP address on the screen when they are hosting a game.

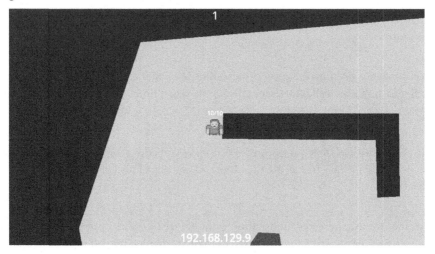

Figure 11.28 – The server has an IP address displayed at the bottom of the screen to connect

In *Figure 11.28*, you can see that we want to show the IP address at the bottom of the screen. Let's get to it:

1. In the main.tscn scene, add CenterContainer with Label as a child, just like we did for the timer. Give them names like in *Figure 11.29*.

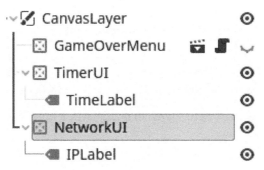

Figure 11.29 – The CanvasLayer node with NetworkUI

2. Now, in the main.gd script, cache IPLabel at the top:

    ```
    @onready var _ip_label = $CanvasLayer/NetworkUI/IPLabel
    ```

3. Next, add this function that shows the local IP address:

```
func show_local_ip_address():
    var addresses = []
    for ip in IP.get_local_addresses():
        if ip.begins_with("10.") or ip.begins_with("172.16.") or
ip.begins_with("192.168."):
            addresses.push_back(ip)

    if not addresses.is_empty():
        _ip_label.text = addresses[0]
```

4. Now, call this function in the _ready() function, but only if we're running on the server:

```
func _ready():
    if multiplayer.is_server():
        show_local_ip_address()
    # …
```

Don't worry too much about the implementation of the show_local_ip_address() function. The basis is that it will search for the local IP address by scanning all the network addresses of the current computer and saving the ones that start with "10.", "172.16.", or "192.168.", which are the know beginnings for local IP addresses. The reasons why it works are a little obscure and beyond the scope of this book.

Now that we know what IP address the server has, let's see how we can actually set everything up to connect two computers together.

Connecting from another computer

The big caveat for now, which we already mentioned in the introduction of the chapter, is that we will not be able to play over the real worldwide internet. This is because of multiple security reasons; you wouldn't want strangers to have direct access to your computer. However, we will be able to play on the same local network. This means that two computers that are connected to the same router, the same Wi-Fi network, and so forth, will be able to connect to each other in the game! All we'll have to do is the following:

1. Transfer the complete Godot project to another computer. You can do this any way you like. With a USB, using an online platform such as Dropbox, Google, Drive, or any other means of transferring files.

2. Make sure both computers are connected to the same local network.

3. Open the project in the same Godot Engine version as you are using.

4. Run a debug instance of the game on each computer.

5. Press play on one computer, making it the server. Use the IP address the server displays to connect to the other clients.

Now, you should be able to play together over the network!

That is all for connecting multiple computers. We'll proceed with a summary of the chapter, but first, here are some additional exercises to solidify our knowledge.

Additional exercises – Sharpening the axe

1. When the game ended, we got a menu with a **Retry** button, but this **Retry** button does not properly work in multiplayer. Can you find a way so that we properly start a new game when all players press this button? The server will have to use the add_player() function for each pair that is connected in the _ready() function of the main.gd script. You can get a list of all the peer IDs with multiplayer.get_peers().

Summary

The joy in playing video games is sharing the experience and nothing makes that easier than directly playing together!

In this chapter, we started by taking a crash course in computer networking where we learned the basics of how computer networks, such as the internet, work. After this, we started to implement multiplayer into our own game using the MultiplayerSpawner and MultiplayerSynchronizer node. Lastly, we tried out playing the game over a real network.

This chapter marks the end of *Part 2* of the book, where we focused on learning how to develop our game and doing so. Starting from the next chapter, we'll learn how to export a game, go a little deeper into more advanced programming topics, and see how we can save or load the game.

Quiz time

- What is the difference between the TCP and UDP?
- If we take the example of a residence with flats, where the port number is the flat number, what does the IP address represent?
- What did we use MultiplayerSpawner for?
- What did we use MultiplayerSynchronizer for?
- What function would we use to check whether the current script is running on the server?

Part 3: Deepening Our Knowledge

After learning how to program and creating your very own game from scratch, you will now take a step back and learn some more advanced programming and game development techniques.

By the end of this final part, you will have exported and distributed your game to various different platforms on the web so that everyone can play it from within their browser. You will also learn more advanced OOP concepts and different programming patterns that will help you in your future game projects. Even the filesystem will be covered so that you can save and load data. The last chapter will guide you through the next steps to take, which resources you could consult to learn more, and how to join the game development community.

This part has the following chapters:

- *Chapter 12, Exporting to Multiple Platforms*
- *Chapter 13, OOP Continued and Advanced Topics*
- *Chapter 14, Advanced Programming Patterns*
- *Chapter 15, Using the File System*
- *Chapter 16, What Next?*

Exporting to Multiple Platforms

After making a game, we should get it into the hands of players. Games are meant to be played, after all! In the old days, this meant burning thousands to millions of CDs and distributing them all over the world to physical game stores, in the hope people would buy them. This cost tremendous amounts of money and manpower. Big studios would often only see 10% of the profits because the rest dissipated in buying physical CDs and paying distribution and store cuts. Even if you developed a successful hit game, the upfront investment to distribute it could stop it in its tracks.

With the rise of the internet and gaming platforms such as **Steam** and **Itch.io**, distribution has become way cheaper, sometimes even free, and easier, with nearly no upfront investment.

Over the course of this chapter, we'll learn everything about exporting production builds for our game and even upload it to Itch.io (if you want to).

In this chapter, we will cover the following main topics:

- Exporting a game for Windows, Mac, and Linux
- Uploading our game to Itch.io
- Exporting our game to other platforms

Technical requirements

As with every chapter, you can find the final code in the GitHub repository in the subfolder for this chapter: `https://github.com/PacktPublishing/Learning-GDScript-by-Developing-a-Game-with-Godot-4/tree/main/chapter12`.

Exporting for Windows, Mac, and Linux

Exporting is the process where we take the game that we have been developing and make it executable outside of Godot. Yes, we can run our game from the engine's editor in debug mode, but ideally, we don't want to share our game's code with players. We also don't want our players to first have to download the whole engine with its editor, and then our game.

When exporting for computers, we'll have to do a separate export for each different operating system, such as Windows, macOS, and Linux. An operating system is software that manages all the hardware and common functionality of a computer.

No matter what kind of **Operating System (OS)** you use, Windows, Mac, or Linux, Godot allows us to export a game to any other platform. This way, we can easily make exports for all our users, no matter what platform they prefer.

Before we can export to any platform though, we'll need to download the export template.

Downloading the export template

To export anything, the Godot engine uses a template that tells it how to actually export our game, which is unique for each Godot Engine version and called the **export template**. Once we have the template, we can export to any of the built-in platforms. We can easily download this export template from within the Godot Editor itself, as follows:

1.   In the top menu bar, open up the **Editor** dropdown and click on **Manage Export Templates...** .

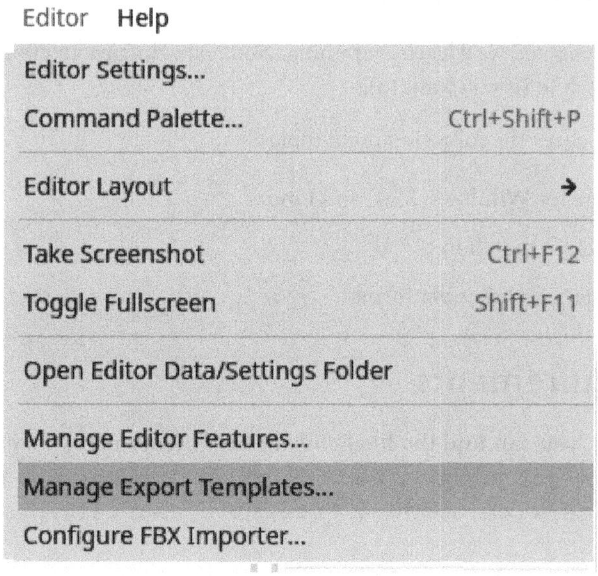

Figure 12.1 – The export templates manager can be accessed through the Editor drop-down menu

2.   Click **Download and Install**.

| Current Version: 4.1.3.stable | Export templates are missing. Download them or install from a file. |

Download from: Best available mirror   ⌄   ⋮   Download and Install
                                                        Install from File

Other Installed Versions:

Close

Figure 12.2 – In the export template manager, we can download and install export templates

It will take some time to download and install the export template, but you only need to do this once for each Godot Engine version you are using. Now, we are ready to do a proper export.

Making the actual exports of the game

With the export template for our given Godot Engine version in place, we can finally export the game. We'll do this using the **Export menu**. Let's get cracking:

1.   In the top menu bar, open up the **Project** dropdown and click on **Export…**.

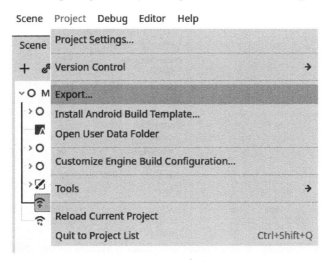

Figure 12.3 – The Export… menu can be accessed through the Project drop-down menu

2. This opens the **Export** menu, which contains the export settings for each export preset. Currently, it does not contain any export presets.

3. Click **Add...** and select the computer platform you are using right now (**Linux/X11**, **macOS**, or **Windows Desktop**).

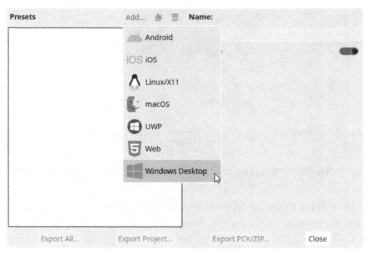

Figure 12.4 – Adding a preset for a certain platform in the Export menu

4. The platform will be added to the **Presets** list.

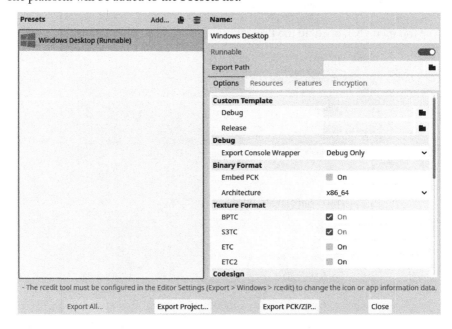

Figure 12.5 – The Windows Desktop platform added as one of the presets

5.   Configure the export depending on the platform you added:

- **For macOS only**: Before you can export the game, you'll need to specify a bundle identifier for your game package. Just fill this field with `com.survivor.game` or something similar.

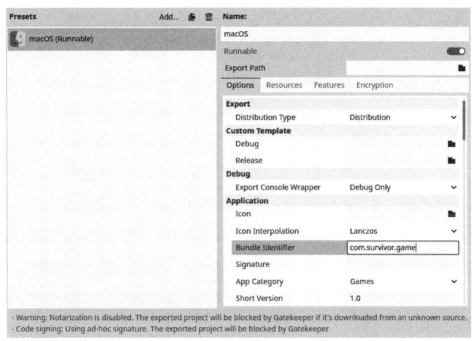

Figure 12.6 – For macOS, you'll have to specify the bundle identifier

- **For Windows and Linux only**: Enable the **Embed PCK** option. This will make sure that our game's PCK file (the package file that contains all the game's data, such as code and art) gets embedded into the executable of the game.

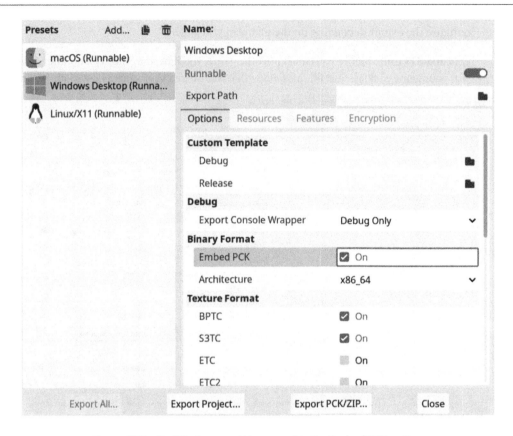

Figure 12.7 – For Windows and Linux, enable the Embed PCK option

6. Now, click **Export Project...** to export the game.

7. Create a new folder called `exports`, under which you can create a folder for each platform. So, if you export for Windows, put it under `exports/windows`. This is just to give some structure to our exports.

8. Disable the **Export With Debug** option.

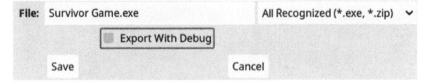

Figure 12.8 – Disabling the Export With Debug option

9. Press **Save**.

We'll now have an export of the game for the target platform in the folder we just created. Repeat the steps in this section for each platform.

Name	Date modified	Type	Size
🎮 Survivor Game.exe	07/12/2023 23:24	Application	68.043 KB

Figure 12.9 – The exported game for Windows

> **Important note**
>
> You might have noticed there is also a button called **Export All…** in the export menu. When all the platforms you want to export to are set up, you can press this button to export all of them simultaneously.

After exporting, it's time to publish the game and share it with the world.

Uploading our game to Itch.io

After making a game, it is a lot of fun to share it with people you know or total strangers to see them interact and play with what you made. In this section, we'll go through the process of putting the game on an online platform called Itch.io. If you don't want to share your game for any reason, then you can skip this section for now; just return to it when you feel ready. But don't worry too much whether it is too early or not to share a game. Player feedback is always a good thing, no matter what point of development you are at, and following these steps to create an Itch.io page is great practice too.

What is Itch.io?

Itch.io is an online platform and store where people can distribute games, assets (to make games), or any other digital resource, file, or program. It is very well known in the game development community because a lot of developers put their small game experiments on there, but you can also find bigger projects.

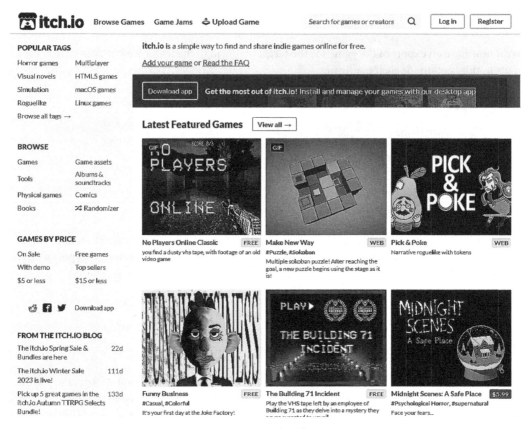

Figure 12.10 – The Itch.io front page

Itch.io is also the place to be to participate in **game jams**. A game jam is a little online event where you build a game within a certain time limit around a certain theme. The time limit and theme differ from game jam to game jam. Afterward, everyone who participated plays each other's games and gives feedback. It is a great way to practice creating games and get feedback from other game developers.

We'll upload our computer builds to the Itch.io platform, but the cool thing is that we can also upload a web build that will be playable from within the browser so that people don't have to download any files – they can just start playing. If we upload both the normal exports and the web export, people can still choose how they want to play, which gives them more options.

Exporting our game to the web

Exporting to the web means that we make an export that can be included in any website and is playable from any browser, even mobile ones.

> **Important note**
>
> Note that when we make a web export, it will only be playable when it is run through a server. You will not be able to directly open the export in your favorite browser without running a server on your computer or hosting it on an online platform. Luckily, we are going to host our game on Itch.io, so you will be able to play it over there.

The first thing we need to do is take out the multiplayer aspect of the game for now.

Removing multiplayer

For security reasons, a website should never have full access to your computer. That is why web exports have some limits, such as slightly worse performance and networking. This means that our game's multiplayer will not work in the web export. There are ways to get multiplayer to work for web exports, but these are out of the scope of this book. With just one small change it will still work fine for a single player:

In the _ready() function of the menu.gd script, add the following line:

```
func _ready():
    _ip_address_line_edit.visible = OS.get_name() != "Web"
    # Rest of the _ready function
```

The OS.get_name() function gives us the name of the operating system the game is currently running on. This makes sure that the input field for the IP address is not visible anymore when the player is playing on the web and cannot get stuck trying to connect, which could break the game for them.

With the multiplayer disables, let's see how we can make the web export.

Making the actual web export

The process of making a web export is equally easy as exporting to the computer platforms; we just add a new preset for the **Web** platform and export the project as normal.

Figure 12.11 – Adding an export preset for the Web platform

One thing that we'll have to ensure is that, when saving the file, we name it index.html, as demonstrated in *Figure 12.12*. Itch.io requires this name because it will be looking for an index. html file to run the game in the browser.

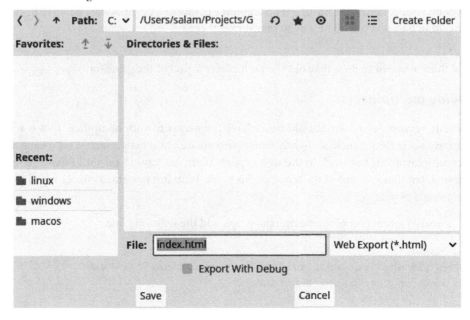

Figure 12.12 – Make sure you save the web export as index.html

Now that we have the export, we'll need to make a zip file out of it. Let's learn how to do that.

Zipping the web export

Itch.io will require a ZIP file that contains all the exported files for the web export. A ZIP file is a file that bundles multiple other files into a compressed format, making it easier to transport them as well as making the content smaller.

Depending on the platform you use, the process is a little different.

For Windows and macOS, follow these steps:

1. Select all the export files.

index.apple-touch-icon.png	07/12/2023 23:24	PNG File	19 KB
index.apple-touch-icon.png.import	07/12/2023 23:09	IMPORT File	1 KB
index.audio.worklet.js	07/12/2023 23:24	JavaScript File	8 KB
index.html	07/12/2023 23:24	Chrome HTML Do...	7 KB
index.icon.png	07/12/2023 23:24	PNG File	4 KB
index.icon.png.import	07/12/2023 23:09	IMPORT File	1 KB
index.js	07/12/2023 23:24	JavaScript File	442 KB
index.pck	07/12/2023 23:24	PCK File	80 KB
index.png	07/12/2023 23:24	PNG File	21 KB
index.png.import	07/12/2023 23:09	IMPORT File	1 KB
index.wasm	07/12/2023 23:24	WASM File	34.581 KB
index.worker.js	07/12/2023 23:24	JavaScript File	6 KB

Figure 12.13 – Selecting all the exported files

2. Now, right-click them so that the **Options** menu appears.

    • **For Windows**: Under **Send to**, select **Compressed (zipped) folder**.

Figure 12.14 – On Windows platforms, select Compressed (zipped) folder

- **For macOS**: Select **Compress**.

Figure 12.15 – On macOS platforms, select Compress

3. Now, name the ZIP file `Survivor Game Web`.

Figure 12.16 – The resulting ZIP file

For Linux, follow these steps:

1. Open the Terminal application on your computer.

2. Use the `cd ~/path/to/game/export/folder` command, with the correct path, to navigate to the web export folder of the game.

3. Now, run `zip -r "Survivor Game Web.zip" .` to create a ZIP file with the contents of this folder.

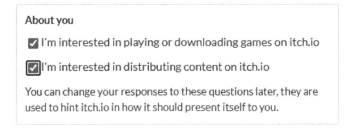

```
web git:(main) × zip -r "Survivor Game Web.zip" .
adding: index.apple-touch-icon.png (deflated 0%)
adding: index.wasm (stored 0%)
adding: index.icon.png (stored 0%)
adding: index.html (deflated 64%)
adding: index.png (deflated 10%)
adding: index.audio.worklet.js (deflated 70%)
adding: index.apple-touch-icon.png.import (deflated 51%)
adding: index.js (deflated 78%)
adding: index.icon.png.import (deflated 50%)
adding: index.worker.js (deflated 59%)
adding: index.pck (deflated 42%)
adding: index.png.import (deflated 50%)
```

Figure 12.17 – The Linux Terminal after running the command to make a ZIP file

With all the exports ready and zipped, it is time to upload the game to Itch.io.

Uploading to Itch.io

Now that everything is ready, we can upload our game to the Itch.io platform and create our own page from which people can play and download the game:

1. Create an account at `https://itch.io/register`. Make sure to check the box next to **I'm interested in distributing content on itch.io** because that is exactly what we want to do.

> **About you**
>
> ☑ I'm interested in playing or downloading games on itch.io
>
> ☑ I'm interested in distributing content on itch.io
>
> You can change your responses to these questions later, they are used to hint itch.io in how it should present itself to you.

Figure 12.18 – When registering for Itch.io, indicate that we want to distribute content

2. Once registered, you'll first have to verify your email address by opening the email that Itch.io sent to the email address you provided for your account and clicking on the button that says **Click to verify your email address**.

Figure 12.19 – Verify your email address

3.   Back in the browser, you should have already been taken to the **Creator Dashboard** page. Click the big red button that says **Create new project**.

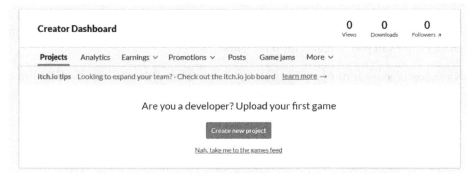

Figure 12.20 – Click on Create new project to start creating the games page

4. Give the project the title `Survivor Game`.

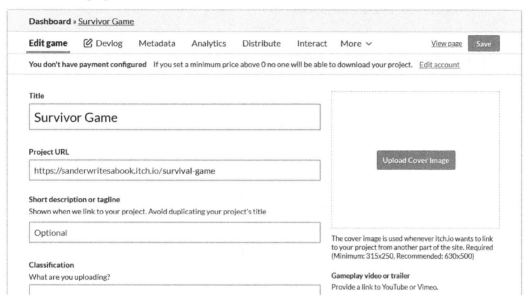

Figure 12.21 – Give the project the title Survivor Game

5. Under **Kind of project**, select **HTML**. This will make sure that people can play the game in their browser.

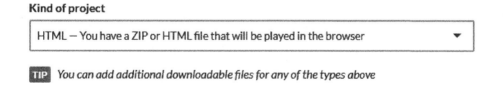

Figure 12.22 – Set Kind of project to HTML

6. Now, under **Uploads**, upload each export ZIP file.

Figure 12.23 – Upload all exports

7. Next, indicate what platform each export file is for. This will help people understand which file they need to download for their platform.

Figure 12.24 – For the Windows, macOS, and Linux platforms, we should indicate the platform

8. For the ZIP file that contains the web export, select **This file will be played in the browser**.

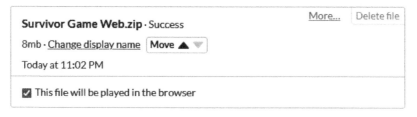

Figure 12.25 – For the Web export ZIP, indicate that it can be played in the browser

9. Under **Embed options**, set **Viewport dimensions** to 1152 px × 648 px. This is the window size of our game on the Itch page. These dimensions are the exact dimensions from our project settings.

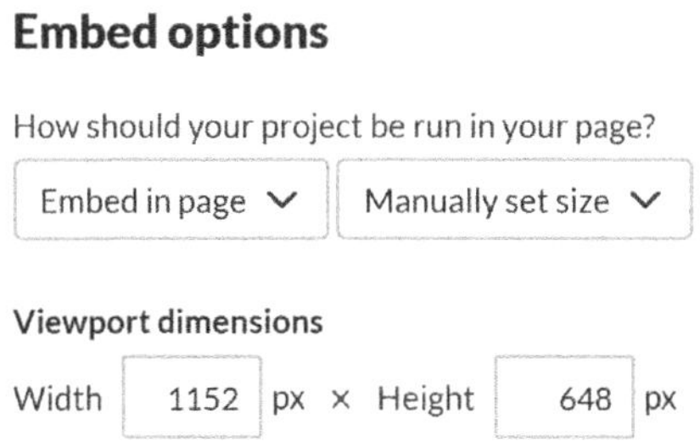

Embed options

How should your project be run in your page?

| Embed in page ∨ | Manually set size ∨ |

Viewport dimensions

Width [1152] px × Height [648] px

Figure 12.26 – For the Web export ZIP, indicate that it can be played in the browser

10. Under **Frame options**, enable **SharedArrayBuffer support**; this is needed for Godot Engine 4 web exports.

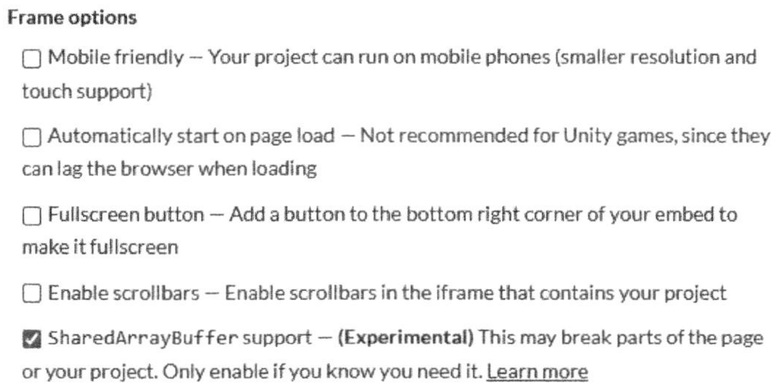

Frame options

☐ Mobile friendly — Your project can run on mobile phones (smaller resolution and touch support)

☐ Automatically start on page load — Not recommended for Unity games, since they can lag the browser when loading

☐ Fullscreen button — Add a button to the bottom right corner of your embed to make it fullscreen

☐ Enable scrollbars — Enable scrollbars in the iframe that contains your project

☑ SharedArrayBuffer support — **(Experimental)** This may break parts of the page or your project. Only enable if you know you need it. Learn more

Figure 12.27 – Enable SharedArrayBuffer support

11. Click **Save & view page**.

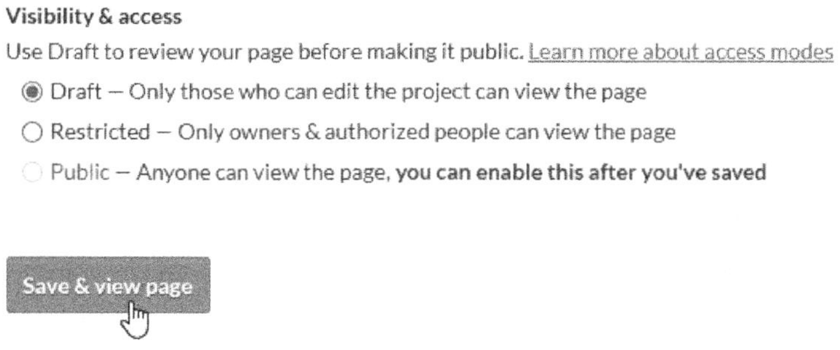

Visibility & access

Use Draft to review your page before making it public. Learn more about access modes

◉ Draft — Only those who can edit the project can view the page

○ Restricted — Only owners & authorized people can view the page

○ Public — Anyone can view the page, **you can enable this after you've saved**

Figure 12.28 – Click Save & view page

12. We'll be taken to a preview of what our page looks like. You'll see that the game needs to load for the first time. To publish it publicly, we need to go back to the **Edit** page.

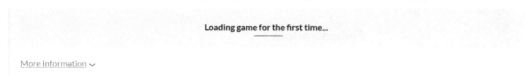

Figure 12.29 – The first time, the game will take some extra time to load

13. This time around, select **Public** under **Visibility & access**.

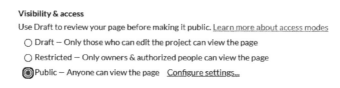

Figure 12.30 – Select Public under Visibility & access

14. Press **Save** again.

The game now has its own page and is online for everyone to see! Send a link to your friend, and share it on social media – you published a game!

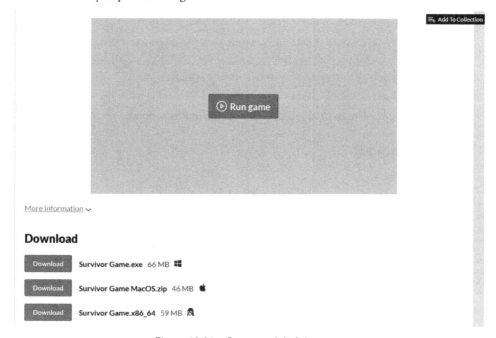

Figure 12.31 – Our game's Itch.io page

Pressing **Run game** will run our game within the browser, while using the download buttons at the bottom of the page help us download the game for any platform we desire.

We know how to do the basic exports for most computers and the web, but what about other platforms, such as mobile and consoles? Let's look at that next.

Exporting our game to other platforms

Now that our game is published and everyone can play it, let's take a quick look at how to export to other platforms that are not regular computers.

Mobile platforms

For mobile devices, such as Android and iOS devices, the process is a little more intricate. However, once the process is set up, it will be very reliable. You can find guides to export to mobile platforms in the official Godot Engine documentation:

- Exporting to Android: `https://docs.godotengine.org/en/stable/tutorials/export/exporting_for_android.html`

- Exporting to iOS: `https://docs.godotengine.org/en/stable/tutorials/export/exporting_for_ios.html`

Next to simply exporting the game, you'll also need to account for the fact that mobile devices, mostly, don't have external buttons, so the gameplay should account for touchscreen controls.

Consoles

Let's address the elephant in the room – what about exporting to consoles, such as **PlayStation**, **Xbox**, or **Nintendo** consoles?

Well, the good news is that it is possible! The bad news is that because the Godot Engine is open source and the code libraries that are needed to export to these consoles are closed source, export options for these cannot be included in the base Godot version. So, by default, they are not in the engine.

However, there are companies that provide a specialized Godot Engine version to export to consoles and/or help port a whole game. These companies include **W4** (a company that employs many of the original Godot Engine developers), **Pineapple Works**, and **Lone Wolf Technology**. You can find an up-to-date list on the Godot documentation site: `https://docs.godotengine.org/en/stable/tutorials/platform/consoles.html`.

Summary

In this chapter, we learned how to export our game to multiple computer platforms such as Windows, Mac, and Linux. We also saw how we can export for the web and upload the game to Itch.io. Now, we are ready to create a whole game and publish it!

In the next chapter, we'll learn more advanced techniques in object-oriented programming.

Quiz time

- What are export templates?

- Why did we enable **Embed PCK** when exporting for Windows and Linux?

- To what platforms can we export using the Godot Engine?

13

OOP Continued and Advanced Topics

We learned so many things about programming over the course of this book, from basic variables, control flows, and classes to things that are GDScript-specific, such as accessing nodes in the scene tree and specific annotations. However, don't be mistaken – there is still so much more knowledge out there that can help solve problems easier and faster.

After many years of studying and professionally applying my programming skills, I can confidently state that computer science is a deep and rewarding field to keep learning. Plus, every few years a new technology pokes out its head, waiting to be studied.

In this chapter, we'll look at a bunch of more advanced techniques and concepts that will elevate your programming skills to new heights!

In this chapter, we will cover the following main topics:

- The `super` keyword
- Static variables and functions
- Enumeration
- Lambda functions
- Passing parameters by value or reference
- The `@tool` annotation

Technical requirements

As with every chapter, you can find the final code in the GitHub repository in the subfolder for this chapter: `https://github.com/PacktPublishing/Learning-GDScript-by-Developing-a-Game-with-Godot-4/tree/main/chapter13`.

The super keyword

In *Chapter 4*, we learned all about inheritance and how we can override functions from a base class in an inherited class. This overriding replaces the function with a whole new body and discards the original implementation of the base class. However, sometimes, we still would like to execute the original logic that was defined in the parent class.

To accomplish this, we can use the `super` keyword. This keyword gives us direct access to all the functions of the parent class on which the current class was based. Consider the following example, where we want to have different kinds of arrows in our game to shoot enemies with:

```
class BaseArrow:
    func describe_damage():
        print("Pierces a person")


class FireArrow extends BaseArrow:
    func describe_damage():
        super()
        print("And sets them ablaze")
```

Here, we define a `BaseArrow` class which is the base for all kinds of arrows. It has one function, `describe_damage()`, which just describes what kind of damage the arrow does by printing out `Pierces a person` to the console.

When we override the `describe_damage()` function of the `FireArrow` class, we first call `super()` as a function. This will execute the original `describe_damage()` function of the `BaseArrow` class before executing the rest.

Let's execute some code that uses these classes:

```
var fire_arrow: FireArrow = FireArrow.new()
fire_arrow.describe_damage()
```

The result will be as follows:

```
Pierces a person
And sets them ablaze
```

You can see that the `describe_damage()` function from the base class has been executed, using the `super()` keyword, as well as the rest of the `FireArrow` class's implementation.

The `super` keyword gives access to the underlying class we inherited from; whether we have overridden that function or not, it will always return to the original one. Let's continue with a look at another new keyword – `static`.

Static variables and functions

The next keyword we will look at is `static`. We can declare a variable or function as static by putting this keyword in front of it:

```
class Enemy:
    static var damage: float = 10.0

    static func do_battle_cry():
        print("Aaaaaargh!")
```

Static variables and functions are declared on the class itself. This means that they can be accessed without creating an instance of the class:

```
print(Enemy.damage)
Enemy.do_battle_cry ()
```

Static variables are made to contain information that is bound to a complete class of objects. But watch out – the following are two big gotchas for static variables and functions:

- In GDScript, static variables can be assigned a new value, and you can change them during the execution of the game. Ideally, you don't want to do this because it can impact your program in ways that are hard to debug.

- From a static function, you can call other functions and use member variables of the class, but only if they are defined as static too. Because static functions are defined on the class itself, they do not have all the context of an initialized object of this class. Static functions need to be very self-contained.

All in all, you won't see static variables and functions that often in GDScript, but it is a well-known concept that many object-oriented programming languages, such as C++ or Java, use. Let's have a look at enums next.

Enumerations

Enums, short for **enumerations**, are a variable type that defines a set of constants that need to be grouped together. Unlike normal constants, where we want to store a certain value, enums automatically assign values to a constant.

In *Chapters 2* and *5*, we saw that it's very important to have well-named variables. This way, we always know what they will contain. We can actually do this for the values of variables too, with named values. Using named values, we can associate a human-readable name with a certain value, making code more readable. It also removes magic numbers from the code. Have a look at this enum:

```
enum DAMAGE_TYPES {
    NONE,
    FIRE,
    ICE
}
```

Here, we create an enum called DAMAGE_TYPES that defines three named values – NONE, FIRE, and ICE. You can access these values like so:

```
DAMAGE_TYPES.FIRE
```

Let's try printing them out:

```
print(DAMAGE_TYPES.NONE)
print(DAMAGE_TYPES.FIRE)
print(DAMAGE_TYPES.ICE)
```

You'll see that it prints out the following:

```
0
1
2
```

This is because each of the names within the enum is associated with an integer value. However, instead of using these rough integers, we can now use nicely readable names. The first named value is associated with 0, and each following one goes up by one.

An enum can also be used to type-hint variables; this way, we know that the variable needs to be assigned an enum value from a certain type:

```
var damage_type: DAMAGE_TYPES = DAMAGE_TYPES.FIRE
match damage_type:
    DAMAGE_TYPES.NONE:
        print("Nothing special happens")
    DAMAGE_TYPES.FIRE:
        print("You catch fire! ")
    DAMAGE_TYPES.ICE:
        print("You freeze!")
```

In this example, we type-hint the damage_type variable as DAMAGE_TYPES. Then, we can, for example, match against this variable and determine what to do.

> **Enums versus strings**
>
> Now, you might think, "*Why don't we use strings if we want to be able to read the value?*" Well, simply, it's because strings are slower and more memory-heavy to work with than integers, the underlying data type of enum values. Another reason is ease of use. An enum has a finite set of values, the ones we defined, while a string can have an arbitrary number of characters. So, when using an enum, we're sure we're only dealing with values we know.

We can also access enums that are defined in one class from a totally different class; like static variables and functions, they can be accessed from the class type directly:

```
class Arrow:
    Enum DAMAGE_TYPES {
        NONE,
        FIRE
    }


func _ready():
    var damage_type: Arrow.DAMAGE_TYPES = Arrow.DAMAGE_TYPES.FIRE
```

Here, we define the DAMAGE_TYPES enum from within the Arrow class. Later, we can access this enum by using Arrow.DAMAGE_TYPES directly.

In this section, we looked at enums, named values that help us by providing human-readable labels. Next, we'll take a look at lambda functions.

Lambda functions

So far, every function we have written belonged to a class or file, which could be treated as a class, but there is actually a way to define functions separately from any class definition. These kinds of functions are called **lambda functions**.

Creating a lambda function

Let's take a look at a lambda function:

```
var print_hello: Callable = func(): print("Hello")
```

You can see that we've defined a function, just as we normally do, but this time without a function name. Instead, we assigned the function to a variable. This variable now contains the function in the form of the Callable object type. We can call a Callable object later on, like this:

```
print_hello.call()
```

This will run the function that we defined and, thus, print out `Hello` to the console.

Lambda functions, just like normal functions, can take arguments too:

```
var print_largest: Callable = func(number_a: float, number_b: float):
    if number_a > number_b:
        print(number_a)
    else:
        print(number_b)
```

In this example, you can also see that lambda functions can contain multiple lines of code in the form of a code block, where each line has the same level of indentation.

Where to use lambda functions

So, where would we use lambda functions? Well, they are very useful in scenarios where you need a relatively small function but don't want to have it as a permanent residence in the class.

One great application of lambda functions is connecting signals. If we have a button for example, then we can connect to its pressed signal using a lambda function, as follows:

```
button.connect("pressed", func(): print("Button pressed!"))
```

Now, every time the button is pressed and emits the `pressed` signal, our lambda function gets executed and prints out `Button pressed!`.

Another one of its use cases are the `filter()` or `sort_custome()` functions that can use lambda function to filter or sort elements in an array:

```
[0, 1, 2, 3, 4].filter(func(number: int): return number % 2 == 0)
[0, 3, 2, 4, 1].sort_custome(func(number_a: int, number_b: int):
return number_a < number_b)
```

Each array has the `filter()` and `sort_custome()` function that takes `Callable` as an argument. The `filter()` function will filter out any element within the array for which the function returns `false`, resulting in an array that only has the elements where the function returns `true`. In the preceding example, this results in an array with only even numbers.

The `sort_custome()` function sorts the elements within the array using the `Callable` we provide it. The lambda function should take two elements and, when the first element should be sorted before the second element, return `true`; otherwise, it should return `false`. This way, we can define our own rules to sort an array's elements.

The resulting arrays after running `filter()` and `sort_custome()` with our lambda functions are as follows:

```
[0, 2, 4]
[0, 1, 2, 3, 4]
```

> **More information**
>
> For more on lambda functions, check out the official documentation: `https://docs.godotengine.org/en/stable/classes/class_callable.html`.

Now that we know what lambda functions are, let's take a look at the different ways in which we can pass values to functions.

Passing parameters by value or reference

When passing parameters to a function, there are actually two different ways in which these parameters can arrive at the body of that function – by value or reference. We, as programmers, do not choose which of the two is used; GDScript makes this decision based on the data type of the value we provide the function. Let's take a deeper look into both the methods for passing values, which data types apply to each, and why it is important to know the difference.

Passing by value

Passing by value means that GDScript sends over an exact copy of a value to a function. This approach is very simple and predictable because we get a new variable in the function that we called. However, because copying over data takes time, it can be quite slow for big data types.

Data types that get passed by value are any of the simpler built-in data types, such as integers, floating point numbers, and Booleans. Some also slightly more complex classes such as strings, `Vector2`, and `Colors` are passed by value. This list is not exhaustive. The general rule of inclusion is anything that is not an array, not a dictionary, and not inherited from the `Object` class.

Let's see what passing by value looks like in practice:

```
func _ready():
    var number: int = 5
    print("Number before the function: ", number)
    function_taking_integers(number)
    print("Number after the function: ", number)

    var string: String = "Hello there!"
    print("String before the function: ", string)
    function_taking_strings(string)
```

```
    print("String after the function: ", string)

func function_taking_integers(number: int):
    number += 10
    print("Number during the function: ", number)

func function_taking_strings(string: String):
    string[0] = "W"
    print("String during the function: ", string)
```

Here, you can see that we have two functions that take an integer and a string respectively, and each modify the value of the parameter during its execution. We also print out the value of this integer and string every step of the way, before, during, and after the function's execution, to see whether the original variable, from the _ready() function, got altered. Running this will print out the following:

```
Number before the function: 5
Number during the function: 15
Number after the function: 5
String before the function: Hello there!
String during the function: Wello there!
String after the function: Hello there!
```

We can see that, although the value got altered in some way during the function's execution, the original value did not change. This is the fun of passing by value; we don't need to worry about side effects.

Side effects of functions

Side effects, in programmer lingo, mean that a function changes the state of a program in ways that are not directly apparent, altering variables outside of its scope. You want to avoid this as much as possible so that it is easy to understand what a function does.

This is how passing by value works – just a straight copy of the data. Now, we'll see the contrasting idea – passing by reference.

Passing by reference

The other way to pass values to a function is by reference. This means that GDScript does not copy over the whole value but, rather, sends a reference that points toward the value. This reference points to where the actual value is stored and can be used to access and change it.

This mode of passing parameters is used for arrays, dictionaries, and any class that inherits from the Object class, which includes all types of nodes. It is essentially used to pass bigger data types, as copying their complete value over would take too much time and slow down the execution of our game.

Here's an example of what passing by reference looks like:

```
func _ready():
    var dictionary: Dictionary = { "value": 5 }
    print("Dictionary before the function: ", dictionary)
    function_taking_dictionary(dictionary)
    print("Dictionary after the function: ", dictionary)


func function_taking_dictionary(dictionary: Dictionary):
    dictionary["a_value"] = "has changed"
    print("Dictionary during the function: ", dictionary)
```

Again, we use the same setup as before to print out our dictionary every step of the way. We run the following code:

```
Dictionary before the function: { "value": 5 }
Dictionary during the function: { "value": 5, "a_value": "has changed"
}
Dictionary after the function: { "value": 5, "a_value": "has changed"
}
```

As expected, we can see that after the function ran, the original dictionary from the _ready() function was altered too! This is a side effect in action.

In general, it is good practice to never alter the values and variables that come into a function, and always make a copy or use them directly to calculate a value for another variable. When in doubt, it's best to test out whether a value is passed by value or reference; this way, you never encounter unintended bugs.

> **Duplicating arrays or dictionaries**
>
> If you really want to make a copy of an array or dictionary, then you can use the duplicate() function that is defined on these data types. This function will return a copy of the array or dictionary that you can alter safely.
>
> See the documentation for more details: https://docs.godotengine.org/fr/4.x/classes/class_array.html#class-array-method-duplicate.

We'll now switch gears and see how we can make tools for the editor from within the editor.

The @tool annotation

As well as using GDScript to run code during our game's execution, we can actually use it to run code in the editor itself. Running code within the editor grants us the power to visualize things, such as the jump height of a character, or automate our workflow. In doing so we extend the Godot editor for our own specific needs. There are multiple ways of running GDScript code within the editor, ranging from running separate scripts to writing whole plugins, but the easiest way is by using the @tool annotation.

The @tool annotation is an annotation that can be added to the top of any script. Its effect is that nodes with that script will run their script within the editor as if they were instanced within a game. This means that all of their code runs from within the editor.

This is very useful when we are editing our scenes and want to preview things within the editor, such as the health of our player, or create new nodes using code.

Knowing this, we can adjust our player script, by adding the @tool annotation to the top to update the health label in the editor:

```
@tool
class_name Player extends CharacterBody2D

const MAX_HEALTH: int = 10

@onready var _health_label: Label = $Health

@export var health: int = 10:
    set(new_value):
        health = new_value
        update_health_label()

func _ready():
    update_health_label()

func update_health_label():
    if not is_instance_valid(_health_label):
        return

    _health_label.text = str(health) + "/" + str(MAX_HEALTH)
```

This example is the minimum amount of code needed to update the health label from within the editor. However, you can just add the @tool annotation at the top of your existing player script, and it will work its magic. You'll see that every time you change the player's health from within the editor now, the health label will automatically reflect this change.

> **The risks of @tool**
>
> The @tool annotation is very powerful but not without danger. It can remove things permanently from a scene and easily change the values of nodes if you don't watch out, so treat it with caution.

However, sometimes you want to use a node in a game and have some code that runs in the editor. When we do that, we need a way to distinguish whether the code is run in the game or the editor. This can be done by using `Engine.is_editor_hint()`. This function on the global `Engine` object returns `true` if we run the code from within the editor and `false` when from within the game:

```
if Engine.is_editor_hint():
    # Code to execute in editor.

if not Engine.is_editor_hint():
    # Code to execute in game.
```

This code example shows us how easy it is to differentiate between running code in the editor or the game.

> **More information**
>
> Want to know more about the `@tool` annotation and running code within the editor? Check out the official documentation: `https://docs.godotengine.org/en/stable/tutorials/plugins/running_code_in_the_editor.html`.

Using the `@tool` annotation wisely, we can make our workflow easier and faster. The possibilities are endless; you can even access and change almost every aspect of the Godot editor from within one of these scripts, but that is out of the scope of this book.

Summary

This chapter took a deeper dive into some of the more advanced topics of programming with GDScript. We expanded our knowledge of object-oriented programming with the `super` and `static` keywords and the difference between passing by value or reference. Then, we saw more features of the GDScript programming language, such as enums and lambda functions. We concluded the chapter with a way to run code within the Godot editor itself, using the `@tool` annotation.

Quiz time

- Imagine we have a class named `Character` that has a function called `move()`. Now, we create a `Player` class that inherits from this `Character` class and overrides this `move()` function. But, instead of completely overriding it, we want to extend the original functionality of the `Character` class's `move()` function. What keyword can we use to call the original `move()` function of the `Character` class from within the `Player` class?

- Can functions that are labeled `static` call functions that are not labeled `static`?

- What will the following snippet of code print out?

```
enum COLLECTIBLE_TYPE {
    HEALTH,
    UPGRADE,
    DAMAGE,
}

print(COLLECTIBLE_TYPES.DAMAGE)
```

- Are container types, such as arrays and dictionaries, the only types that get passed by reference?

- What annotation do we use at the top of a script if we want to run it in the editor?

14

Advanced Programming Patterns

Although computer science as a scientific field is pretty new, being less than 80 years old, many smart people have studied it. This means that most programming problems have already been encountered in one way or another. These are problems such as how to connect parts of a program without them being hardwired or how to create and destroy thousands of objects, such as bullets for example, without slowing down a game.

These smart people, often called software architects, came up with smart solutions that solve these problems in an elegant manner. Then, they realized that they could generalize these solutions into a sort of recipe, a template that others could use too. This is what we call a programming pattern. In this chapter, we'll learn what programming patterns are exactly and have a look at the three most used patterns in game development.

The bigger your vocabulary of programming patterns, the easier it will be for you to solve your own problems and communicate your ideas to others.

In this chapter, we will cover the following main topics:

- The basics of programming patterns
- The Event Bus
- Object Pooling
- State Machines

Technical requirements

As with every chapter, you can find the final code on the GitHub repository in the subfolder for this chapter: https://github.com/PacktPublishing/Learning-GDScript-by-Developing-a-Game-with-Godot-4/tree/main/chapter14.

You can find the code required for implementing Object Pooling in our game here: https://github.com/PacktPublishing/Learning-GDScript-by-Developing-a-Game-with-Godot-4/tree/main/chapter14-objectpool.

What are programming patterns?

I'll be honest – we are not the first people to create games, or to write software for that matter. But this is actually a good thing; it means that many others before us encountered the same problems that we might have too. They thought up solutions to these problems in one way or another, and we can now make use of these solutions in our own games and software.

Programming patterns, or software design patterns, are descriptions or templates that tell us how we can solve certain problems while programming. They are not completely implemented solutions; they just give us directions on how we could tackle whatever we are trying to solve. A programming pattern tells us how we can organize our code for different outcomes.

To express these patterns, there are different parts that are important:

- **The name**: How the pattern is called.
- **The problem**: What the pattern is trying to solve.
- **The solution**: How the pattern will work.

Other than just providing a solution, programming patterns also give us a means to talk about our software. Communicating what we did can be hard when, as in software development, every problem can be tackled in a multitude of different ways. Design patterns give us a way of talking about the solution without going too deep into the actual implementation.

Lastly, if we structure our code according to one or multiple patterns, we know what to expect. We know how the code will react to new changes and communicate to other parts of a program. This helps us to understand how we can make changes, be it solving a bug, adding new functionality, or rewriting old code.

> **Rewriting old code**
> Sometimes, you will find that the way you solved a problem is not fast, extensible, or sufficient enough. At this point, you can choose to rewrite some code. We call this refactoring code.

Believe it or not, anything can be a pattern, and you could have been using an existing pattern, even if you didn't realize it.

However, it is not as simple as picking any pattern and forcing it into our game's code. We should carefully consider whether to use one pattern or another. When we use a certain pattern that is ill-fitting for the problem we are trying to solve and actually makes our software worse, we call that an **anti-pattern**.

In the interest of not overextending this chapter, the code examples will function more as an introduction and demonstration of how a pattern can be used. We will not implement all the patterns in our game as this would require too much text for some. The real goal of this chapter is to make you aware of the most useful programming patterns.

Let's get started with our first pattern – the Event Bus.

Exploring the Event Bus

The first programming pattern we'll look at is the **Event Bus**. It will help us to decouple code, meaning that two pieces of code don't need to rely on each other too much while still being able to communicate.

Let's take a look at what problem the Event Bus pattern tries to solve.

The problem

If we decouple different classes and parts of our code, they are easier to reuse later on. We did this earlier, in *Chapter 9* for example, with the signals that we can connect provided by Godot Engine. The piece of code that publishes the signal does not care about who is listening or wants to receive that signal.

But signals only work very locally, and using them globally can turn out to be a challenge. The classic example is an achievement system. Achievements are little rewards that a player gets when accomplishing certain tasks within a game. These could even be linked to external achievement systems like the ones from Steam or PlayStation Network. The tasks necessary to unlock these achievements are often bound to very different systems within the game – *"defeat the end boss," "jump 250 times," "play backwards for 2 minutes,"* and so on. Because of this variation in different achievements, the achievement system needs to get information from many different parts of the code. However, we don't want to access the achievement system directly from within the code of each system or vice versa, as this would create a hard dependency for the achievement system to be present at all times. On the Nintendo Switch, for example, there is no achievement system, so all of this achievement code would be useless.

Now that we know what kind of problem we are trying to solve, let's dive into the solution that is the Event Bus.

The solution

This is where the Event Bus pattern comes in. It's a class we autoload, where other pieces of code can subscribe to or publish events. The basic structure looks like this:

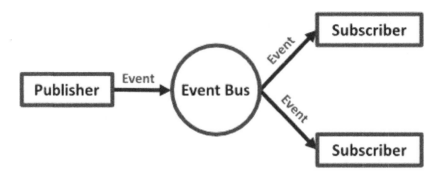

Figure 14.1 – The basic structure of how the Event Bus works

It is very similar to signals, but this time on a global scale. Let's look at a very simple example:

```
extends Node

var _observers: Dictionary = {}

func subscribe(event_name: String, callback: Callable):
    if not event_name in _observers:
        _observers[event_name] = []

    _observers[event_name].append(callback)

func publish(event_name: String):
    if not event_name in _observers:
        return

    for callable: Callable in _observers[event_name]:
        callable.call()
```

Add this previous script to the project's autoloads, as we did for the highscore manager in *Chapter 10*, so that we can access it globally.

Let's assume a very simplistic example of a boss fight, where we have one node that has a script that looks like this:

```
extends Node

func _ready():
    while randf() < 0.99:
        print("You're still fighting the boss!")
    print("The boss dies x.x")
    EventBus.publish("killed_boss")
```

You can see that we just compare a random value until that value is bigger than 0.99, which should average around 100 tries. Ultimately, the boss battle is over, and we publish an event to the Event Bus that is called `killed_boss`.

Now, we can create a little achievement system and subscribe to this event, to be notified when the boss battle is over:

```
extends Node

func _ready():
    EventBus.subscribe("killed_boss", on_boss_killed)

func on_boss_killed():
    print("Achievement Unlocked: Kill the Boss")
```

Add this script as an autoload, named `AchievementSystem`, and then you can run the project. In the console, you'll see that it works perfectly:

```
You're fighting the boss!
...
You're fighting the boss!
The boss dies x.x
Achievement Unlocked: Kill the Boss
```

The signals, which are default in Godot, and the Event Bus patterns are both close cousins of the Observer pattern. The big difference between signals and the Event Bus is that with signals, you can only subscribe to one specific entity, such as when we subscribe to one enemy's `died` signal to signify that the enemy died, whereas an Event Bus is global. It doesn't matter what node or object threw the event; everyone who is subscribed to the event will get notified, such as when any node (it doesn't matter which) throws the `game_over` event to signify that the game ended. The Observer pattern and all its different forms are widely known.

> **Learn more**
>
> Learn more about the Observer pattern here: `https://gameprogrammingpatterns.com/observer.html`.

The Event Bus programming pattern is ideal for decoupling your code. Let's now explore a pattern that has a completely different purpose, namely optimizing load times.

Understanding Object Pooling

The second programming pattern we'll see is Object Pooling. The purpose of this pattern is to keep up the frame rate of our game while still being able to create and destroy many objects or nodes. Let's take a deeper dive into what we are trying to solve – that is, the problem.

The problem

In some games, we want to be able to spawn and remove objects really quickly. In the little game that we have constructed over the course of the book, for example, we want to be able to spawn and remove projectiles and arrows fast and reliably. With the rates our arrows are being shot at now, this is not a big issue, but it could become one if we increased this rate, especially in multiplayer. Creating new nodes – for example, by using the `instantiate()` function we saw in *Chapter 10* and adding them to the scene tree – is pretty slow. The game needs to load the scene file from disk and then allocate new memory every time we create a new node. Then, when the node gets freed, the game has to free up that memory again.

To optimize this process, we can use an Object Pool, which we will discuss in the next section.

The solution

Theses loading problems can be solved by the Object Pooling pattern. Object Pooling basically means that we keep a list, also called a pool, of already initialized nodes somewhere. For example, with a bunch of arrows, when we need an arrow, we can simple take one from this list. When it is not needed anymore, we return it to that list so that it can be reused later on.

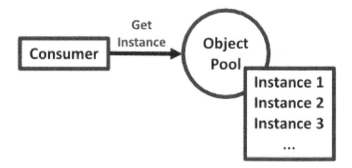

Figure 14.2 – Any class that wants an instance can ask the Object Pool

Because we do not actually delete or remove the arrow node from the scene tree, we will need to make sure, through code, that the node stops working in the background when it is supposed to be stored away in the Object Pool. When an object is in use, we say it is alive because it lives within the game. When it is in the Object Pool, it is dead because it is not in use anymore. When we want to return a live object to the pool, we say that it gets killed.

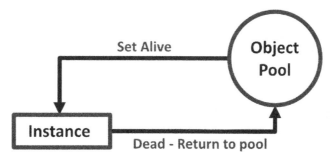

Figure 14.3 – The Object Pool sets an instance as alive. When the instance is dead, it returns to the pool

Here is an example of what an Object Pool's script could look like:

```
class_name ObjectPool extends Object

var _pool: Array

func _init(scene: PackedScene, pool_size: int, root_node: Node):
    for _i in pool_size:
        var new_node: Node = scene.instantiate()
        _pool.append(new_node)
        new_node.died.connect(kill_node.bind(new_node))
        root_node.add_child(new_node)

func kill_node(node: Node):
    node.set_dead()
    _pool.append(node)

func get_dead_node() -> Node:
    if _pool.is_empty():
        return null
    var node: Node = _pool.pop_back()
    node.set_alive()
    return node

func free_nodes():
    for node in _pool:
            node.queue_free()
```

You can see that we keep an array, called _pool, which will contain all of our dead nodes. First, we create a number of objects within the _init() function of type scene and add these new objects as children to root_node, which we can pass to this _init() function. The number of objects we populate the pool with is defined by pool_size.

In the _init() function, we also connect to the died signal of each node using the kill_node() function. This means that the node, when it dies, needs to emit the died signal. The kill_node() function, in turn, will call the set_dead() function on that node. This function should disable the node and will be different for each kind of node, so we need to implement that later on in the definition of the node script itself. After this, the node is returned to the _pool.

You can also see that I called a function called bind() on the kill_node callable – kill_node.bind(new_node). This binds arguments to Callable, which means that if the signal is emitted and this Callable gets called, the arguments we bind here are given to the kill_node() function. This way, we know what object is being killed in the set_dead() function.

When we need an instance from the pool, we call the get_dead_node() function, which will first check whether there are still objects in the pool; if not, we return nothing. If there are still objects in the pool, we remove the first element from e _pool, set it as alive, and then return it.

Lastly, we implemented a free_nodes() function that frees all the nodes that are present in the pool. This way, we can free them all conveniently when we stop the game.

Implementing the Object Pool in our game

Let's implement the Object Pool in our own game! The obvious nodes to pool from our Vampire Survivor like game are the projectile and the enemy. We'll use a pool to deal with the projectiles here. You can always take a stab at making an Object Pool that deals with the enemies:

Create a script, object_pool.gd, that has the exact content of the script from the previous section. Save it under a new folder, parts/object_pool.

Let's prepare the projectile.gd script so that it can be in a pool:

1. At the top, add a new custom signal, died. This will be called when the projectile can go back into the pool.

    ```
    signal died
    ```

2. Then, add two functions, set_alive() and set_dead(), which we call from the Object Pool:

    ```
    func set_alive():
        if multiplayer.is_server():
            set_physics_process(true)
            _enemy_detection_area.monitoring = true
        show()
    ```

```
func set_dead():
    set_physics_process(false)
    _enemy_detection_area.set_deferred("monitoring", false)
    hide()
```

The `set_alive` function turns on the `_physics_process` and the collision detection for the projectile, but only if this code is run from the server. Then it shows the projectile, no matter if we are running from the server or not so that everyone can see it. The `set_dead` function undoes all these changes to make sure the projectile is unusable while dead.

> **Important note**
>
> We use the `set_deferred()` function on the `_enemy_detection_area` to set `monitoring` to `true` or `false` because this change has to be incorporated by the physics engine and we need to wait until all physics calculations for that frame are executed. The `set_deferred()` function sets the value to our desired value at the end of the current frame.

3. Now, replace the original `_ready()` function with the one in the next code snipper which makes sure new instances don't start acting when they are created and put into the scene tree:

```
func _ready():
    set_dead()
```

4. Lastly, replace the mentions of `queue_free()` with `died.emit()` because the Object Pool will manage how the node gets created:

```
func _physics_process(delta: float):
    if not is_instance_valid(target):
        died.emit()
        return
    # Rest of _physics_process

func _on_enemy_detection_area_body_entered(body: Node2D) ->
void:
    body.get_hit()
    died.emit()
```

5. Next, let's change the `main.gd` script to have an Object Pool of projectiles.

   At the top, add a `projectile_pool` variable and preload the `projectile.tscn` scene:

```
var projectile_pool: ObjectPool
var projectile_scene: PackedScene = preload("res://parts/
projectile/projectile.tscn")
```

6. Now, we only want to initialize this variable when we run from the server. The server will manage all the projectiles. Add the following line to `_ready()`:

```
Func _ready():
    # ...
    if multiplayer.is_server():
        # Code for server setup

        projectile_pool = ObjectPool.new(projectile_scene, 50,
self)
```

7. The Object Pool will not free itself when we close the game, so we will have to do that manually in the `_exit_tree()` function of the main script:

```
func _exit_tree():
    if projectile_pool:
        projectile_pool.free_nodes()
        projectile_pool.free()
```

> **Important note**
>
> Nodes in the scene tree will be freed automatically when we close the game. But objects that are not inside of the tree, like our `projectile_pool` or nodes we take out of the scene tree, are not managed by the same process. So, we need to manage when to delete them ourselves.

8. Lastly, we'll need to update the `player.gd` script to access the Object Pool for a projectile and set its target and position. Replace the original way we created a new projectile with this code:

```
func _on_shoot_timer_timeout():
    # Shooting code to select a target enemy

    var new_projectile: Projectile = get_parent().projectile_
pool.get_dead_node()
    if new_ projectile:
        new_projectile.target = closest_enemy
        new_projectile.position = global_position
```

This is all we need to do to implement our Object Pool in our multiplayer game. When you look at the **Remote Tree** while running the game, you'll see that 50 projectiles have been created at the start, ready to be launched by the players.

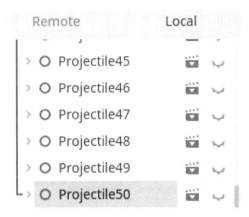

Figure 14.4 – 50 projectiles are created, ready to be used

That's it for the Object Pool pattern. It is very useful to keep frame rates in check when you need lots of objects to spawn and disappear often. Let's look at yet another completely different pattern in the next section.

Working with State Machines

Games are massive pieces of code that can get quite complex. To lower the complexity of code, we can try to separate different pieces so that they only perform one action very well. That is exactly what we are going to do with a State Machine. Let's first start with a better problem statement.

The problem

Agents, such as the player or enemies, often have to operate in very different scenarios. In a platformer game, such as **Super Mario Bros** for example, the character needs to be able to walk, run, jump, dive, wall slide, fly, and so on. This is a lot of different kinds of code. If we try to fit this into one big class for the player, we'll end up with a jumble of code that is very hard to understand, debug, or extend.

Ultimately, we want our game's code to be easily understood and maintained. That's why we will learn about the State Machine in the next section.

The solution

A great way to combat this complexity is by separating the behavior for each of these wanted behaviors (walking, jumping, etc.) into different files and classes. This is exactly what the State Machine pattern does. The State Machine swaps out part or the complete behavior of an object with a different behavior, depending on the state it is in.

Each of the behaviors we identified earlier (walking, jumping, etc.) is defined as a totally independent state that alters the behavior of the agent and is saved in a separate file.

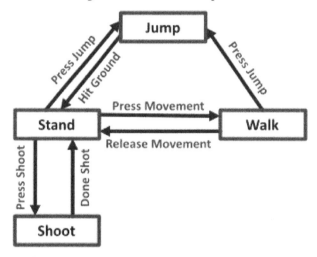

Figure 14.5 – An example of how states could connect with each other

The State Machine can only have one active state at one time. This rule makes sure that we don't mix up behaviors or code.

Each of these states knows which other states it can transition to. This transition gets triggered from the code of that state by asking the State Machine directly to transition.

Now that we have a surface-level idea of what a State Machine can do, let's quickly list all the things it should do. The State Machine should do the following:

- Have a list of all possible states
- Designate one active state
- Be able to transition from one state to another
- Update the current active state and provide it with direct input

With that in mind, let's take a look at the code for the actual State Machine itself:

```
class_name StateMachine extends Node

@export var starting_state: String

var states: Dictionary
var current_state: State

func _ready():
```

```
    for child in get_children():
        states[child.name] = child
        child.state_machine = self
    if not starting_state.is_empty:
        transition_to(starting_state)

func transition(state_name: String):
    if current_state:
        current_state.exit()

    current_state = states[state_name]
    current_state.enter()

func _physics_process(delta: float):
    if not current_state: return
    current_state.process(delta)

func _input(event: InputEvent):
    if not current_state: return
    current_state.input(event)
```

You can see that in the _ready() function, we scan all the children of the State Machine and add it to a dictionary of states. This dictionary will help us to quickly look up states when we need them in the transition() function. This also means that we will add each state as a child node to the State Machine itself, like so:

Figure 14.6 – The State Machine with each state as a child node

At the end of the _ready() function, we transition to starting_state, which is an export variable that we can use to set the initial state of the State Machine.

In the transition() function that is used to transition to a new state, we first check whether we have current_state; if we do, we'll first have to call the exit() function on it to make sure it can clean itself up. After that, we use state_name, which is provided as an argument to look up the next state, assign it as current_state, and call the enter() function on it.

The `_physics_process()` and `_input()` methods are used to directly feed into the `process()` and `input()` functions of `current_state`, if there is a current state.

Now, let's have a look at the `state` class itself:

```
class_name State extends Node

var _state_machine: StateMachine

func enter():
    pass

func exit():
    pass

func process(delta: float):
    pass

func input(event: InputEvent):
    pass
```

The state class is a simple skeleton with functions that we have to implement when we inherit from it. This means that if we have a jump state, for example, we'll need to make sure that the `enter()`, `exit()`, `input()` and `process()` functions all work as they should during the jumping behavior of our character.

If we want to go from one state to another, we can simply use `_state_machine.transition()` from within the state and provide the name of the state we want to transition to.

We can now create specialized states and connect them through code, by calling the `transition()` function on the `_state_machine` object.

An example state

Let's take a quick look at an example state, `Walk`, for the player. This is the state when the player moves freely around:

```
extends State

var _player: Player = owner

@export var max_speed: float = 500.0
@export var acceleration: float = 2500.0
@export var deceleration: float = 1500.0
```

```
func process(delta: float):
    var input_direction: Vector2 = Input.get_vector("move_left", "move_
right", "move_up", "move_down")
    if input_direction != Vector2.ZERO:
    _player.velocity = _player.velocity.move_toward(input_direction *
max_speed, acceleration * delta)
    else:
        _player.velocity = _player.velocity.move_toward(Vector2.ZERO,
deceleration * delta)

    _player.move_and_slide()

func input(event: InputEvent):
    if event.is_action_pressed("jump"):
        _state_machine.transition("Jump")
```

You can see we extend the State script from earlier. Then, we implement the process() function to do our movement calculations, which are specific to walking around, and the input() function to detect when we want to transition from this state to the Jump state.

We don't need to override every function from the State script, just the ones that we need, which in this case are the process() and input() functions.

State Machines, in one way or another, are used in almost every game you ever played. It is a very important concept to understand. They abstract complex behavior into separate classes that are easy to understand and maintain.

Let's conclude the chapter with some additional exercises.

Additional exercises – Sharpening the axe

1. The implementation of our Event Bus makes it possible to subscribe to an event, but not to unsubscribe when the receiver doesn't want to be subscribed anymore. Implement an unsubscribe() function that unsubscribes a Callable from an event:

    ```
    func unsubscribe(event_name: String, callback: Callable):
        # Your code
    ```

2. The Object Pool we have implemented returns nothing when we try to call get_dead_node() while the pool is empty. A smarter way of dealing with this would be to create a new object, basically extending the Object Pool on the fly. Create a new function, get_dead_node_or_create_new(), in such a way that when the pool is empty, it creates a new object that is correctly connected and returned to the pool when it dies.

Summary

After learning how to program and make a game, we finally took a step back and learned about higher-level patterns that help us structure our project and code nicely. First, we learned about what programming patterns are in general. Then, we learned about the Event Bus, Object Pool, and State Machine patterns that can help us in different ways. These three are some of the widely used patterns in gaming and are applied outside of game development too.

From here, you can start to investigate more niche programming patterns, such as the following:

- **Components, also known as Composition**: `https://gameprogrammingpatterns.com/component.html`

- **Commands**: `https://gameprogrammingpatterns.com/command.html`

- **Service Locators**: `https://gameprogrammingpatterns.com/service-locator.html`

In the next chapter, we'll look at the filesystem and learn how to save the state of our game so that our players can start a game from where they left off.

Quiz time

- Programming patterns are standardized ways of solving problems in a program or game. What is the advantage of knowing them?

- Any piece of code can be considered as a pattern. But when we call something an anti-pattern, does this mean that it works in our favor?

- The Signals and Event Bus patterns are very similar because, in both, we subscribe to events, but what is their fundamental difference?

- Why would we use an Object Pool pattern in our game?

- What is the line of code with which we can transition from one state to another using the State Machine pattern?

15

Using the File System

In the early days, arcade games would never store the progress of players. Every time you put in a quarter, the game would start from zero, unless there was a system that would let you buy more lives within the same run. But in general, you could not return the day after and start playing where you left off the day before.

Even early console games had limited functionality in terms of saving your progress. Some games would have a code system with which you got a secret code from the moment you had beaten a level. Later, you could use this code to start directly from there. But these games still didn't really save your progress.

This restriction was partly because storage space, like hard drives or flash memory, was very expensive. Nowadays, almost every computer and console comes standard with a few hundred gigabytes, if not terabytes, of storage. Saving data has become very cheap and easy and players have come to expect that some kind of progress is tracked between play sessions.

In this chapter, we will cover the following main topics:

- What is the file system?
- Creating a save system

Technical requirements

As with every chapter, you can find the final code in the GitHub repository in the subfolder for this chapter: `https://github.com/PacktPublishing/Learning-GDScript-by-Developing-a-Game-with-Godot-4/tree/main/chapter15`

What is the file system?

A file system is a system that manages files, their contents, as well as the metadata of these files. For example, a file system would manage in what folders the files are stored. It makes sure that we can access these files to read the content and metadata and write new data back. For Godot, this means that Godot Engine manages all resources that we could need in our game, from scenes to scripts, as well as images and sounds.

> **Metadata**
>
> When we have data, such as a text file, it is often accompanied by metadata. This is data about the data. While the text file contains the actual data, that is, the text, the metadata contains information such as the date of creation, who the author was, where it is stored, and what accounts have access to the file.

Let's start our exploration of file systems with file paths in the next section.

File paths

To be able to locate a file, the file system gives a unique path to each file. On our computer, we can find files through folders, also called directories, where we store them in a nice order. This path could look like this on a Windows-based system:

```
C:\Users\user_name\Documents\my_text_file.txt
```

Or it could look like this on macOS and Linux-based systems:

```
~/Documents/my_text_file.txt
```

For resource and other project-related files, Godot Engine's paths work relative to the position where the project's `project.godot` file is located. This file's path is considered as the root directory. The paths within the Godot file system to access resource files always start with `res://`. To access one of the files within the project, for example, a path could look like this:

```
res://parts/player/player.tscn
```

> **Important note**
>
> For convenience and compatibility, the Godot file system always uses forward slashes (/). Even on Windows-based systems, where the backward slash (\) is normally used.

We actually already used one of these paths when we preloaded the projectiles in *Chapter 10*.

User path

The fact that we can easily access all project files using the `res://` path is very convenient, but there is a problem. We cannot write to any file in the `res://` domain; when the game is running from an exported build, we can only read files from it. To help developers out with this problem, Godot Engine provides another root path, `user://`, which files can be written to and then read from.

Godot Engine automatically makes a folder somewhere on the computer to store this user data. The location of this folder is dependent on the system the game is running on, so it will be at a different for each OS:

- Windows: `%APPDATA%\Godot\app_userdata\<project name>`

- macOS: `~/Library/Application Support/Godot/app_userdata/ <project name>`

- Linux: `~/.local/share/godot/app_userdata/ <project name>`

> **Important note**
>
> In the project settings, we can even specify where to locate this folder for each of the three OSs, but that is not needed for now, as Godot handles this for us and hides the folders away somewhere safe.

You can access the `user://` folder for a given project by opening up the **Project** menu and choosing **Open User Data Folder**.

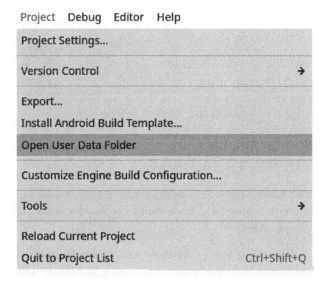

Figure 15.1 - Open User Data Folder takes us to the user:// folder

The `user://` path is what we are going to use to write our save data to in the next section of this chapter. So, let's get to the actual implementation of our own little save system.

Creating a save system

In theory, all we need to do is open a file, write the data we want to save to it, and then, later on, read that same file whenever we need the data. As it turns out, in the Godot Engine, it is indeed easy to read and write files.

We're first going to see how to write to an external file.

Writing data to the disk

Let's get to it by creating a new script called `save_manager.gd` under the `autoloads` folder. Then, to save data, put this code in the script:

```
extends Node

const SAVE_FILE_PATH: String = "user://save_data.json"

var save_data: Dictionary = {
    "highscore": 0
}

func write_save_data():
    var json_string: String = JSON.stringify(save_data)

    var save_file: FileAccess = FileAccess.open(SAVE_FILE_PATH,
FileAccess.WRITE)

    if save_file == null:
        print("Could not open save file.")
        return

    save_file.store_string(json_string)
```

At the top of the script, we define a dictionary, called `save_data`, that we'll use to store all the data in. For now, it only contains `highscore`. If we want to access the saved data later on during the game, we can just use this variable.

Then we have the `write_save_data()` function, which actually writes our data to a file. This function starts by converting our `save_data` dictionary to a JSON string using the `JSON.stringify()` function.

The JSON standard

JSON is a data format that is widely used on the web and other platforms. The name **JSON** stands for **JavaScript Object Notation**. It is a very lightweight way of storing data and has the added benefit of being easy to read and adjust once our data is stored in the file.

Next, we use the `FileAccess` class to open the file in which we would like to write our data. We stored the path to the file as a constant, `SAVE_FILE_PATH`, at the top of the script. Because we want to write to the file, we need to open it with write access by providing `File.Access.WRITE` to the `open()` function. This mode of accessing the file will also create the file for us if it doesn't exist yet. The opened file gets stored in the `save_file` variable.

Next, we check whether `save_file` opened properly. If, for any reason, the file could not be opened, this variable's value will be `null` and we should stop executing the function.

> **More information**
>
> For more on the `FileAccess` class, check out the official documentation: `https://docs.godotengine.org/en/stable/classes/class_fileaccess.html`.

The last thing we need to do, when the file is properly opened, is actually write the JSON data to it. We do this using `store_string()` on `save_file`, passing along `json_string`.

That is all we need to write data to a file in the `user://` folder. Now we can write a function that reads this data back in.

Reading data from disk

To read data from the `user://` folder, we follow the same steps as writing it, but in reverse. Add this function to the `save_manager.gd` script:

```
func read_save_data():
    var save_file: FileAccess = FileAccess.open(SAVE_FILE_PATH,
FileAccess.READ)

    if save_file == null:
        print("Could not open save file.")
        return

    var file_content: String = save_file.get_as_text()
    save_data = JSON.parse_string(file_content)
```

The `read_save_data` function loads the saved file and parses the content so that we can use it in the game. Firstly, we open the saved file with `FileAccess.open`, providing the file's path and `FileAccess.READ` to indicate that we only want to read it. After this, we check to make sure the file is opened properly, else we need to exit the function again.

Next, we read out the complete file as a string into a variable called `file_content`. We'll have to parse this string from the JSON format it was saved in, to the format that GDScript can handle, a dictionary. The parsed value is directly stored in the `save_data` variable that we defined in the previous section.

> **More information**
>
> For more on saving and loading data in Godot Engine, check out the official documentation: `https://docs.godotengine.org/en/stable/tutorials/io/saving_games.html`.

This is great, we have two functions that are able to write and read the saved data for our little game. Now we still need to add some functions to make sure the script is usable by the game.

Preparing the save manager for use in the game

The save manager is almost ready, but we still need to add these two functions:

```
func _ready():
    read_save_data()

func save_highscore(new_highscore: float):
    save_data.highscore = new_highscore
    write_save_data()
```

The first function, the _ready() function, makes sure that we load the saved data from the moment the player starts up the game.

The second function adds a convenient way of storing a new high score. It adds the new high score to the save_data dictionary and then writes the data to disk.

Now, to make sure we can access the save manager from anywhere, add this script to the project's autoloads. What we want is for our save manager to be the first autoload that gets executed, which will make sure that the saved data gets loaded before any other part of the game executes. To do this, make sure the save_manager.gd script is at the top of the list of autoloads. You can do this by dragging and dropping the entry of **SaveManager** or by clicking the arrows on the right until it is at the top.

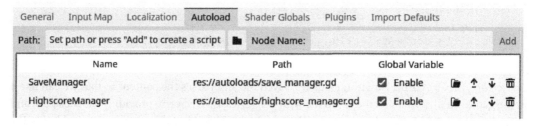

Figure 15.2 - Make sure SaveManager is the first autoload in the list

With this script finished and in place as an autoload, we can finally hook up the game to use it. Let's do that in the next section.

Adjusting the game to use the save manager

Now, all we need to do is to get the high score from **SaveManager** when we load the highscore_manager.gd script and save the high score every time the player attains a new one. Add the

following _ready function to the highscore_manager.gd script and add the SaveManager.
save_highscore() function call:

```
func _ready():
    highscore = SaveManager.save_data.highscore

func set_new_highscore(value: int):
    if value > highscore:
        highscore = value
        SaveManager.save_highscore(highscore)
```

With these in place, we can finally play the game a bit, get a high score, close the game, and, when we reopen it, see our previous high score come up.

Figure 15.3 - The high score gets loaded when we open the game

Now our game is really ready for users to strive over beating their high score over multiple days without having to keep track of it themselves. In the next section, we'll take a glance at the actual content of the save file itself.

Having a look at the save file

For now, we have treated the save file as a black box, without knowing its actual contents. We save data to it, in JSON format, and read it back in, parsing it back to data that is usable by GDScript.

> **Black box**
>
> We say we interact with a black box when we don't have an idea of how the thing itself actually works. We provide the system with input and it spits out some output.

Of course, we can also take a look at the contents of the save file with a text editor, such as Notepad on Windows. Just open the `user://` folder, as we did in the *User path* section, earlier in this chapter. From here, open up the `save_data.save` file that we created in the save manager.

You'll see that the data within this file is very easily readable, and looks a lot like the actual dictionary that we defined in the `save_manager.gd` script. This is because JSON also has a notion of the dictionary data structure and the syntax is very similar to that of dictionaries in GDScript. The file looks like this:

```
{"highscore":56}
```

If you want, you can change the save data from here and cheat, by filling in an impossibly high score. Unfortunately, users will also be able to do this if they know where to look for the save file.

> **More information**
>
> There are ways to encrypt save files, but these are out of the scope of this book. See the official documentation for more: `https://docs.godotengine.org/en/stable/classes/class_fileaccess.html#class-fileaccess-method-open-encrypted`.

Awesome, with our game saving the player's high score, we have come to the end of this chapter. There are still many tricks to be learned about loading and saving the game state, but for now, this will surely do.

Summary

In this chapter, we learned all about the file system of Godot and computers in general. It allowed us to write a little save system that keeps the high score of our game and loads it every time we start up the game.

This was the last chapter for this part of the book. Over the course of the last five chapters, we took a deeper dive into programming concepts, patterns, and the file system.

You are all ready to go and develop some games of your own. But before you do so, I want to give you some last pointers and steps on what to do next in the last chapter of this book. See you there.

Quiz time

- What is the difference between the `res://` and `user://` file paths within Godot Engine?

- To save data, we used the JSON format. Is JSON a format unique to Godot Engine? In what other domain is the JSON format widely used?

16
What Next?

What a journey! We went from knowing nothing about programming to having an intermediate understanding and creating a whole game from scratch within one book. I know that it isn't always easy to understand everything on the first go, but that is how we learn. We have to fail at something and try it over and over – each time getting better at the thing we are trying to learn.

Starting a new project is always a struggle. It's like the white canvas of a painter or the blank page of a writer. Starting something new is hard. That is why I like to provide some ideas to get you started. And don't worry about what project is the ideal one. From here on out, any project that interests you is a good one to try out. Just make sure to keep them small and finish them so that people can play what you have made.

In this chapter, we will cover the following main topics:

- Ideas for your next project
- Learning new topics
- Joining the community

Ideas for your next projects

As mentioned in the introduction of this chapter, the fear of an empty project is a real thing. Where to begin and what to make is always a struggle. Let's take a closer look at both problems.

Starting a new project

Here are some tips I learned the hard way about starting a new project that will help you focus on creating the game you want to create:

- **Start by creating the main gameplay loop**: The first thing you should do is create the gameplay on which the game is based. If you are creating a platformer, make sure that moving and jumping around is fun to do on its own before you start adding more intricate systems.

- **Make it functional before you make it beautiful**: It's easy to get lost in making your game overly beautiful, but this will slow down the production of the game significantly. Even worse, if the game is not fun and you need to redo a lot of systems, you'll also need to redo all the things you did to make it beautiful.

- **Focus on the thing you want to learn**: If there is a specific topic you want to learn about, such as menus and the UI, then make this the focus of your project. There are more UI-focused game genres, such as visual novels or strategy games, that you can make.

- **Keep it small**: Most people appreciate playing a small, fun game more than a long, half-baked experience. This will also make sure that you'll be able to finish the game. Any game you ever played was finished (or deemed finished enough), while the unfinished ones were never played by anyone.

- **Make a GDD**: At the start of a project, create a short game design document. This could be a one-pager, just to state the general intentions of the project. It will guide you while developing and help make decisions later on.

These were some high-level tips on how to tackle any new project. It's easy to get caught up in the details, so the most important thing is to just begin. Learning happens when we make mistakes, after all. We'll now move on to more concrete ideas of what to do next.

Extending the survivor-like game

The logical next step is to extend the game we create throughout this book. Some ideas could be as follows:

- **Introducing new enemy types**: Maybe an enemy that is slow but deals a lot of damage, or a bomb that stays in place and explodes after 5 seconds.

- **Creating different projectile types**: Maybe a dagger that has a shorter range but deals more damage to enemies.

- **Adding more items to pick up**: Maybe a shield that protects the player for five seconds, or boots that make the player move around faster.

However, one warning I have for you is that you should not stay on one project for too long. When learning to create and design games, it is best to keep projects small and not over-polish a single game. It is often better to consider something as done, let people play it, and then move on to the next project – this is until you feel confident enough in your skills to tackle a bigger game.

> **Polish in video games**
>
> In video game development, we call anything that is not the core experience of the game **polish** – things that are not integral to the experience, but make it look nicer or feel smoother. Polish is very important for the final experience of the game.

On the subject of creating many smaller games, let's look at some game ideas you could work on next.

Creating another game

In the game developer community, we often say *your first 10 games will suck*, which is a harsh way to say that the first 10 projects you create will not be great. And that's OK. We have all been there. But every project you get under your belt will teach you something.

Maybe you'll focus on creating an engaging gameplay loop in one project, while focusing on creating clear menus in another.

Try to make many small projects, each of which teaches you something useful; this way, you will be able to grow your skills while also having something to show for it.

Some game ideas you could try to tackle next are as follows:

- **A platformer**: Learn how to work with 2D physics where gravity pulls the player down.
- **A turn-based strategy game**: Learn how to divide gameplay up into discrete steps.
- **A card game**: Learn how to work with a more intricate UI and how to abstract card abilities.
- **A puzzle game**: Learn how to design interesting puzzles that are not too hard or too easy.
- **A visual novel**: Learn all about menus and how to integrate dialog into a game.
- **An endless runner**: Learn how to generate random levels on the fly.

While working on one of these projects, look up the parts you don't know how to do or don't understand. The information in this book is a great starting point, but it won't suffice to solve everything. A book that would try to do that would be unwieldy long.

Free game assets

If you are not a visual artist or musician, then creating assets to put in your game can be hard. Luckily, there are many free options around; check out these links:

- **Kenney**: An awesome free 2D, 3D, and audio asset created in the Netherlands. The sprites used in this book come from Kenney: `https://kenney.nl/assets`.
- **OpenGameArt**: A community of game developers and artists providing free and open source assets: `https://opengameart.org/`.
- **Itch.io**: The platform we used to published our game on is also a great resource for free assets of all kinds: `https://itch.io/game-assets/free`.

With these, you'll be able to make a beautiful game in no time.

Even though these assets are free, it is often required to credit the creator of the assets somewhere in the game or on the game's store page. So, don't forget to do that; this way, you get free assets and they get exposure. Everyone wins!

Knowing what to learn is the first step, which you hopefully identify while doing the projects suggested in this section. From there, the question is, how do we learn these things? Let's look at that in the next section.

Learning about new topics

There are many great resources out there to learn more about programming and game design. In this section, we'll go over some different types of resources that could help you out.

Following specific tutorials

When you know what you would like to learn, there will most certainly be a tutorial on that topic in video or text format. All you need to do is use your favorite search engine, such as Google or YouTube, and search for whatever topic you are looking for. Some of my favorite sources of great Godot Engine tutorials are the following:

- **GDQuest**: This provides great video tutorials on a wide variety of topics and even provides whole courses: `https://www.youtube.com/@Gdquest`.

- **Hearbeast**: A YouTube channel with complete game projects but also shorter tutorials on different Godot Engine-related topics: `https://www.youtube.com/@uheartbeast`.

- **The Godot Engine docs**: There is a whole page in the documentation that introduces different third-party tutorials: `https://docs.godotengine.org/en/stable/community/tutorials.html`.

- **KidsCanCode**: This has many great articles on a variety of Godot-related topics: `https://kidscancode.org/godot_recipes/4.x/`.

- **Game Maker's Toolkit**: A channel with great video essays about game design: `https://www.youtube.com/@GMTK`.

There is no shortage of online tutorials on the Godot Engine.

Reading more books

Another way to deepen your knowledge is by reading other books on more specialized and advanced topics. Here are some of my favorites:

- *The Art of Game Design: A Book of Lenses*, by Jesse Schell. This book is a very thorough introduction to everything game design-related.

- *Game Programming Patterns*, by Robert Nystrom. Want to learn more about the programming patterns applied in games? Then this is the book for you.

- *Theory of Fun for Game Design*, by Raph Koster. A short book about what makes games fun and their cultural importance.

- *Godot 4 Game Development Projects*, by Chris Bradfield.

- *GAMEDEV: 10 Steps to Making Your First Game Successful*, by Wlad Marhulets.

Any of these will help you on your way to becoming a game developer and designer.

Reading the Godot Engine documentation

Next to third-party resources, there is, of course, also the official **Godot Engine documentation**. This is a very exhaustive source of information on all the different classes and nodes and contains manuals on all the different subsystems related to the engine.

You can access the documentation here: `https://docs.godotengine.org/`.

Whenever you search for how to use a certain part of the engine, you should start by consulting the documentation.

Looking at the game code of other people's projects

A great way to learn is by looking at other people's game projects and code. Because the Godot Engine is an open source project, many games with the engine are open source too. This means that the full project is available online for anyone to see and play around with.

Some great projects include the following:

- **Godot Engine demo projects**: These are fully open source, small projects that range from tech demos to full games: `https://github.com/godotengine/godot-demo-projects`.

- **GDQuest's open RPG**: A demo of a 2D, open-world RPG game: `https://github.com/gdquest-demos/godot-open-rpg`.

Note that these projects are often still under development or could have been made with an older Godot Engine version, but it doesn't hurt to take a look how people solved certain problems.

Learning new topics is a great way to improve your game development; it will allow you to do more, faster. However, another important, yet overlooked, way to improve is by joining a community of like-minded people who love sharing, giving feedback, and supporting each other. Let's have a look at how we could join such a community.

Joining the community

Lastly, I would want to encourage you to join the game development community. In general, it is a very welcoming and friendly bunch of people who love to hear from you and your games. Don't hesitate to approach people and ask them questions. Most people are very helpful and will encourage you on your journey.

Joining the Forum, Discord, Reddit, or any other platform

There are many different communities that have sprung up related to creating games on many different platforms. It doesn't matter what social media you are most active on; there is likely a lively game developer community based there. Here are some of the outlets you can join:

- **The official Godot Engine Forum**: It's the perfect place to ask questions, help out others, and show off your projects: `https://forum.godotengine.org/`.

- **The official Godot Engine Discord**: Here, you can encounter like-minded game developers who work with Godot: `https://discord.com/invite/4JBkykG`.

- **Godot Engine Reddit**: Here, you can share your project and look at other people's progress: `https://www.reddit.com/r/godot/`.

- **Godot developers on Twitch**: If you're into streaming or watching streamers, then there is a Godot tag you could check out: `https://www.twitch.tv/directory/all/tags/godot`.

- **Any of the social platforms**: Many people post on social platforms such as **Instagram**, **Twitter**, **Mastodon**, **Bluesky**, or **TikTok**. Just look under the `#GodotEngine`, `#IndieDev`, and `#GameDev` hashtags.

Sharing your progress, seeing other people's progress, and discussing game development with others can be a very motivating and satisfying way of building a little community around you.

Contributing to the Godot Engine project

Because the Godot Engine is open source and you now know how to work with it, you can help out, if you want to. Here are some of the ways in which you could do so:

- **Log issues**: The Godot Engine, like any piece of software, is unfortunately not without its bugs, but there are a lot of people solving them. If you find a bug in the engine, you can always open an issue on the GitHub page for the engine: `https://github.com/godotengine/godot/issues`.

- **Write documentation**: Whenever you are reading the documentation and you feel like it is a bit lacking on the page you are on, don't hesitate to add your own improvements and help out anyone else who is new to the Godot Engine. There is a link on every documentation page that will take you directly to where you can edit the page.

Figure 16.1 - Click on Edit on GitHub to propose a change to the Godot documentation page

- **Translate parts of the engine**: Want to help localize the engine or its documentation to other languages so that more people have access to this great tool? If so, you'll find everything you need to know here: `https://docs.godotengine.org/en/latest/contributing/documentation/editor_and_docs_localization.html#doc-editor-and-docs-localization`.

- **Contribute code to the engine directly**: Once you feel confident enough in your coding abilities, you can give coding directly in the core of the engine a shot. You can find more information here: `https://docs.godotengine.org/en/latest/contributing/development/index.html`.

These are some of the biggest ways you can contribute back to the Godot project and community. Let's now return to creating games in the next section.

Joining a game jam

A big part of being a game developer is, of course, developing games. And nothing is more fun than to develop games with others. That is exactly what **game jams** are for. Game jams are events where you create a game from scratch over a small period of time, often a weekend, but it can go up to a month or more.

The goal is to create a little game that is then played by the other participants of the jam. This is a great way to get lots of feedback and play the games of many other people during the jam. What's more, you can enter these jams with a team. This way, you create connections within the game development world and learn to work with multiple people on something. However, you can also just participate on your own.

One of the biggest platforms that provide game jams is `itch.io`, which we used to upload our game in *Chapter 12*. Just visit `https://itch.io/jams` and look for a game jam that interests you. There are always many game jams going on at any given point in time.

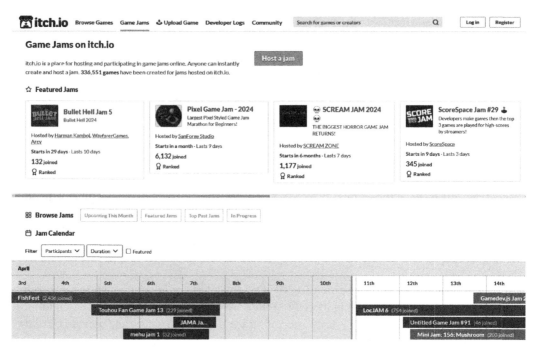

Figure 16.2 - The game jams page on Itch.io

Some great jams that you could join are as follows:

- **Godot Wild Jam**: A monthly game jam specifically for Godot game developers: `https://godotwildjam.com/`.

- **Global Game Jam**: A physical game jam organized globally. Check out the site to find a location near you: `https://globalgamejam.org/`.

- **The GMTK Game Jam**: A yearly game jam organized by the **Game Developer's Toolkit** YouTube channel. This one doesn't have a stable website linked to it, but it's always announced on the YouTube channel: `https://www.youtube.com/@GMTK`.

Now, you know how to integrate yourself into the game developer's community and start sharing your awesome games with thousands of other like-minded people.

Goodbyes

In this chapter, we concluded the book by showing you what is next on your journey to creating great games. We saw what possible projects we could work on next, how to learn new things, and how to join the community.

The intention of this whole book was to get new people to start creating games in the Godot Engine. We went from knowing absolutely nothing about programming or game development to a very solid and intermediate understanding of both.

At the start, we learned how to us GDScript as our language of choice, learning about the basic concepts, such as variables and loops, and progressing to more intermediate topics, such as classes and proper programming guidelines. We eventually made our way to advanced topics, such as the super keyword and programming patterns.

During the book, we also developed our own game, a small survival game modeled after *Vampire Survivors*. We saw what nodes are and which ones we should use in all kinds of different situations. We even made the game multiplayer and published it on **Itch.io**, ready to be played by anyone who would like to do so!

I hope you had a great time learning how to program and use the Godot Engine, and I would like to thank you from the bottom of my heart for sticking around until the end. Now go out there and create some awesome games!

Index

packtpub.com

Subscribe to our online digital library for full access to over 7,000 books and videos, as well as industry leading tools to help you plan your personal development and advance your career. For more information, please visit our website.

Why subscribe?

- Spend less time learning and more time coding with practical eBooks and Videos from over 4,000 industry professionals

- Improve your learning with Skill Plans built especially for you

- Get a free eBook or video every month

- Fully searchable for easy access to vital information

- Copy and paste, print, and bookmark content

Did you know that Packt offers eBook versions of every book published, with PDF and ePub files available? You can upgrade to the eBook version at packtpub.com and as a print book customer, you are entitled to a discount on the eBook copy. Get in touch with us at customercare@packtpub.com for more details.

At www.packtpub.com, you can also read a collection of free technical articles, sign up for a range of free newsletters, and receive exclusive discounts and offers on Packt books and eBooks.

Other Books You May Enjoy

If you enjoyed this book, you may be interested in these other books by Packt:

Godot 4 Game Development Projects

Chris Bradfield

ISBN: 978-1-80461-040-4

- Get acquainted with the Godot game engine and editor if you're a beginner
- Explore the new features of Godot 4.0
- Build games in 2D and 3D using design and coding best practices
- Use Godot's node and scene system to design robust, reusable game objects
- Use GDScript, Godot's built-in scripting language, to create complex game systems
- Implement user interfaces to display information
- Create visual effects to spice up your game
- Publish your game to desktop and mobile platforms

The Essential Guide to Creating Multiplayer Games with Godot 4.0

Henrique Campos

ISBN: 978-1-80323-261-4

- Understand the fundamentals of networking and remote data exchange between computers
- Use the Godot game engine's built-in API to set up a network for players
- Master remote procedure calls and learn how to make function calls on objects remotely
- Enhance your GDScript proficiency to get the most out of this powerful language
- Explore industry-standard solutions for common online multiplayer challenges
- Improve your networking skills and discover how to turn single-player games into multiplayer experiences

Packt is searching for authors like you

If you're interested in becoming an author for Packt, please visit authors.packtpub.com and apply today. We have worked with thousands of developers and tech professionals, just like you, to help them share their insight with the global tech community. You can make a general application, apply for a specific hot topic that we are recruiting an author for, or submit your own idea.

Share Your Thoughts

Now you've finished *Learning GDScript by developing a game with Godot 4*, we'd love to hear your thoughts! Scan the QR code below to go straight to the Amazon review page for this book and share your feedback or leave a review on the site that you purchased it from.

https://packt.link/r/1-804-61698-2

Your review is important to us and the tech community and will help us make sure we're delivering excellent quality content.

Download a free PDF copy of this book

Thanks for purchasing this book!

Do you like to read on the go but are unable to carry your print books everywhere?

Is your eBook purchase not compatible with the device of your choice?

Don't worry, now with every Packt book you get a DRM-free PDF version of that book at no cost.

Read anywhere, any place, on any device. Search, copy, and paste code from your favorite technical books directly into your application.

The perks don't stop there, you can get exclusive access to discounts, newsletters, and great free content in your inbox daily

Follow these simple steps to get the benefits:

1. Scan the QR code or visit the link below

https://packt.link/free-ebook/978-1-80461-698-7

2. Submit your proof of purchase
3. That's it! We'll send your free PDF and other benefits to your email directly

Made in the USA
Las Vegas, NV
15 May 2024